GIBBOUS MOON OVER LAGOS

PURSUING A DREAM ON AFRICA'S WILD SIDE

Chris and Kate !

This might bring back
some Nigerian memories !

Pamela x

PAMELA WATSON

Hardie Grant

BOOKS

Published in 2020 by Hardie Grant Books,
an imprint of Hardie Grant Publishing

Hardie Grant Books (London)
5th & 6th Floors
52–54 Southwark Street
London SE1 1UN

Hardie Grant Books (Melbourne)
Building 1, 658 Church Street
Richmond, Victoria 3121

hardiegrantbooks.com

British Library Cataloguing-in-Publication Data.
A catalogue record for this book is available from the British Library.

Gibbous Moon Over Lagos: Pursuing a Dream on Africa's Wild Side

ISBN 9781743795606

Publishing management by Courtney Nicholls
Edited by Leanne Tolra
Cover artwork by Sylvester Aguddah
Text design and typeset by Megan Ellis
Author photo by Jay Clark
Maps by Jason Sankovic
Printed and bound in Great Britain by Clays Ltd, Elcograf S.p.A.

To AJ, my partner in life's adventures

MAP 1: AFRICA SHOWING NIGERIA

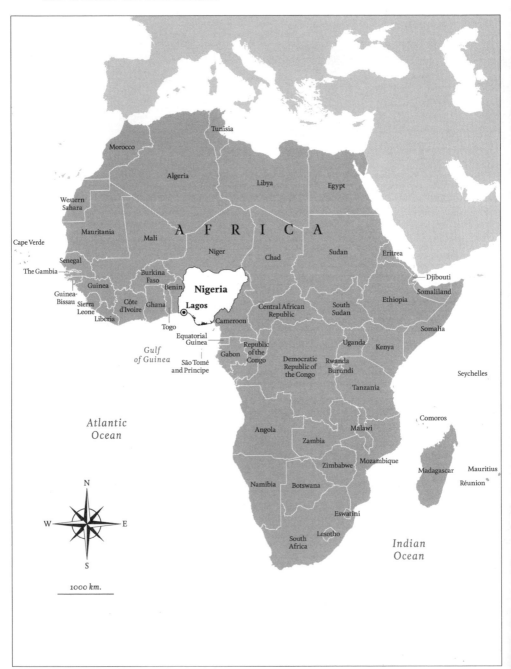

MAP 2: NIGERIA

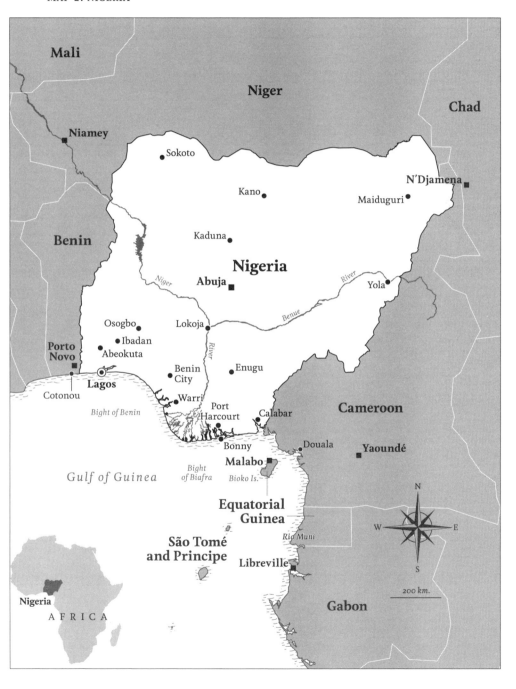

MAP 3: LAGOS STATE

MAP 4: LAGOS ISLANDS

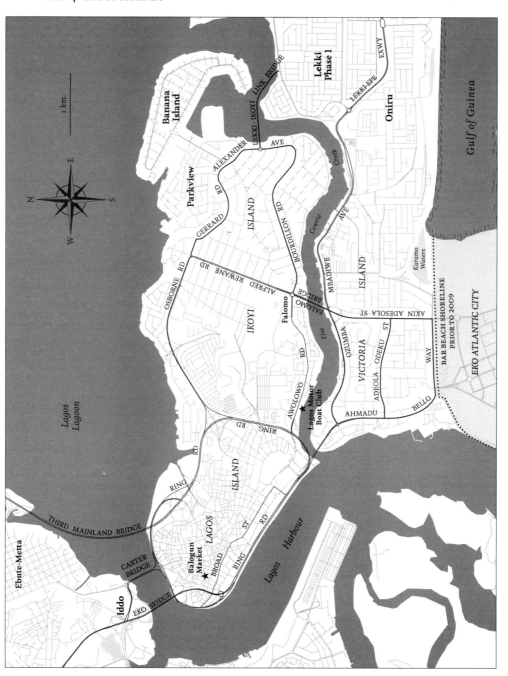

Timeline

Year	Event
1992–94	Cycled alone and unsupported for 18 months, 14,500 km across Africa from Dakar, Senegal to Dar es Salaam, Tanzania.
1999	Published *Esprit de Battuta: Alone Across Africa by Bicycle* (Aurum Press), my account of the above trip.
1999	Moved to Lagos, Nigeria with my partner, Alec.
2000–01	Worked as Associate Director of Strategy at international consulting firm in Lagos.
2002	Founded Strategyworks, a consultancy firm specialising in strategy and change management for private and public sector organisations, in Lagos.
2003	Year spent with my staff, Peter, Remi and Sonny, experimenting with paper making.
2004	Founded Ekologika Papers in Lagos.
End of 2004	My partner Alec left Lagos. I stayed, running Strategyworks and Ekologika Papers.
2005	Appointed Honorary Consul for Australia in Lagos.
2009	Left Lagos for London.

About This Story

This story focuses on events between 2004 and 2009, when I was running Strategyworks and Ekologika Papers. Most conversations are based on my best recollections. Names, including those of my businesses, have been changed and some characters are composites of several real people. While the events depicted are true, in some cases I have compressed or rearranged them to simplify a story that unrolled over five years and to place more focus on the drama rather than the miscellaneous sub-plots of my life.

Ten years on, I am based in London but regularly visit intoxicating Lagos and enticing Africa for business and adventures. Change and the movement of people to cities such as Lagos are rapid and relentless – and my optimism for this megacity and its inhabitants' future waxes and sometimes wanes like the moon. Hype about business prospects in Lagos and Africa goes hand in hand with debilitating hiatus, and many ventures fail. Corruption, lack of access to justice and poor, self-interested political leadership remain disappointingly strong, creating many obstacles to success. China's enormous public and private investment in Africa and Nigeria brings both benefits and concerns. But, generally, the continent's and nation's people are wealthier, healthier and more hopeful than they were twenty-five years ago when I rode my bicycle alone on Africa's roads. Indeed, what seems most astonishing is the tenacious hold of the rural, impoverished, needy African stereotype ingrained in so many western minds.

Being fascinated by the complexity and wondering how it will all turn out, I watch, speak, write and advise about business and adventures in this exciting, rapidly urbanising, inexorably westernising continent of fifty-four nations.

People in Lagos still ask about my paper company. 'What happened?' they ask. Here is its story.

Principal Characters

Note: Names have been changed, some characters are composites of several real people.

Name	About them
Aaron	Australian managing director of a multinational soft drinks company, not in a rush to hire a consultant
Alec	Scottish executive with a multinational oil and gas company, dashing in a kilt
Alhaji	Gateman who has completed the haj to Mecca, sometimes kept on his toes by his boss
André	Lebanese friend of Jean, with gorgeous wife Vanessa
Mr Atta	Helpful and wise lawyer with glaucoma
Ayo	Upright lawyer, husband of Toks
Mr Babatunde	Enterprising operator of a large punching and binding service in Lagos
Bola	Creative accountant who works for Wale
Bruce	Generous Australian wine distributor
Caroline	Hard-working young Congolese woman
Chuks	Ekologika Papers conversion officer, a smart engineering graduate, cost control not his strength
Cliff	Shady Australian businessman
Colin	Naïve Australian farmer with a buxom girlfriend, Deirdre
Dapo	Printer, dubious about most things, husband of Esther
David	Barman at Lagos Motor Boat Club (LMBC) with a growing family
Deirdre	Colin's aid worker girlfriend

Name	About them
Dennis (deceased)	Ginger tom cat, curious and brave, brother to Tippy
Deola	Self-confident Strategyworks consultant, seeking new horizons
Edith	Strategyworks analyst who puts vacation first
Edward	Steward who likes cooking for crowds
Esther	Hard-working manager and wife of Dapo
Father Jim	Australian Catholic priest, long-serving in Lagos, fond of beer
Feyi	Bright, young Strategyworks consultant and mother of two
Gail	Canadian general manager (GM) of Ekologika Papers, apparent friend to all
Gloria	Assertive personal assistant (PA), with an invaluable ability to find just about anything
Haresh	Oxford-educated, successful Indian entrepreneur, client, friend and mentor
Helmut	Unlikely rescuer in Mali
Hew (deceased)	Alec's younger brother
The High Commissioner	Australian High Commissioner to Nigeria who knew the capital Abuja and its diplomatic world better than Lagos and its commercial realities
Ibrahim	Sword seller at Agaja beach
Ismail	Snappily dressed and slippery sheriff of a Lagos court
James	Cheerful young graduate and Ekologika Papers papermaker
Jean	Young Lebanese guy with a wicked sense of humour, also in the printing business
John	Mature Strategyworks senior consultant who did not last long
Josh	British West African correspondent, a courageous but possibly blinkered journalist

Name	About them
Kevin	Sports-mad and energetic Australian banker, excellent client and friend
Kola	Senior experienced Ekologika Papers sales professional, hard to manage
Kunle	Strategyworks analyst with a liking for music
Luke	Caretaker at Agaja beach hut, builder and brave swimmer
Max	French–Lebanese businessman with a cool Parisian style, business partner to Jean
Michelle	Australian businesswoman with wide-ranging interests
Mike	Australian Deputy High Commissioner who has seen it all
Molly	Self-starting business graduate with creative flair, responsible for paper conversion and sales
Moustafa	Likeable gateman with a watchful eye
My girl	Long-serving and capable personal assistant to the Australian High Commissioner
Mr and Mrs Olumide	Happily married couple – but unhappy with Ekologika Papers
Pamela	Consultant and entrepreneur with a taste for adventure, but has she bitten off more than she can chew?
Patience	No-nonsense accountant, a source of common sense
Patrick	Independent and entrepreneurial graphic design professional
Peter	Boat mechanic and Ekologika Papers's first employee, papermaker and leader, suspicious of women as employees
Philippe	'No wahala' landlord
Remi	Lead Ekologika Papers papermaker, with looks and strength like Atlas, a foundation employee
Reti	Strategyworks analyst, briefly

Name	About them
Segun	Nigerian MD of a Nigerian–Australian joint venture, a man with a problem
Sonny	Ekologika Papers craftsman and cool dresser, a foundation employee
Sophie	Inexperienced but promising Strategyworks consultant
Steve	Senior executive with an oil and gas multinational; a hard-headed, blunt-speaking but savvy Aussie
Tayo	Willing, able and loyal driver
Theodora	Capable lawyer who ran and founded a shelter for abused and homeless women
Thomas	'Just in time' handyman
Tippy	Timid but hungry white female cat, sister to Dennis
Tokunbo (Toks)	Stylish Lagos property developer, friend and philanthropist
Tola	A friend of Dapo's, in the hospitality business, pious by his own measure
Vanessa	André's glamorous wife, hard to get out of the kitchen
Wale	Gentleman landlord at Agaja and good cricketer
William	Company driver
Yinka	Talented Ekologika Papers graphic designer with a temper (possibly for good reason)
Zainab	Strategyworks senior consultant with ambition

Nigerian National Leaders Post-Independence[1]

Name	Position	Term	Exit
First Republic 1963–66			
Sir Abubakar Tafawa Balewa	*Prime Minister*	1963–66	Murdered
Military Rule 1966–79			
Major General Johnson Aguiyi-Ironsi	*Head of State*	1966	Assassinated
General Yakubu Gowon	*Head of State*	1966–75	Deposed
General Murtala Mohammed	*Head of State*	1975–76	Assassinated
Major General Olusegun Obasanjo	*Head of State*	1976–79	Lapsed
Second Republic 1979–83			
Shehu Shagari	*President*	1979–83	Deposed
Military Rule 1983			
Major General Muhammadu Buhari	*Head of State*	1983–85	Deposed
General Ibrahim Babangida	*Head of State*	1985–93	Resigned
Third Republic 1993			
Ernest Shonekan	*Head of State*	1993	Deposed
Military Rule 1993–99			
General Sani Abacha	*Head of State*	1993–98	Died in office
General Abdulsami Abubakar	*Head of State*	1999	Resigned
Fourth Republic 1999–present			
Olusegun Obasanjo	*President*	1999–2007	End of term
Umaru Musa Yar'Adua	*President*	2007–10	Died in office
Goodluck Jonathan	*President*	2010–15	End of term
Muhammadu Buhari	*President*	2015–	

Contents

Phases of the Moon (2019)

Half of the moon is always bathed in sunlight, but how much we can see depends on our own location relative to the moon—it is what we can see that determines what we refer to as the phase of the moon.[1]

Prologue

Little by little is how the pig's nose enters the yard.
— Nigerian proverb

In the quiet hour before dusk, when shadows lengthen and views are painted with a rosy hue, the ghosts from adventures past come to greet me. Alone on the deck of the Lagos Motor Boat Club I sipped a cold drink and watched the gleaming motorboats bob gently in the wake of a passing vessel. The scene was milky and soft-edged from an unseasonably late harmattan, the northeast wind from the Sahara that whips up blurring dust to deposit across West Africa. There was not even the whisper of a breeze under the shade of the spreading branches of a tropical almond tree to relieve the heavy humidity.

But, having spent many evenings at this club, I knew that on a normal weekday everything would soon change. Within an hour the temperature would mellow as the sun sank and the outdoor bar would vibrate with greetings and laughter. Business people, some women but mainly men, in well-cut suits or traditional lace *agbadas* and wax-fabric *boubous* would arrive. Shoulders would be clasped, and hands shaken vigorously in enthusiastic bonhomie.

Drinks would be ordered from familiar waiters and a buzz of exchanges about business or politics would fill the club.

But for now, the deck resonated only with my memories.

I had spent ten years living in Lagos, from 1999 to 2009. I returned as a visitor in 2019, having started a different life in London. Coming back to my old haunt, as I had done many times in the intervening years, I again felt a wash of nostalgia for the club in which I had celebrated so many exhilarating successes and had my worries soothed by well-meant advice and glasses of wine. In my mind's eye, I could still see the thrown-back heads and shimmering smiles of my friends.

Some angels – and devils – are pervasive.

I looked at my watch. There were still a couple of hours before my friends arrived from the mainland. Time enough to drink in all the details I had forgotten in over ten years.

A young mechanic in grease-stained overalls passed from a jetty to the deck. Even today when he should have been voting and when movement was to have been restricted, it seemed he had been working on a club member's boat and was now on his way home.

'Good afternoon Madam,' he said as he passed and, for a moment, his soulful brown eyes were those of my former skipper and boat mechanic, Peter.

I could not escape my ghosts in Lagos. I waved to him and time turned backwards to where it all began.

O

Africa. Many westerners think of it as a single country and they pronounce it with a false accent – Af-ri-kaa – as though they are Karen Blixen remembering her lover and lost farm in Kenya. It is a word that conjures romance and adventure – and I know its draw well. My childhood in Perth, Western Australia, was filled with evenings spent watching sunsets over the Indian Ocean and wondering what it would be like under the blazing sun on another, distant continent. Even at a young age, cocooned in a pleasant and safe part of the world, I thought life in Africa would have more edge and meaning.

After university I had my chance. Backpacking down the Nile, I got an unquenchable taste for wide skies, dust in my nostrils and not knowing how each day would end. But a Master's degree in Business Administration brought me into the corporate world, away from the red dust and heat of adventure.

It would give me a long-lasting career in business strategy and change management consulting – but in the eighties it was not something that was going to take me to Africa.

By the mid-eighties my life and career were in London, but I was delighted to grab a chance to slip away to Madagascar. On assignment, I worked with a string of moribund, nationalised companies and farms, asset-stripped by their former Marxist government, to be revived under private ownership. Despite my hopes to make a positive difference for the deeply impoverished Malagasy, the intrigues of international aid agencies and the new government dispelled any romance or sense of fulfilment in this kind of work.

And so I returned to London for six years, earning well but working long hours for my clients. My colleagues and I were yuppies – young upwardly mobile professionals – and we worked hard. So hard, that in rare moments of relaxation who of us didn't start dreaming of escape from the daily grind, from the grey skies of England, for some meaning and fun to life?

Instead of heading for Provence as Peter Mayle had done, I went to Monday evening lectures at the revered Royal Geographical Society in London and absorbed tales of modern derring-do. Thoroughly captivated, I swapped desk for dust and took my bicycle on my own epic expedition for eighteen months. Alone and unsupported, I cycled 14,500 kilometres through seventeen African countries.

Life-changing, adventure non-stop, but not a way to make a living.

With funds burnt through, I returned to London and my career – but plotted my next escape.

Like many Europeans dreaming of Africa, I conjured sub-Saharan Africa. I smelt the cloves of exotic Zanzibar and saw the wide Serengeti plains and migrating wildebeest, the conical snow-covered Mount Kilimanjaro reaching into an afternoon halo of clouds, the spray and mist clouds billowing above the crashing Victoria Falls and the out-of-this-world beauty of Table Mountain at dawn. These sub-Saharan African images were repeated in my piled-up copies of *National Geographic* and *Condé Nast Traveller* and recalled from documentaries narrated by David Attenborough. They were also in movies about courageous Victorian explorers or a sometimes-inglorious colonial past. These images were not only sub-Saharan but also came from eastern and southern Africa.

West Africa featured much less vividly in our romantic mind's eye of the continent. Music lovers might hear the haunting rifts from land-locked Mali and cognoscenti might remember the beaches of Gambia and Senegal and the former slave forts of Ghana.

Few westerners, however, had romantic images of Nigeria – but I was one of them.

In 1993, while cycling in Nigeria, I had thought I would die. Lagos is enormous and I avoided cycling there (I went via Ibadan instead) in fear of its intense traffic. But vast numbers of people being transported at high speeds in dilapidated vehicles meant I saw a lot of crashes and dead bodies along my route through the south of the country. I developed a twitch in my eye as cars and trucks sped by me and I took to cycling on the wrong side of the road, so I could see the deadly traffic coming.

This, I thought, was Africa's wild side.

Yet in the late nineties, as I eyed a way to build a professional life on the continent I loved, Lagos stood out from everywhere else.

In 1999, Nigeria emerged from a lost decade during which a long-term military leader, General Ibrahim Babangida (1985–93), proved reluctant to make way for democracy and another leader, General Sani Abacha (1993–98), displayed unprecedented greed and ruthless political control. There was now a new constitution and a return to an elected civilian government under President Olusegun Obasanjo (1999–2007). Foreign investment was arriving and business was unleashed – at least in Lagos, the country's commercial capital.

So in late 1999, my dream of living in Africa took shape. What Lagos lacked in romantic aura, it offered in size and commercial potential. Management consultants were in demand. Yes, it was a cacophonous coastal city, overcrowded and chaotic with an unsavoury reputation, home to many millions with more arriving daily.[2] Lagos was intimidating to visit, let alone as a place to live and start a business. But at last, I thought, I could contribute professionally and help in a tiny way to shape a more prosperous African future.

I decided to give it a go.

There was a complication.

While plotting my African future, I had taken a short-term contract with a multinational oil company and met Scottish Alec, a senior gas executive. He worked on the other side of the world, in fact, in Perth, my old home town. We had a fresh but strong relationship, begun only that year and I worried I'd be forced to choose between a man and fulfilment – such a clichéd situation for the modern, independent woman – I thought to myself. But just as I was arranging to relocate, by incredible coincidence Alec was also transferred to Lagos as managing director (MD) of an indigenous gas company.

What a relief – we could go together.

Nervous about stories of the corrupt and challenging business environment in Nigeria, I joined a large international consulting firm and worked as associate director of strategy. Despite the tentative start, during my first two years I fell in love with my adopted city of Lagos. I became excited that at last I could use my professional skills to help emerging companies, and I was optimistic that the developing private business and entrepreneurial energy could pull Nigeria up by its bootstraps. Its vibrant, creative and energetic inhabitants soon captivated me, too.

Frustrated that my expatriate status blocked me from a top role in my employer's firm, in 2002 I founded a small consultancy practice, Strategyworks, which offered pragmatic strategy and change management services. Soon I employed two consultants and expected some big opportunities in Lagos's growing private sector.

At this time, I was also approached by the Australian High Commission in Abuja to become the Honorary Consul for Australia in Lagos. My romantic notions about the role derived almost entirely from reading about Sir Richard Burton, the intrepid Victorian explorer and linguist. In 1861, following his most significant African journeys, Burton was appointed consul in nearby Fernando Po (now Bioko), the island capital of today's Equatorial Guinea, an oil-producing neighbour to Nigeria in the Gulf of Benin. I found it appealing to be offered the chance to become a contemporary explorer and to represent my country in a modern-day West African entrepot Lagos. In reality, it was a role that was to put me more closely in touch with my fellow Australians, as an expatriate, than I had been in decades.

But by 2003 I had another dream to add to an already busy life. I wanted to make a philanthropic, positive social impact in Lagos, my new home. My immediate concern was for the urban poor rather than the rural poor – for women more than men – and I wanted to help by providing jobs rather than handouts. My strategy was to invest to create a small, self-funding social enterprise. I did not expect to change Lagos, or the world, with my vision for a small venture. But as founder and investor (and optimistically expecting to turn a profit) I decided I would not take out any dividends. Instead,

I would reinvest the bulk of profits to grow and create more jobs and donate ten per cent to support disadvantaged women.

Why had this become my passion?

In the new twenty-first century, sub-Saharan Africa was urbanising fast. In rural areas aid-provided pumps delivered drinkable water, but it was still carried in a bucket on a girl's head. Women could grow extra produce to support their children using aid-provided micro-credit, but selling the produce meant carrying a heavy load (and one's baby) for several kilometres to market. Many Africans knew life could be better and sought to alleviate their suffering by moving to cities. In Lagos this accelerating influx was leaving millions jobless or under-employed. I felt that western aid donors, obsessed with the rural poor, were missing this point.

During my previous cycling adventure, I had passed through many villages and gratefully guzzled litres of water from aid-provided pumps. During those thousands of kilometres of cycling from Senegal to Tanzania, I came across some fantastically managed non-governmental organisations (NGOs) doing good in creative ways, including those working with communities for long-term and systemic change. Overall, however, I was rather scathing about the glut of NGOs. They seemed conferred with an unchallengeable aura of goodness, even though many were so small that good governance and transparency were non-existent. It was impossible to track how efficiently and effectively they met their goals. Indeed, over my years of exposure to their work, I concluded donor agencies and NGOs were much like anti-inflammatory steroids. They seemed a good idea but many treated symptoms rather than problems, creating unintended side-effects that were sometimes worse than the original complaint.

For example, the provision of micro-credit to enhance women's earning potential seemed a good thing. But without broader entrepreneurial opportunities or distribution support, many women took loans to enter the same business, such as growing tomatoes.

When an increased volume of produce came onto the market at the same time, prices dropped and their ventures were no longer viable. Worse, illiterate women who did not understand the concept of interest could further impoverish themselves by borrowing money from their neighbours to make interest repayments. Furthermore, the NGOs' provision of micro-credit sometimes increased the level of societal domestic violence – from husbands threatened by their wives' increased independence or from fellow wives in polygamous households who were jealous of a co-wife's success. Micro-credit was not a bad idea, but it needed sensitive administration by agencies working in a community long-term. It also needed to be accompanied by community education initiatives and backed by an enforceable legal framework. In my experience, this was not often the case, and the unintended side-effects persisted.

During my cycling journey, I had felt solidarity with the African women in villages. I observed in country after country, village after village, that men owned the assets and made decisions while women did most of the work and brought up the children. Coming from the corporate world, this situation resonated with me. By 2003 I'd worked for more than twenty years for a number of global consulting firms and I bore scars from encounters with misogyny, sexual harassment, unequal pay and glass ceilings. Without the momentum and support of the global #MeToo movement that began in 2017, the 30% Club, begun in the United Kingdom in 2010, and other groundswells for social and political change, I had abandoned the then unfair corporate rat race and, like so many women, was choosing instead to make my mark with my own firm – and philanthropic activity.

I was supportive of NGOs that aimed to help hard-working but marginalised village women claim their rights and those of their children, but through my own social enterprise in Lagos, I was keen to simply create jobs for some of the women I had seen begging on Lagos's roadways – many made destitute after fleeing abusive relationships – and for the girls who had left school without prospects.

Confucius may have said, 'Give a man a fish and you'll feed him for a day, but teach him to fish and you'll feed him for a lifetime' but, in my experience, a woman would rather have a job and a washing machine.

But what kind of jobs would I create? What business could employ relatively unskilled and under-educated women? I had a few ideas, but in 2003 handmade paper was a hot prospect. I loved handmade paper and making it was low-technology, low-investment and labour-intensive work. It also had the virtue of using recycled paper as a key ingredient so I could help the environment while creating jobs.

Then my dream took a new form.

Peter, a marine mechanic and our skipper at the Lagos Motor Boat Club, approached me. Alec and I kept a small boat, which Peter maintained, and he accompanied us down the lagoon to our beach hut in the small village of Agaja most weekends during the dry season. But he had a problem that he brought to my attention.

'I cannot earn enough from just maintaining your boat, and there is no other work,' he said. 'Is there anything else I can do for you?'

I thought about it. Peter was slightly reserved, methodical rather than fast, of a solid build and round-faced with appealing brown eyes. I trusted his serious approach to his work and thought he might be just the person I needed. 'I want to try building another small business,' I told him. 'Maybe you could work for me.'

He wasn't the woman I had in mind to run my Nigerian start-up social enterprise, but he had proved reliable and I liked him. I decided to hire him, somehow.

'I'd like to try making handmade paper,' I said. 'Would you be willing to help me experiment?'

He agreed and it was a start; the venture had unofficially begun. It was only much later that I wondered why I had thought a boat mechanic might want to work as a papermaker.

O

My foundation team consisted of three men, Peter, Remi and Sonny – a noticeable lack of women. But while we were only developing the company's product and concept, I thought this imbalance would not matter too much. I employed several women in Strategyworks and there would still be an opportunity to get some women on board in my new venture.

I asked Peter if he knew some women who would be interested in working for me. He instead suggested I employ his 'brother' Remi. I never did discover their true relationship as the terms 'brother' and 'sister' might be applied to any relative, or even a friend from the same community. Remi was sturdy, a Nigerian Atlas for whom no job was unpalatable or too difficult.

Then there was Sonny, who came from the same impoverished area of Lagos – Ajegunle – but was not a relative, truly or figuratively, of the other two men; he was their friend. Sonny was Remi's opposite – a lanky but talented craft-worker and artist whose favourite attire of psychedelic hand-painted T-shirts suggested a detour from Woodstock.

In the spare time I snatched from my consulting work, the three young men and I spent a happy but dedicated year perfecting our paper recipes and techniques. Peter took the lead in experimenting, using shredded office paper (in ample supply in commercial Lagos) and different plant fibres and flowers found in my lush garden. I purchased our only specialised piece of equipment, a Hollander beater, to separate and stretch the plant fibres for paper pulp, from a supplier in New Zealand. We developed full-fibre papers, fibre-and-flower paper, a mix of recycled and fibre paper, pure-recycled paper and flower paper. We then moved on to working with natural dyes.

The variants multiplied. We had a number of eye-catching products, but would the sales follow?

Although the first customers murmured appreciatively at our decorative papers, they always chose the plain ones. We loved the products of our experiments but, if we were to make a business, the logical decision was to narrow our range.

O

In early 2004, it was time to get serious – to incorporate the business and invest more money. I took the team to the beach for a day and we brainstormed ideas for a business name over a lunch beneath palm trees.

'Nigerian Papers,' suggested Peter.

'Too limiting,' I countered. 'Let's think bigger than Nigeria.'

Actually, I had other reasons for my reservations. Although Nigeria was not a small market – its 2005 population was approximately 140 million and expected to reach about 400 million by 2050 – it did not have a warm international image. As I had discovered during my long bicycle trip, its African neighbours sometimes offered opinions that Nigerians were competitive and too successful, by fair means or foul. A paucity of sincere leadership and abundant examples of venal leaders looking after themselves and their cronies had corroded institutions, eroded the justice system and made corruption seem pervasive. Although I knew Nigeria was not alone in having such issues, it made foreigners who only heard the calamitous news stories wary of what Nigeria and Nigerians stood for. As a result, if we wanted to export, I did not think including Nigeria in the business name would contribute to international sales.

Remi's expressive face crinkled into a broad grin. 'What about Africa Papers? We can sell throughout Africa.' This got murmurs of approval, but it did not quite capture our imagination.

'Eko Papers,' suggested Sonny, ever the creative one. 'Eko is the original name for Lagos.'

'Our paper is environmentally friendly,' I mused. 'So how about Ekologika Papers?'

The guys loved it and the social enterprise was christened.

Actually, it was a limited liability company. Social enterprise, in which profits were made but reinvested for growth or used for a defined social purpose, did not exist as a corporate form in Nigeria. I was advised legal vehicles for social or not-for-profit entities existed but did not permit profits; the alternative was to be incorporated. Given my reservations about NGOs and aim to create a sustainable enterprise that funded itself, I chose the latter. I did not then realise what problems this might create for us. On the contrary, with our goals to create employment, help the environment and contribute philanthropically, I figured Ekologika Papers truly qualified as a social enterprise and the legal form of our operation was but a small detail.

Anyway, I had a more immediate concern. To achieve our social goals, we first had to find customers and make a profit.

O

'Madam, would you like anything else?'

A waiter's voice pulled me from my thoughts. While I had been lost in the past, dusk's deep shadows and dark corners had enveloped the club's deck. Night falls quickly and quietly in this part of Africa. The brutish damp air was now leavened by the feathery touch of a cool breeze, and the evening's banter at the brightly lit bar had begun.

'A Star, please,' I said. This was the local brand of beer I preferred. It was time for a sundowner – and sensible reality not lyrical dreams.

I found it hard to relate to my former self. I had spent ten years in Lagos from 1999 to 2009, but it was during the last five that I experienced an extraordinary business adventure. It would neither bring me wealth nor make the philanthropic impact I hoped, but it possibly had a bigger impact on me than all my previous work or travel life. Compared to cycling solo across Africa, it was a far wilder and more perplexing journey.

Like a naïve wildebeest on its first migration, I had felt both as unsteady as a newborn calf and as exhilarated as a young adult thundering over the grass-covered plains in the company of a million others. And, sometimes, I felt like a weary animal snapped at by the jaws of hungry crocodiles.

Despite being in my consulting profession for so many years, my business adventure had taught me sharp lessons about the vicissitudes of running a small business; the mismatch between how we see ourselves and our actions, and how others see us. It also had taught me about my limitations as a manager and an entrepreneur. I was exposed to the full spectrum of human nature, from amazing generosity, friendship, mentorship and philanthropy to the more base aspects of greed and betrayal. Deep relationships had been built and shattered along the way.

Now ten years since I left, and as Nigeria arrived once again in westerners' consciousness as both a venal, violent dystopia and a land of economic opportunity and energetic entrepreneurialism, I pondered why my story had unfolded the way it did.

My experiences gave me an unshakeable belief in Lagosians and Nigerian women and men in general to make a positive impact on their world. I was hopeful new visionary and honest leaders would transform the rules of the game by which Nigerians lived. There was too much vivacity, intelligence and too strong a sense of justice for it all to be held back by bad leaders and a corrupt system.

However, I had been naïve about corruption and the extent and nature of its debilitating spread. I came to understand that people, including foreigners, adapt their behaviours to the cultural, social, legal and economic system in which they find themselves. The Australians and other expatriates I met through my role as Honorary

Consul and my work were as varied in their responses to Nigerian opportunities and corrupt practices as were Nigerians themselves.

Everyone, I concluded, has choices but not all people's situations allow them to make the moral and ethical choice. It was more complicated than that.

I looked back towards the clubhouse restaurant, impatiently wondering when my friends would arrive. My eye caught a gossamer white glow shining through the haze-filled night sky above the building's roofline. It was the soft outline of the moon.

So many phases of the moon had passed during my years in Lagos as I followed my dream. I had watched the moon from this deck and from my beloved beach hut at Agaja against a backdrop of silhouetted palm trees and massed stars. And I had watched it from the balcony of my apartment as I listened to the muezzin hauntingly call the faithful to evening prayer. It was a familiar orb waxing and waning, changing regularly from the hint of renewal in a new moon, to the bright optimism of a full moon and then slowly ebbing back to the dark side. It was, I reflected, just like the fortunes of Lagos and the rhythms of my life – sometimes bright and sometimes bleak – in this pulsating megacity.

PART ONE

Earth Shine (2005)

Earth Shine is sunlight reflected back from the earth's surface, which allows us to discern the full shape of the moon, albeit dully, even though most of the moon's directly sunlit surface is away from us.[1]

CHAPTER ONE

Fresh Meat

Preparing cocoyams for planting does not mean that they are already planted.
— Nigerian proverb

'What about me?' I said as I closed the front door. We had barely said goodbye to Alec's boss, our dinner guest, but the bombshell he'd delivered had left me stunned. 'You didn't think to tell me that you were being transferred?'

The unwelcome news of yet another international job transfer – this time from Nigeria to Holland – had come out after Alec's boss had asked about the length of the lease on the company-sponsored house we shared.

'I think your successor wants to live in an apartment,' he added, giving me my first hint that life was about to change radically.

'I only found out today,' Alec protested. His resemblance to his compatriot Alex Ferguson (the famous and successful Scottish former manager of Manchester United Football Club) in his prime, swiftly changed to one where his team had conceded a goal to Chelsea. 'I was going to tell you.'

By late 2004 Alec and I had been living and working in Nigeria for nearly five years. As a senior gas executive and chemical engineer working thirty years for the same oil and gas multinational, Alec was used to a life of moving on whenever the company required it and, to him, five years was long for an expatriate assignment. But I was used to making my own career decisions as a management consultant who had never worked for anyone for longer than three years. Moreover, over the past two years I had invested in two Nigerian companies and my appointment as Honorary Consul for Australia in Lagos was being processed by Canberra.

I had a life in Lagos. While it had been intimidating and difficult at first, I now felt established. I was finally creating a fulfilling career in Africa, something I'd striven for so long to achieve. I might still be romanticising the opportunities, and thinking of myself as a modern Sir Richard Burton, but I knew the alternative route was not romantic at all. Was I now going to turn my back on Africa and run off to Europe like some woman in a Tammy Wynette song, standing by her man?

A fight was approaching like a swirling dust storm across a dry plain.

'Do you think I'm going to be a *haus frau* in Holland?' I asked. 'What about my businesses? Am I meant to close them down?'

It was Alec's way to avoid dissension in our relationship, and in his non-committal response I felt my resistance was being 'managed'. I tried to think calmly about the situation.

Over the past two years, the young professionals I had employed at Strategyworks had developed well under my leadership. If I left, they could probably look after themselves. Ekologika Papers, however, had been incorporated only earlier that year. If I shut up shop and put my staff out of work now, how would I feel? What about my motivation to create a business that provided stable and sustainable jobs? What about the underprivileged women I still intended to support? I had told my staff we were building something original and important? I needed to be credible, not just to outsiders but to myself, and if I closed down and followed Alec I'd feel like a fraud.

Beyond that, the opportunities for both businesses felt boundless. I was excited about consulting work opportunities that could result in a greater impact than comparable work for established European firms in mature markets. The edge, the risks and not knowing how the story would end enthralled me.

Yet I loved Alec. Our five years together in Lagos had been tumultuous as well as fun, and our relationship was deeper than ever. Beyond the relocation, I understood that his new role would involve a lot of travel. Being with him in Holland, I would still not see much of him, especially if I also travelled in a new consulting role. I found the alternative, an 'accompanying spouse', abhorrent.

The old prediction of my former Lagos boss also rang in my ears.

'You'll be a two-year expatriate,' the country partner at the international consulting firm had forecast. I had been a local-hire associate director and, having sold and delivered major consulting assignments, we were discussing my prospects with his firm. I protested that my future was in Africa as my career choices had been primarily Africa-focused since the mid-eighties, but he thought otherwise.

'You will leave when Alec leaves.'

I was captivated by my technicolour life in Lagos. Constantly inspired by what I was doing and achieving, I had dreams and ambitions and I would not let my staff down. I would not be a two-year or five-year expatriate. It took less than five minutes after Alec's boss's departure for my mind to be made up.

'I'm not leaving,' I said.

O

Saying these words had been easy. In the cold light of day, I needed to think again. Where would I live? How would I cope without all the household services and staff provided by Alec's company? Could

I make enough money to survive, let alone prosper in this expensive, tantalising city?

I had benefitted by living under the protective umbrella of Alec's corporate system. We had a lovely home with a lush garden, pool and a guesthouse that I had turned into my office. The paper workshop was located near the tennis court. We had an embarrassingly large domestic support team, all provided by the company and given a 'thirteenth month' gift of salary at Christmas to help cover the expense of going home to their villages – not to mention gifts such as rice sacks or home appliances. Our personal staff included one steward, two drivers, several gardeners, two generator operators, a pool cleaner and many gate security guards. Sixteen people supported the domestic life of two expatriates and two cats.

Living like this was not unusual for expatriates in a so-called 'hardship posting', where public services were eroded and personal security was not assured. Still, I had felt guilty living in gilded luxury and, to salve my conscience, I tipped my domestic staff well, offered gifts regularly on top of their company-provided salary and gave them ample time off. Indeed, I was so involved in their welfare that the large retinue sometimes also felt like an emotional burden and a source of stress.

If I stayed and faced a future without Alec's corporate perks or staff, I'd have a smaller retinue and a more humble lifestyle. This would not be unwelcome, but could I survive the general 'hardships' without a full staff and their services?

In my five years in Lagos, I had learned that every day an unexpected ball could suddenly spin into view. You batted it away or got hit in the face, but either way your day would not be the one you had planned. Nigerians and expatriates alike weathered inconveniences with a good bit of swearing and stoical flexibility but, for the expatriate employee, support staff undertook their resolution and the costs were borne by whatever firm employed them. Daily obstacles and irritants were as diverse as they were frequent.

'We've run out of water. Again.'

When there was no mains water or when our water tank ran dry, Alec would shout and I'd call his PA. For that morning, we would have to make do with a 'bucket shower' – throwing cups of water over ourselves – but later that day a tanker would arrive to refill our water tank.

'NEPA has taken the light, Madam.'

Our steward made this somewhat unnecessary announcement about electricity cuts whenever he served dinner by candlelight. The erratic service of the Nigerian Electric Power Authority, drolly known as Never Expect Power Again, was the reason we had generators. (Following restructuring it became known as PHCN, the Power Holding Company of Nigeria, and resilient Nigerian humorists then referred to it as Problem Has Changed Name.[1]) But even with a full-time generator operator, an uninterrupted power supply was not guaranteed.

'The generator man says we are out of fuel.'

That meant suffering a sweaty, sleepless night without air-conditioning, while Alec sprayed foul-smelling insecticide each hour to combat the mosquitoes that bit him (but not me). The next morning I'd call Alec's ever-willing PA to organise a fresh supply of diesel.

'The car needs new tyres, Madam.'

My driver regularly declared my vehicle in need of servicing or repairs. Lagos roads were as rough on a vehicle as spring gardening on manicured nails. I'd rearrange my plans and he'd organise the work by the company garage.

And, as for Lagosians, things were different and harder. Much, much harder.

Many had no water tank, no back-up generator and no car. From my workers, I knew that when there was no domestic water available, it would have to be carried in a bucket from a public pipe. When electricity was cut, they'd have a cold dinner and, as soon as it came back on (possibly several days later) they'd get up to iron their work clothes – even at three in the morning. When there was a petrol shortage the roads became clogged with vehicles queueing at filling stations. They spilled out like an extended used car lot and Danfo, the distinctive yellow minibuses and Molue, also bright yellow but larger buses, which then comprised Lagos public transport, were too few and far between to offer any other means of getting to work. I'd be amazed when my staff made it to the office – and then made it in the next day too.

'How long did it take you to get home last night?' I'd ask, knowing the 'go slow' – the traffic snarl – would have delayed them.

'Three hours.'

Three hours! If I were to lead an independent future, I'd need to absorb these new costs myself and be nearly as self-reliant and resilient as a Lagosian. For a start, I needed to learn how much a tanker of water cost, how to maintain a generator and how to find a good mechanic. After all, I knew I was not willing to carry water, do my ironing in the middle of the night or suffer a three-hour commute.

I wondered how much of this expatriate lifestyle I could truly live without.

O

It was not long after these reflections that my driver William, provided by Alec's company, announced he needed the weekend off to attend a funeral in his distant village. It was awkward timing as I had a Saturday client meeting scheduled. In Lagos, it seemed, people worked harder than God. Business carried on for six days and the seventh was reserved not for rest but for networking, either at a church or mosque for Lagosians, or at the beach or bar for expatriates.

My meeting was in Apapa, a mixed industrial and residential area adjoining the congested container port of Tin Can Island. To me it seemed a rough sailor's neighbourhood that I usually avoided. It was several miles from my home on Victoria Island, accessible by the expressway that went through Lagos Island. How would I get there? In the mood to see what services I could do without, I decided to drive myself. It couldn't be that hard, I thought, and let William go to his village.

The home I shared with Alec was on Victoria Island, universally referred to as VI. The island smelt of the Atlantic Ocean and had the bright, blinding light of an uninterrupted coastal sky. It was essentially a low-lying breakwater protecting the other islands of Lagos Lagoon and the mainland from the strong swells that travelled northwards, uninterrupted, from the Antarctic and arrived as crashing waves. VI had once been marshland but was in-filled to reduce mosquito infestation during colonial times, and a land bridge had been created between VI and the Lekki Peninsula to the east. The island was developed as an upscale residential area for homeowners and guesthouse patrons to enjoy the playground of Bar Beach, made famous in the classic sixties surfing movie *Endless Summer*.

Being something of a beach bum (or coastal connoisseur), when I first came to Lagos in 1999, I went in search of the best waves and sand. The enlargement of the port at Apapa and Tin Can Island demanded the development of a western breakwater, but this in turn had changed the prevailing wave patterns and resulted in dramatic erosion. The entire beach was gone – something that later was to become significant for me.

The state government's failure to maintain drainage systems all over Lagos meant mosquitoes once more were a problem as they bred in the stagnant water in blocked drains. On VI, during the wet season, it also meant the salty scent of the Atlantic Ocean was overlaid with the less fragrant smell of leaking raw sewage.

Yet despite the weak infrastructure of the place, there had been an influx of new money during the years I was in Lagos. It transformed VI from a run-down holiday resort to a bustling, congested commercial and retail centre. Every month would bring change: new restaurants and clubs, residences re-leased as commercial offices or bulldozed for redevelopment, unpaved roads sealed, and the main thoroughfares turned into divided highways. Its lustre in the dry season was dusty and the finish often rough, but this was the unruly, rhinestone style of Los Angeles in Lagos[2].

On VI, I felt optimistic about the future of Lagos and Nigeria and could believe in the locals' affirmation to relax. 'Every problem has an expiry date,' they promised.

Today, however, my journey would take me through some of the seedier parts of Lagos. In my compact four-wheel-drive car, and dressed in a smart suit, I headed out towards Independence Bridge and crossed over Five Cowrie Creek. My plan was to join the ring road along the south side of Lagos Island and then cross over another bridge to Apapa. I had done the journey with my driver several times before – surely it would be easy.

The first problem was the heavy, stop-start traffic with cars weaving in and out and hawkers trying to sell everything from snacks to gaudily framed mirrors and toilet seats. I hoped they would move out of my way fast enough when the time came.

'*Oyibo!*' one cried, spotting me driving near him. (*Oyibo* was a name given to white people.) Other hawkers saw me, too.

'*Oyibo!*' they also cried.

I reached over to lock my doors as I realised what an obvious spectacle I was in that part of town.

Once across the bridge I avoided the turn for Ikoyi and Awolowo Road, the residential area at the eastern end of Lagos Island. This elite remnant of colonial times now consisted of leafy roads named after pre-independence leaders, and verdant compounds that featured graceful, gently decaying mansions. Ikoyi possessed the style of Louisiana's old plantations transported to Lagos. But with new economic growth, developers' greed and corrupt planning authorities, these grand old homes were being bulldozed and replaced with high-rise, luxury apartment blocks and garish mansions. Traditional gardens were less prized by the ostentatious super-rich than concrete and glass. Many of my expatriate and Nigerian friends lived in Ikoyi, but I was not headed there that day. I took the ring road alongside Lagos Island's historic and commercial heart.

My foreign friends dismayed me when they revealed their own vision of Lagos, which resembled a large village of mud huts and thatched rooves. This was also wrong. Lagos, especially on this patch on Lagos Island, was a veritable African Manhattan. On one side of the elevated highway was Lagos Harbour and a view to the cranes, container ships and mountains of containers of Tin Can Island. On the other side was an impressive cityscape of high-rise buildings.

Lagos Island had been the original commercial district since Portuguese slave trading commenced in the fifteenth century and it continued to bustle with business throughout British colonialism's heyday in the nineteenth and early twentieth centuries. Broad Street, the main artery along which these skyscrapers were clustered, was Lagos's Wall Street – or had been. From the mid-nineties, due to failing infrastructure, rotten planning and a lack of civic services and controls, many banks and other businesses had abandoned the island and started again on VI. Lagos Island was not as salubrious up close as it looked from a distance. Today I would simply skirt by it – or so I thought.

A signboard offered a choice – a turnoff for Carter Bridge or continue straight ahead for Eko Bridge. But which of these two bridges took me west to Apapa? I chose Carter Bridge. It was not long before I realised this was a mistake.

Lagos Island has a Brazilian quarter where returning slaves had lived. Sadly, the once-impressive buildings were crumbling and covered in green and black mould. I now found myself amongst them.

On Saturdays, Lagos Island has a vibrant market in Balogun Street and the adjoining area. Traders spread goods onto already narrow roadways, and thoroughfares are thick with customers and petty traders. Alec and I had previously visited the market, pushed

our way through the crowds, and come away laden with gorgeous
bolts of mud cloth from Mali, locally produced waxed cloth and a
glorious selection of beads and baskets. But we had visited it on foot.
Now it seemed I was unwittingly visiting it in my car.

I struggled for an hour to navigate the roads, trying to find a way
out. I moved slowly along streets filled with men and women wearing
sober suits or jeans and T-shirts and steered clear of bemused traders
and their laid-out wares. I noticed traditionally attired men in dull
white and brown *agbadas* and women in wrappers and magnificently
flared head-ties like butterflies flashing in a rainforest canopy.

'*Oyibo!*' one man shouted at me through my closed window.
'Do you know where you are going?' I wound down my window
somewhat anxiously.

'Let me show you the way,' he offered.

Although grateful for some help, I would not let him in the car.
After some haggling, I agreed to a generous 'dash' (a tip or petty
bribe) and to pay his fare on an *okada* (a motorbike taxi) to travel
ahead of me through the maze of streets. An hour later, I emerged
shaken and rather shame-faced, onto Eko Bridge and made it to
my meeting rather late. I did not tell my client about my detour. I
figured that such an escapade, while fun on a bicycle journey, was
probably best avoided when trying to build credibility with a client.

But some good had come out of my little adventure. I knew that
once Alec left and William returned to the company pool of drivers,
I needed to employ a new driver.

While sitting in my garden paradise, I fingered the two draft business
plans I had worked hard at developing in the month since Alec's
announcement. I had made what I hoped were realistic assumptions
about investments and running costs for both businesses. I had tried
to be frugal and allowed myself a small domestic staff and an office

support team. As well as a driver and steward, I decided I needed a new accountant and someone like Alec's stalwart PA who would hound others to solve our problems – or fix them herself.

Looking at the future projected in the documents I held, I knew my life would certainly change. But would it be for the better? What further adventures or misadventures might I have? I wanted to stick by my original decision to stay, but I still had doubts.

Now I found unexpected emotional reassurance in the financial projections. Was that odd? Turning these dry plans into reality involved transferring my life's savings to a Nigerian bank. Contemplating a move to a rundown property, in a shabby neighbourhood of a disreputable city, in a country known for corruption, on a continent still perceived by outsiders as a basket case, I needed the comfort of projected profit.

Strategyworks, my core business, would support my modest salary, housing and living allowance if it grew. I employed only two young Nigerian consultants, but investments and higher outgoings demanded a larger operation. Significant investments for leases on a home and office, a generator and a personal vehicle were initially factored into my plan until I discovered that lease charges would cost more than a contemporary London pad. These were payable three years in advance and would house me only in a decrepit shell in need of wiring, lighting, tiling, large appliances and air-conditioning. It would certainly not be like my current Eden. I decided it would be ideal to find a single location for living and working to save money.

Service charges, although payable in advance annually, did not resemble those in London for a uniformed concierge and cleaning. Here in Lagos, a modest portion covered the costs of gatemen and maintenance, but mainly the charges were for generator diesel.

I was confident I understood the market opportunities and that the growth potential of my business could justify these investments, but could I get clients?

There was another opaque impediment, too.

'How will you cope with all the corruption?' asked friends and colleagues. I thought they echoed each other in a clichéd view of Nigeria. I felt more optimistic.

Corruption, to me, seemed an ugly and dismal game played by an elite group of public officials, extraordinarily wealthy business people and unprincipled politicians, which limited the economic potential of this powerful African country. Corruption provided sensational, titillating and discouraging stories but they seemed remote compared to my world. In my five years in Nigeria, I had been burned trying to get consulting contracts from federal agencies and had failed to win jobs due to my unwillingness to pay bribes. But I also witnessed corruption and self-interested behaviour amongst the personnel of foreign companies and international aid agencies. It took two hands to clap and corruption was not a failing unique to Nigerians.

By choosing the right private sector clients for Strategyworks and serving them well, I planned to operate cleanly. Yes, I needed a lucky break with one or two large consulting assignments but, given my market knowledge and promising leads, I believed that lucky break was just over the horizon.

Ekologika Papers was more problematic. Following Alec's departure, I developed a business plan that was essentially an educated guess. After only a year of rather tentative operation, I had rapidly gathered more detailed estimates of the costs of paper and products still under development and talked to potential customers to assess the market. I decided to let Ekologika Papers be subsidised by Strategyworks, sharing its premises for a nominal rent and giving a small share of my time for no salary. The good news was that we had uncovered substantial demand in the corporate seasonal gift market for products made with our paper. Instead of simply being a handmade paper company, we would convert our paper into Christmas cards, gift boxes, notelets, calendars and bound notebooks.

Instead of my normal, professional data-driven approach, I allowed myself to be propelled by a combination of instinct, experience and passion, although this was sacrilege for an analytical strategy consultant. I thought that if we delivered terrific handmade products to customers we'd be rewarded with more work and the profits would come quickly. I also believed that respect for my team and inclusiveness would deliver loyalty, strong teamwork and excellent results. I worried my heart was ruling my head. Would I really take the plunge and experience Lagos life outside this luxurious cage?

O

Two months after our dinner with Alec's boss, it was the beginning of a new year and rumours were rife about Alec leaving. I knew my staff was uncertain about their future. Alec was making a formal announcement to his staff soon, so I needed to make mine. What would I say? Even after all my research and planning, I still hesitated. What would happen to Alec and me? We had committed to see each other every six weeks, mainly in London where I kept a flat as a base, but with work pressures would it actually happen? With all the high overheads, would I be able to survive financially? Could I manage two businesses and the risks alone?

Alec was surprisingly silent with his opinions, although silence can communicate clearly too.

My friend Dapo had been more forthright.

I had known Dapo since I arrived in Lagos, through an introduction from a mutual friend. He ran a small printing business and his experience and expertise was often relevant to Ekologika Papers. A snappy dresser in his late forties, Dapo often sported a fedora that made him resemble an African Indiana Jones. He proved a sardonic observer of society and was scrupulously honest. True to form, however, when I shared my plans with him, he was sceptical about my chances of success.

'You will be fresh meat,' he said – meaning that I would be eaten alive.

With this daunting thought in mind, the day came to let my staff know my plans. Feeling nervous, I started with my senior Ekologika Papers staff and invited Peter, Remi and Sonny to a meeting in our garden workshop.

I looked at Peter, who avoided my eyes and fiddled with an oily rag. He was my touch paper, both the first employee in this enterprise and symbolic of its core purpose of creating jobs for those who needed them most. I might not yet have the female employees I intended, but in the very first year Peter and I had successfully experimented with making papers and forged a strong bond. I had seen his character up close and wanted to be as dependable as him.

I took a deep breath.

'I am not leaving Lagos,' I said. 'I am staying, and your jobs are safe.' There; it was done. There was no going back now.

As I continued talking – about my plans and how I needed their commitment – I saw the anxiety fall from their faces.

'We'll make this work,' interrupted Peter.

'Together,' Remi and Sonny chimed in. We laughed and courage once more welled up inside me.

I was in the mood for adventure and I *would* prove Dapo wrong, I vowed. This time I'd exchange my cycling gear for a business suit, and instead of a solo journey it was going to be a fabulous team ride.

But secretly I did wonder. Would I be steak tartare?

CHAPTER TWO

No *Wahala!*

One must row in whatever boat one finds oneself.
– Nigerian proverb

'No *wahala!*' said Philippe, my new Lebanese landlord, a large, avuncular and seemingly unflappable man as he examined my front door.

Alec left in late February and had been gone several weeks. My new solo life in Lagos had begun. It was Sunday evening, the first weekend after moving into the furnished flat. Philippe had come around to discuss various issues, including a damaged lock. *Wahala*, a Yoruba word for 'problem' or 'trouble' and used all over Nigeria in pidgin English, was something Philippe apparently dealt with imperturbably.

We went to the kitchen and I showed him the microwave that would not work.

'No *wahala*, I will replace it,' he announced.

Philippe had rented me two separate flats – a furnished one for my own apartment and an unfurnished one for my office and paper workshop. Although about three kilometres apart, both were on VI, with full services provided. He owned and operated the generators and back-up generators at both sites, and organised the security, water supply and all maintenance.

Philippe had driven a hard bargain.

For nearly six weeks I had negotiated with a different landlord to rent a rundown house that would house me and both my businesses – my ideal scenario for saving money. The renovation plans had been drawn up and a builder readied to begin, all awaiting the signing of the lease. Then, without warning, that landlord reneged on our deal.

With Alec leaving and me being evicted from our former home, I'd had few alternatives, so when I saw Philippe's properties my bargaining power was weak and my nerves were shredded. But the sum he demanded for fifteen months' rent for two apartments was what I had planned to pay for a three-year lease of the house, including refurbishment, and have a generator at the end of it.

It upped the ante even further in what was, for me, a high-stakes game.

'You want to focus on your businesses, Pamela, and getting money in,' Dapo had advised, adopting a role as counsellor. He thought it wise to accept Philippe's terms and he offered some compelling reasons. 'You don't want to spend time with generator maintenance men or tracking who stole the diesel.'

My first impression had been that the apartment was dull. Decoration seemed to be from the seventies, in shades of brown and cream. But it was clean and neat and far surpassed any other living space I had seen on offer. I was still unpacking and getting used to it, as was Tippy my tortoiseshell cat, who was staying with me.

'No *wahala*,' Philippe had said about Tippy. I had met quite a few Nigerians who didn't like cats, and some prospective landlords had already vetoed her occupancy. Philippe's relaxed attitude, even more than Dapo's advice, had sealed the deal.

'Philippe is very correct—he will look after you,' another friend had promised when she had heard I was in the market for premises.

It was a curious expression, meaning that his word was reliable and that he did things 'correctly'.

'All the people here are my friends,' Philippe assured me. 'I used to live in a different compound where nothing ever worked and the landlord would never fix it. So I have taken on the head lease here, made the improvements and run the services myself, and all my friends have come to stay.'

Indeed, I felt a stranger. The other residents seemed to be young Lebanese men, some with families, who left for work early with their drivers in their company Peugeots and came back late. I had always mixed with my Nigerian staff, colleagues, clients, friends and Anglo expatriates who worked in oil and gas from Alec's business world. Now this was an unfamiliar milieu, but perhaps not an unfriendly one. Lebanese were the backbone of West African foreign-owned, medium-sized enterprise, and often enthusiastic patrons of the late-night clubbing circuit. I looked forward to getting to know them.

Philippe, when marketing the property to me, had seemed especially proud of his power supply system. 'We have two generators,' he said and went on to explain his switchover system. '*Alhaji* will sleep through a mortar attack. I have organised a loud alarm to wake him.'

Many Lagos gatemen, responsible for opening the gates and flipping between NEPA and a generator during the night as the mains power came and went, were northern, poorly educated but pious Muslims. Some, despite their relative poverty, had somehow assembled the resources to make the once-in-a-lifetime haj to Mecca and gained the respected title of *Alhaji*. Philippe was confident that his gateman, whom I only knew as *Alhaji*, could be trusted to look after the generators.

'There are two different noises—one so that he knows to flip from NEPA to generator, and another to switch from the main generator to the back-up,' Philippe said.

In my first week at the flat I had become used to waking to the loud cries of the alarm, sometimes a double clang, and other times something like an air raid siren. Inevitably, a few minutes later, I would hear Philippe add his alarm call to the noise. '*Alhaji*! The generator.'

Despite his claim, it did not seem that even these elaborate alarms could wake the gateman up.

This Sunday evening, I showed Philippe the gas stove and hob in the tiny kitchen. 'I cannot make it work,' I said, a little ruefully, suspecting the solution might be in a concealed power switch, but tired of a week of cold meals.

'No *wahala*,' he said. 'Have you connected a gas bottle?'

I grinned sheepishly and blushed. If water is delivered in a truck why did I think gas should be supplied through the mains? I guessed one of the sixteen staff in my old life had handled this.

O

The following Monday morning the wet season announced its early April arrival with a massive crack of thunder and a lightning show, which turned to heavy and persistent rain. My commute through VI, unlike that of my staff who lived on the mainland, was usually short. My new driver, Tayo, was a serious, mature man with experience behind the wheel, but I knew that this weather meant trouble.

We set off but made little headway. A battered Mercedes taxi and a yellow Danfo, both with flooded engines, blocked all progress at the major intersection of Adeola Odeku and Akin Adesola. The street drains overflowed and the intersection was so deeply underwater that it looked as though VI was returning to its origins as a bog. The traffic policeman in charge of marshalling us had not arrived; he was probably caught in the chaos too. Vehicles from all directions weaved around the stalled traffic. Their drivers, skilled at manoeuvring cars through the narrowest of openings, were undisciplined and competitive, sometimes blocking the way themselves. Horns blared, drivers shouted intimidatingly and screamed their indignation. It was a Lagosian concerto I would have been happy to miss.

We eventually managed to crawl along a badly potholed side street in front of the Lagos campus of the Nigerian Law School. The car rocked and jolted as we fell into submerged pits. I dropped my newspaper and grabbed at the roof strap. Even being a passenger was hard work. The journey felt as though we were in the bush, not in a rush-hour commute of the commercial heart of sub-Saharan Africa's largest city.

I watched Lagosians emerge from their Danfo with rolled-up trouser legs, or dresses hitched above the knees, holding jackets, briefcases or handbags over their heads to pick their way through the flooded streets. One woman staggered as her leg dropped into a flooded, muddy drain but she picked herself up and kept going. I saw an aggressive Danfo living up to its name – Danfo in Yoruba means 'hurry'. Its speedy progress through a deep puddle sent a wave of water crashing onto an office worker seated on the back of an *okada*.

A loud siren prompted Tayo and the other drivers to edge right and allow a dark blue police car through. Not an emergency vehicle, it was the Mopol, or Mobile Police, who were assigned as a security escort (and a faster means of travel) for some 'Big Man'. Big Men were those who held senior positions or were very wealthy and powerful. The term was also an epithet full of envy and opprobrium. The police in the escorting vehicle wore dark blue uniforms and, despite the dull day, dark sunglasses, and brandished large automatic weapons outside their open windows. The muzzles drifted carelessly and menacingly towards road users.

I had been wary of Mopol after hearing about several incidents in which pedestrians were shot by the accidental discharge of these weapons. Tayo knew I was antsy and waited for the following black LandCruiser with dark tinted windows – the vehicle of choice for the Big Men – to pass.

Finally, we turned into the street where my office was located. It was a narrow, unpaved road filled with parked cars and NEPA poles draped in tangled strands of wire and fixed with hand-written signboards advertising welders and electricians. Street vendors sat patiently, damp under their umbrellas and rust-roofed shacks, selling recharge cards for mobiles and sweet bread or plantain chips to hungry workers. There were even plastic shoes and buckets for sale, which would be useful items in this weather.

Our journey of less than three kilometres had taken one hour. I wondered how my employees coped with their longer commutes without my vehicle's air-conditioning.

This jerky, slow and frustrating ride had exhausted me.

We reached our compound, which was identifiable by two great black gates. It showed an anonymous face to the street and was secured by high walls topped with razor wire. Tayo tooted and the gates were opened by the gateman.

Strategyworks and Ekologika Papers now occupied the second floor of an old apartment building. Philippe had his office on the ground floor. Noisy construction work hammered nearby. Only on weekends, when the traffic and work stopped, did it feel as it once had as a fully residential area: peaceful.

Leaving the cold, dry car and stepping into the damp, clammy air outside, I knew my curly hair would immediately spring into an unflattering, frizzy mop. Lagos workdays started early, often by 7.30am, but certainly by 8am. Now it was 8.30am and I was late.

'Thank you, Tayo,' I said. 'Tomorrow let's try to leave by 7am.'

'Yes, Madam,' he replied.

Tayo never questioned my demands, although I sometimes questioned them myself. How could I ask him to pick me up even earlier?

But another voice admonished me. It's his job.

Tayo had long hours on the job but spent many of them sleeping. I reasoned that if I started trying to 'save' my workers from the difficulties of their daily lives, we would not have a business, and without a business there would be no jobs. It was, however, a difficult balance to strike.

O

I walked into my office, once a three-bedroom apartment and the second property rented from Philippe. We had used my old sofa and a potted plant to demarcate the reception by the front door. The dining area contained our circular conference table and the living room became an open-plan office area for my Strategyworks consultants. The first and largest bedroom was for Ekologika Papers's graphic design, sales and conversion work – the process of printing our paper and using it to create cards, calendars and notebooks. The workshop for making and storing paper was downstairs at the rear of the property in what had been the staff quarters. The second bedroom now housed my new PA and accountant, while I worked out of the smallest bedroom in the far corner.

Despite the rainy start, the morning light (always bright on VI) illuminated our meeting space and, as I put my umbrella away, I gazed around proudly. It had been a rush job to have Philippe finish the painting and tiling before we moved in, but while the office was still a bit bare, the potted plants softened the space and the new wooden desks arranged into two three-person workstations looked very professional.

Deola and Feyi, my two bright consultants, looked up expectantly from their desks.

'Good morning. How are you?'

'Good morning. I'm fine. How are you?'

These polite salutations may have stemmed from colonial days or were a reflection of Nigeria's mannered, hierarchical and formal society. But they were always exchanged prior to any engagement, whether in person with a friend, colleague or stranger, or over the phone.

'Let's get together at 9am,' I then reminded them. A Monday morning team meeting was scheduled, and I was anxious to get the day started. Deola volunteered to call the senior team together.

Deola, self-confident and experienced in strategy consulting, and Feyi, a recent MBA graduate, were my new recruits and the entire Strategyworks consultancy team. I had expected to hire four consultants by now. Unfortunately, my two original consultants – fearing I was not serious about staying in Nigeria – had sent out their resumes and accepted jobs too good to refuse. I was pleased that their experience with my tiny firm had landed them such prime roles, but disappointed to lose their capabilities. Given my plans for growth, it was a setback to square one.

I went on to greet Patience, my new accountant, a middle-aged woman whose small stature belied a steely bark I had seen her use on Peter. I was pleased to have her on my team as her predecessor was so lazy and incompetent that he hadn't even developed a proper chart of accounts. She was thrifty with company money, had a huge appetite for work and I looked forward to having my finances in proper order.

'It was not raining on the mainland,' she explained as to how she and the others made it in before me. To avoid the longest commutes, many of my staff left their homes as early as 5am. They left the office between 4pm and 5pm in the afternoon while I usually left between 7pm and 8pm. I did not ask them to work harder or longer hours than I worked myself.

I looked into the Ekologika Papers office.

The company had grown from the foundation team of three. There were three casual staff in the papermaking workshop including James, a cheerful young man with a ready smile, who seemed a hard worker. Chuks, another staff member introduced by Peter, worked in the large conversion room. He was an engineering graduate, more highly educated and computer literate than his peers, necessary for the more technical work of printing and making paper products.

While Remi was most often to be found downstairs in the workshop with James and the other casuals I now employed, Chuks, Peter and Sonny mainly laboured in the conversion room. That morning no one was there. Had they been delayed by the traffic?

'They are in the workshop,' called Patience, reading my mind. I set my bag down in my own office, turned on my computer and gazed out the window to the dense foliage of the mango tree outside. It had stopped raining, but I knew traffic chaos would reign for the rest of the day.

Soon, it was time for the meeting to begin. I was very keen on treating everyone equally and having a flexible approach to both organisations. I asked the consulting staff to help plan and run Ekologika Papers as necessary, and the paper staff to help with printing documents or readying equipment for Strategyworks workshops. A single team brought efficiencies and encouraged mutual respect, and a weekly meeting was the right place to plan for both businesses.

Deola, Feyi and I gathered at the round meeting table. Where were the others? I had seen Patience talking on the telephone, but Peter and his colleagues were still absent.

Deola said she had sent Tayo to summon them.

Patience joined us and, after several minutes of exchanging pleasantries, I decided to get started.

'Here's the agenda,' I said and handed out a prepared sheet.

We were interrupted as Peter arrived, then again as Gloria joined us. My right-hand woman and PA, Gloria, had only been working for me a few weeks, but I wondered how I had done anything without her. Aggressive and assertive by nature, she could source anything in a Lagos market and complete any task the same day. Alone, she bullied Philippe into getting the office refurbished on time, then organised and supervised our move, including the purchase of new equipment. As I had learned from working with Alec's PA, having someone who could get things done in a professional environment was invaluable.

'Madam. Madam!'

It was difficult to get people to call me by my first name. All my staff referred to me as Madam or Ma or Aunty. I had learned that in Nigerian culture using the first name of someone who was your boss or your elder was perceived as rude. I felt it made me too distant and was not in keeping with my intention to create a flatter hierarchy. But while I explained my reasoning and persisted in asking, they persisted with their use of their preferred polite title for me.

I turned around. Would I never be allowed to get on with this meeting? It was Edward, my steward, who reported to the office to clean it first thing in the morning and then used my driver to take him back to the flat to clean there.

'I have finished the cleaning here and will now go to your apartment, but Mr Tayo needs fuel money,' he said.

'Thanks Edward,' I said and fished in my bag for the money. A cross thought fleeted by – why hadn't Tayo asked for payment on my arrival?

It was now after 10am. I took a deep breath and sat down.

Remi, Sonny and Chuks finally joined us. The whole team gathered at the meeting table, looking as committed as a gang of crested cockatoos waiting to swoop down on the wheat field. What was an hour's delay?

Suddenly a grinding sound filled the air, followed by loud explosions. We all let out startled squawks.

In a horrible instant, floor tiles cracked and pushed up jaggedly from the floor, popping sequentially in a line of debris across the formerly neat office space. The explosion rippled towards the reception and under the potted plant by the door, making it tilt at a disturbing angle.

Were we in the midst of an earthquake? Was the concrete foundation breaking? We leapt up, screeching as loudly as the breaking floor.

'Outside!' I shouted.

Deola and Feyi high-tailed it out the front door, followed rapidly by Patience, Gloria, Peter and the other staff members.

But the disruption was soon over, and the only noise came from the air-conditioners. I was alone with more unanswered questions.

Was the floor about to cave in? I'd investigate later. I swiftly followed my team downstairs. They were huddled in the rainy driveway just as Philippe, having heard the pandemonium, emerged from his office.

'I think the concrete slab on our floor has cracked,' I told him.

'Let's go and see,' he said sombrely and offered no opinion. I followed him gingerly up the stairs and opened the door to see a long line of tiles buckled and broken.

'It is the air-conditioning,' Philippe pronounced. 'The office was humid when we laid the tiles, and now the drier cold air has contracted the adhesive.' He sounded like a judge passing sentence on our air-conditioners. 'The adhesive contracted but the tiles had nowhere to go—so they buckled.' Then a smile twitched at his lips.

I could now see that the concrete slab below was visible and not cracked. Presumably he was right. I could only see the mess. Would I learn to take any of this new and independent life in my stride?

'We will lay new ones,' said Philippe, his features breaking into a grin. 'No problem, Pamela. No *wahala.*'

CHAPTER THREE

Everyone Worked Hard

It is the work of one's hands that determines what one eats for dinner—for some it is pounded yam, for others it is pounded plantain or nothing.

– Nigerian proverb

It was May, two months after my new independent life in Lagos had begun. I'd just arrived at the Lagos Motor Boat Club after an intense three-day workshop. The friendly security guard had waved my car through to the busy parking area behind the low boundary wall, which was pitted by vehicle swipes and years of neglect. The shabby two-storey clubhouse dating from the colonial period suggested a club on its uppers, but appearances were deceptive.

As we drove in, I saw the stylish vehicles – four-wheel-drives and Mercedes – and the forty-foot-plus powerful motorboats on trailers under newly built pens. There was serious money in this watering hole, even if the mentality came straight from the fifties.

Walking through the clubhouse to the waterside patio, I spotted Dapo at the round, thatched bar that overlooked the more elegant boats moored at the club's jetties in Five Cowrie Creek. The club's ambience was very different from bars or hotels in Abuja, the country's capital. There, illicitly leaked oil revenues lubricated all relationships and a busy furtiveness suggested the Monday to Friday customers comprised grifters or those there for hard graft. Indiana

Jones would not look out of place in the Hilton Abuja's lobby while he waited to take off in his biplane to search for the Lost Ark.

'Everyone worked hard but nothing was achieved,' I heard Dapo say as I greeted another member I knew. Dapo enjoyed his own comment and laughed as he rocked back and forth on his bar stool then reached for his glass and took a long draught of golden Gulder beer. Dapo's printing business still used offset equipment and served a stable of regular business customers with forms, brochures and, in the last quarter of any year, calendars. I enjoyed talking with him about our businesses and today would be no exception.

'David,' Dapo called to the dapper barman, who seemed to know all the regulars by name. 'A Star for Madam.'

Dapo was a Gulder man but he knew my favourite tipple. Although I seldom drank beer elsewhere, I'd gained a taste for cold African beer during my bicycle journey just over a decade before. David put down the beer and glass and I saw that both were already encased in condensation forming in the humid evening air. As I felt like Lawrence of Arabia emerging from the Empty Quarter, I gladly accepted his round.

'How are you, David?' I asked. 'How's the family?'

He filled my glass. 'My wife is expecting our fifth baby,' he said quietly. I wondered how he could afford it on the club's basic wage.

'Will you bring something for me, Madam?' he murmured while he wiped the bar near me.

Members were not permitted under club rules to offer tips to staff. But only by breaking the rules could family men like David survive.

A few years previously, I had been on the committee of the club. While other committee roles were elected by members and derived their title from their responsibility – such as mooring member or entertainment member – this old-fashioned club only seconded a sole woman to the committee.

She was the 'Lady Member'.

I took on the appointment cautiously, not knowing what it would entail. I should have guessed. I was responsible for staff uniforms and table linen. That said, I did not allow the committee's bias to inhibit my actions and ended up on a sub-committee managing the club's refurbishment. Our collective efforts had lifted the club from an even more rundown state at the turn of the millennium.

'Lady member. How are you?'

I left my beer and went over to shake the hand of the club's secretary. He lunged at me and lifted me off my feet. Sloshed like a deck in a force ten gale, I thought. Landed, I unruffled my feathers.

'Are you not going to greet me now?' exclaimed the treasurer, another of my committee friends, less inebriated but still jolly.

'Your excellency, how are you?' said another businessman I knew well. I was chuffed by the grand epithet but also taken aback. Dapo knew about my prospective appointment as Honorary Consul and, a bit prematurely, must have let some other members know.

I had recently received word from the Australian High Commissioner in Abuja that my appointment was delayed – again. Since the role had been mooted over two years before, delays in my appointment had occurred due to the need to find premises for the new Australian High Commission in Abuja, the appointment of a new High Commissioner to Nigeria, security checks and now, I learned, to a strategy review of the Department of Foreign Affairs and Trade (DFAT). McKinsey & Company, an international consulting firm, was undertaking it. As strategy consulting assignments like those I undertook for my clients often delayed decisions, I could hardly complain. But after this much time I was starting to wonder if I would ever be appointed.

I moved on with a series of handshakes and air kisses. Despite its tired chauvinism, I felt at home and welcome at this bar. Although, I was largely oblivious to the ethnic origins of people I knew, I had learned that club membership was principally drawn from the elite of Lagos's Yoruba, one of Nigeria's largest ethnic groups.

Nigeria was formed as a federation of the British colonial northern and southern protectorates in 1914, and the protectorates themselves were only created at the beginning of the twentieth century during the great carve-up of Africa by European powers.

In 1870, only ten per cent of Africa had been under European control. Following a conference convened in Berlin in 1884 to discuss humanitarian issues such as slavery (but really to resolve rules for African colonisation), the unseemly scramble to partition Africa began. By 1914, an incredible ninety per cent was under European control. Thus, the Federation of Nigeria, like so many African nations, was entirely a foreign conqueror's construct. But, unlike many other African nations, its national boundaries enclosed a human diversity greater than that found in the whole of Europe.

Within its one million square kilometres, Nigeria enclosed hundreds of different ethnic and linguistic groups (some having populations in the hundreds, some in the millions), as well as Islamic, Christian and pagan religions, various cultural practices, and several sophisticated, powerful kingdoms and empires (and the history of those that preceded them). In the north, principally populated by Hausa and Fulani people, were the 1000-year-old Kingdom of Bornu and the Sokoto Caliphate, an affiliation of largely independent emirates pledging allegiance to the Sultan of Sokoto. The Caliphate became a supreme political force in the 100 years prior to conquest by Britain.

The southwest of Nigeria, together with southern parts of modern-day Togo and Benin, was Yoruba country. The origin of the Yoruba people, related in their own oral history, was as remarkable as it was disputed[1]. It included a story that Oduduwa, the ancestor from which all Yoruba are descended, fled from Mecca at some time after Mohammed's death, and was a Nubian, Phoenician, Chadian, Jew or Christian, depending on one's interpretation and source, and settled in Ife (also known as Ile-Ife), a town some hours' drive north of Lagos. As the Yoruba people spread over the forests and plains towards the coast and created multiple kingdoms, the *Oòni* (or King) of Ife, claiming direct descent from Oduduwa, remained as the first amongst Yoruba kings. Ife was a substantial settlement between the twelfth and fourteenth centuries and clay, copper and bronze heads and masks and glass beads from the period are testament to the artistic and technical advancement of the kingdom.

With time, power struggles and trade with Europeans (from the fourteenth to eighteenth centuries the principal trade was slaves and gold exchanged for European manufactured goods), kingdoms with access to the Guinea coast became more powerful. The Benin Kingdom (centred on modern day Benin City and not the neighbouring country of Benin) of the Edo people reached its zenith in the fifteenth century and is known for its iconic bronze wall plaques and the life-size bronze heads of its Oba. It remained a significant power until British annexation in 1897. The neighbouring Oyo Empire of the Yoruba peaked in the eighteenth century and its decline in the nineteenth century was marked by court intrigues and war amongst vassal kingdoms. It too became a British protectorate in 1888.

Meanwhile, the southeast was home to the more loosely organised but very populous Igbo people, whose history was undoubtedly as complex and as disputed as the Yoruba. The Niger Delta was also home to many smaller ethnic groups, of which the Itsekiri and Ijaw are just two.

What a complicated ethnic diversity. Its subtleties and disputed histories fascinated me, though I could never hope to fully understand. And world history suggested such marvellous diversity was difficult to cohere and rule, not unlike the less diverse European Union.

Lagos started life as a Yoruba fishing village called Eko but, as the entry point for the first European settlers and with its trade economy and status as the Federation of Nigeria's first capital, it became a melting pot of the country's inhabitants. But the Yoruba people remained dominant – certainly in the city's power structures – and today, back at the boat club, membership was principally Yoruba.

My friends at the club were bankers, Senior Advocates of Nigeria (SANs) and businessmen. These people were working hard and achieving things mainly in business and politics, bringing investment, growth and jobs to this city-state. The sharp suits, British public-school accents and murmured conversations suggested an outdated British Overseas Airways Corporation departure lounge, perhaps at the old Croydon Aerodrome (London Airport), while they waited to be called for a Constellation flight to Cyprus. I always listened to their conversations with interest and fascination. Now, as I took a bar stool beside him, I returned to Dapo's comment.

'So, what have you been working hard at without achieving anything?' I asked.

'Well, very little, Pamela,' said Dapo, with a grimace. 'My workers!' he sighed. 'We had a major stationery order to deliver—by today. We completed it, but no thanks to them.'

Harsh, Dapo, I thought, picking up my beer.

'All through the week, there was one problem after another,' he continued. 'The machine broke down because they misused it. Paper was trimmed incorrectly. The wrong paper was used. They even chose the wrong plate. I ended up on the factory floor supervising it myself.'

I laughed at his diatribe against his workers and toasted his efforts. I then told him about my latest troubles in Strategyworks when running a client workshop. I started the story from my first phone call from the handyman.

O

'Sorry Madam.'

My heart sank. What could be the problem now? Thomas, my Nigerian handyman, had been out of touch all day and I had been trying to reach him urgently.

'My phone ran out of credit,' he explained.

I pressed on. 'Is the wall constructed now?'

'No, Madam. We had a problem.'

Thomas had fixed nearly every carpentry, plumbing and electrical problem I had suffered during my years in Nigeria. He had recently been employed to construct a prefabricated wooden wall for the final team-building exercise to be used on a Strategyworks retreat focused on strategy and team-cohesion.

Taking place tomorrow.

The workshop was for the senior management team of a Lagos subsidiary of an international bank and the stakes were high for Strategyworks – and me. Having invested so much, I badly needed this retreat to be a success to build our reputation and lead to more work.

But conceptual strategy seemed to be taking a back seat to carpentry chaos. We had had a trial erection of the wall – a four-metre high obstacle, which executives would climb over *if* they worked effectively together – at the office the day before. Now disassembled, the wall was Thomas's job to transport and re-erect at the venue, a beach resort an hour or so east along the Lekki Peninsula.

Thomas had left our office at 10am. I had given him an ample budget to transport the pieces to the site.

Belts and braces, I thought. What had gone wrong?

'We got stopped by the police, Madam, several times. The driver did not have his papers. They wanted us to go to the station. We had to pay, Madam.'

It was now 6pm.

'We just got to the hotel, Madam. The truck broke down. It was too bad.'

Thomas had gone to Lekki Market to buy a new part for the truck and got stuck in traffic. To save time, he and the driver had fixed the truck by the side of the road.

'That driver, I told him his truck was no good,' he added. 'It has cost me much money.'

I assured him I would pay for these extras. But was the wall erected?

'It is too dark, Madam. There are no lights on the beach. This place is not safe. We will unload the wood tonight and I will come back tomorrow to erect it then.'

The line 'dropped', as the local expression went. Thomas was gone.

The next morning my ever on-time driver Tayo, reliable PA Gloria and I stuffed ourselves into my CRV for the trip to the resort. In addition to our kit for the other outdoor team-building exercises, we brought workbooks, caps and T-shirts for the participants, Strategyworks signs, various stationery including a flipchart stand and paper, a projector, laptops and our overnight bags. We were packed tight as peppercorns in an over-filled grinder and the journey took its toll. We arrived at 10am, three hours ahead of our client, as finely crushed black and white pepper.

I saw the planks of the deconstructed wall piled under a palm tree on the beach. There was no sign of Thomas.

There was also no sign of Deola or Feyi, who had assured me they could make their own way. Where were they? I tried to ring them.

'This number is not available. Please try again later.'

This was a familiar message. Mobiles were a wonderful innovation in Nigeria, but I knew this message by heart. Unexpectedly popular subscriber growth meant the network infrastructure struggled to keep up and coverage was often patchy. There were other issues, too. Excessive voice traffic at peak times caused connection failure and 'dropped' lines. Without reliable power, people also struggled to keep their handsets charged. As most people were on pay-as-you-go contracts they often ran out of credit and so 'flashed' me instead, ringing once or twice before hanging up, and expected me to ring them back.

In addition to this, basic human nature was at work. If people did not want to be contacted, they simply switched their phones off.

Tayo unloaded the car while Gloria and I went to the reception and then to the conference room. Gloria, Deola and I had searched the Lagos hotels for a good venue that offered suitable outdoor space for the exercises we'd planned, food agreeable to a mixed Nigerian and expatriate group, quality bedrooms with air-conditioning and modern conference facilities. The neighbouring country of Benin, a former French colony, had a cool aesthetic – a melange of French chic and rich and long traditional culture and styles – and offered venues that ticked all the boxes. Savvy travellers seeking style would like Benin's commercial coastal city of Cotonou, but my client thought it was too far away, so we had stayed in Lagos.

The choice there, especially for venues with outdoor space, was limited. Our conference room was fine – if I was a Kalgoorlie goldrush brothel keeper.

Red velvet curtains made the room dark and the air was humid and close. It was small for a group of twelve executives. The walls were covered in blistered off-white plaster, and the lighting totalled about forty watts. The conference table – also covered in red velvet – wobbled, and inspection showed it was plywood on flimsy legs. The floor was carpeted in red nylon tuft with brown patches, evidence of a leaking ceiling, and was also mouldy. At least we had a beachside setting.

Gloria and I both screwed up our noses at the smell of the room. We sprang into action and tied back curtains, switched on the air-conditioning, removed the velvet tablecloth and replaced it with a bright tie-dyed cotton one in blue.

Cynthia, the young events coordinator of the hotel, entered the room as we laid out the participants' workbooks. 'The flipchart stands you ordered are coming from VI,' she announced. 'But the van might be caught in traffic.'

Would I ever see the additional flipchart stands?

Being crushed in the car by all our equipment had been worth it. I sent Tayo to bring in my own stand. At least, I would have one flipchart.

It was time to set up the laptop, projector and screen, but this too presented a problem.

'Where are the UPS, extension cord and screen we ordered?' asked Gloria. She was referring to the Uninterruptible Power Supply, an essential piece of kit for operating sensitive electronic equipment, providing emergency stored power when there were mains or generator interruptions or fluctuations.

'We don't have them,' Cynthia said without apology.

We would just have to manage, which meant probable blackouts during power outages and surges that might destroy the electrical equipment while we projected onto the bubbled plaster wall. Making a mental note to add these items to future logistics lists, I plugged my laptop power cable into the wall socket.

A shock surged up my arm.

O

'Madam! I am here.'

Thomas walked in easy strides down the beach towards me with a broad smile. Having sent efficient Gloria to check on lunch, I was still rubbing my numb arm while I checked on the whereabouts of my team. It was noon.

'It was the traffic, Madam. It is too bad near Lekki Market.'

I left him to start construction of the wall and went to greet Deola and Feyi, who had just arrived.

'It was the traffic, Pamela,' said Deola. Despite the midday sun, I was a bit cool. Why hadn't they left earlier, like me? After all, preparation was something I relied on them for. I took them to the beach to run them through the team-building exercises and found Thomas in a dither.

'Why haven't you started, Thomas?'

'I cannot find the bolts,' he replied. 'I think in the dark last night, I must have left the bolts on the truck.'

My surface calm was as thin as cracking ice. My credibility and business were at stake. I gave Thomas the money to buy more bolts at Lekki Market and sent him to Tayo to be driven, quickly I hoped. Having done a fraught dry run of the team-building exercises with Deola and Feyi, I rushed up the path from the beach to the hotel. The client's mini bus had arrived.

Slowing down, I greeted Kevin, the MD, and his group of Nigerian and expatriate executives with a bright smile and handshakes for all.

Inwardly I heard my own wail: 'What the hell am I going to do without a wall?' I needed a big team-building finale and the wall was *it*.

'We're looking forward to this,' Kevin grinned. He had the immense energy of a new arrival to Nigeria and was ambitious to lead the bank's growth during his tenure. His boyish enthusiasm, however, belied a steely resolve to get his own way. Having been a captain in the navy, he liked to be in charge, which rankled certain Nigerian executives. Yet Kevin's success would depend on getting his senior team behind him. A rousing, sporting role model was usually trotted out by MDs in these circumstances. I had heard all the athletic expressions before, about the team watching his back, bringing forward the ball or hoisting the jib together, but I had also observed how such dominant and talkative leaders could think they had agreement from their team when they really only had collective silence.

'You have to understand, Pamela,' one of Kevin's senior Nigerian team had confessed to me privately, 'that we see these expatriate MDs come for two years. They have big agendas for the changes they want to happen while they are here, but we are here for the long haul. We must deal with the consequences of their plans and build long-term relationships with our teams.' This fundamental difference in outlook, timescales and criteria was what our retreat was trying to tackle, but I also had no idea then how relevant his words would be to me.

For the moment I was focused on getting through the day.

My plan was to help Kevin and his team tackle both the significant strategy issues and the subtler cultural ones, building their trust and improving communication during the first afternoon. Over the next two days we would create a space in which to talk, listen to each other's perspectives and forge a shared plan. I had put together a highly structured agenda to achieve these goals and the timings were tight. Kevin had other plans.

'I have a super opening speech,' said Kevin, as we sat together. 'I'm going to describe a great team—Jonny Wilkinson and England's rugby team who won The Rugby World Cup.'

'Great,' I said, but thought 'Bingo!' having heard it all before.

'I might need a bit longer than you had allocated in the agenda.'

Usually I would have been unsettled that my detailed timings were being derailed so soon, but not this afternoon. I planned to use 'Going over the Wall' as both a good metaphor and an experiential learning exercise for demonstrating that this team could work well together and was up to the challenges ahead. Also, I needed all the time I could get to put the wall in place.

'No problem,' I said quickly and held crossed fingers behind my back. 'No *wahala*.'

O

'It's WAWA, Pamela,' said Dapo, interrupting my story before I could tell him how it turned out. WAWA – West Africa Wins Again – was a concept we were both familiar with. 'You know that Thomas made a lot of money creating those problems?'

Dapo was truly cynical. Before I could object and continue, he guffawed and shouted a comment toward the club treasurer. I drank my beer while the bar erupted in a discussion about the oil price subsidy. This was a controversial and long-standing policy, which resulted in fuel shortages yet was the only tangible benefit of Nigeria's oil economy that ordinary Nigerians could see. The treasurer was arguing for its removal.

I sighed and parked my story, resigned to the way conversations went at this bar – freewheeling commentary that sometimes led to mayhem, with everyone up in arms and shouting different views. Lagosians' passion and loudness sometimes suggested that brawling might follow, but this was just their style. I reflected on Dapo's comment about WAWA, a widely shared piece of West African wisdom.

It certainly seemed that any struggle in Nigeria to go two steps forward was inexorably followed by one, two or three steps backwards. In all my efforts to get a place to live and work (never mind having it tiled) and to get a wall built for my team-building event, everyone worked hard but less was achieved than one would think for the effort expended.

This could be the story of Nigeria itself.

O

Size matters. With one in five sub-Saharan Africans a Nigerian, and the country's population three times that of South Africa, Nigeria was Africa's heavyweight. About ninety-five per cent of its foreign exchange earnings came from oil, a shift that began with exploitation from the late fifties. It soon became the eleventh largest producer in the world. But Nigeria's vast human pool ensured the country still had a diversified economy, and the informal economy was large. Manufacturing, banking, telecommunications and other services were expected, in a planned GDP rebasing exercise, to make Nigeria officially what we already suspected – the biggest economy in Africa.[2]

Nigerians, if the evidence of Lagosians was anything to go by, also had entrepreneurial flair and a resolution to succeed, unlike some other nationalities I had seen on my travels through Africa. In 1858, Thomas Hutchinson, a visitor to Lagos, described them:

'But whatever sex they are, the people of Lagos impressed me—
[they] walked along as if he had a feat to accomplish as well as a
determination to complete it'.[3]

It had not changed since.

Many Nigerians seemed very keen on higher education. Even
amongst my job applicants, resumes ran to several pages and applicants described multiple (if dubious quality) degrees. Business education and American-style self-help books, such as *You Can Be
Rich* were popular reading matter. Indeed, many Nigerians seemed
so enterprising and ambitious that in Lagos one did not speak of
unemployment but instead of under-employment. People became
entrepreneurs, even if it was only hawking phone charging cards or
water purification sachets on the traffic-clogged roads.

Everyone was working hard but it was not being converted into
wealth, equality or the economic growth expected. Seventy million
people lived in poverty, the third largest number of poor people after
India and China. Even if its revenue were spread equally, oil would
not deliver wealth. Instead, an estimated eighty per cent of the oil
bonanza went to the super-rich – one per cent of the population,
who spent large sums in the world property market, on luxury yachts
and in London's New Bond Street.

There was a promising hint of growth for a new, professional
middle class, but for most Nigerians the decades since independence
in 1960 had seen them become poorer, both relatively and absolutely.

So what had gone wrong?

O

I was jolted from my reflections by the voices of my club companions,
growing louder still.

'*Den dey chop more money-o*,' said Dapo contributing to the oil
subsidy debate now in full swing at the bar. Chop meant 'to eat' and
this was a reference to what would happen to the additional retail

oil revenue if the price subsidy were removed. It could also refer to all Nigeria's corrupt leadership. Political and military leadership, and their Big Men associates, had failed Nigerians for too many years. A series of bad leaders had condemned many of Nigeria's citizens to dire poverty and a lack of justice and basic rights.

With the return of democracy, there was hope. But was Nigeria unmanageable? Would it ever be different?

Alone in my thoughts, I returned to the results of the corporate workshop, ended only a few hours ago.

O

Kevin's opening speech, with a rugby scrum analogy, had worked well. My earlier scorn had been misplaced and the executives seemed fired up to score their equivalent of a try, or even to win a cup. Through the days of the workshop, Kevin's enthusiasm, energy and knowledge motivated the group to think bigger and beyond their individual functions and, with the help of our training and strategy framework, conversations got richer and deeper, and disagreements were expressed and explored. My goals for Kevin had been achieved, but did he think so?

When the workshop was over, we had all wanted to get on the road to beat the Friday 'go slows'. While I was busy with loading my vehicle, Kevin walked up to me.

'Our team has gone over the wall,' he exclaimed and vigorously shook my hand.

My mind flew back to the end of the first day. As sunset approached, I led the group of twelve towards a clearing shaded by palm trees where the four-metre wall stood. Yes, it was all there, looking just as it had in our compound.

I was almost as surprised as my clients.

Despite my doubts about Thomas, despite the anxiety he created, he had worked hard and delivered – just in time.

'Your challenge now,' I said to the perspiring, mainly overweight black and white office bodies, 'is to get every team member over the wall without any tools or equipment'.

They had been surprised but had got the final executive over, with some difficulty, in the dark. There had been high fives and everyone had been ecstatic.

'I don't mean simply over *your* wall,' Kevin continued, breaking my reverie. 'I am really confident now we have the basis for our growth plans.'

I nodded, holding my breath.

'We will need your help, Pamela. Strategyworks can do a lot more useful work for us I am sure.'

It had been a success after all.

Everyone in my team had worked hard and there was hope for our consulting future.

So, what about the future of Nigeria? My optimism for the place, founded in the energy and entrepreneurialism of its people, was also tempered by the quality of its leadership. Would new leaders, who tackled corruption and created policies that worked not for the vested interests but for the greater good, actually emerge and be effective?

O

I finished my beer, ordered some 'small chop' and offered Dapo a Gulder. He accepted and we picked up our conversation.

'WAWA, Pamela. That is how it is. And that is how we like it.'

In a way, I could see Dapo's point. The challenge created a thrill that captivated me.

'It's why we say, "No food for lazy man",' continued Dapo.

I saw this slogan painted on trucks and Danfo all over the place. Everyone worked hard because they had to, I thought, as I sipped my beer. But although people in Nigeria all worked hard, it hadn't delivered the best collective outcomes.

I gazed out at the expensive motorboats. The moon glowed yellow in the cloud-filled sky and a gaunt fisherman in a shallow wooden canoe glided between the boats. He stood to cast his net, which blossomed into a circular shroud and fell into the water. But with no fish captured, the fisherman carefully lowered himself back down into the canoe and silently paddled away to a more promising location. He would have a long night ahead.

I mentally saluted the fisherman and hoped his efforts, like mine, would bring the desired outcomes. I did not know then how much tougher everything would get before the journey's end.

CHAPTER FOUR

Ekologika Saturday

It takes a whole village to raise a child.

– Nigerian proverb

A week later, I had the start of a cold and was going through tissues nearly as fast as a runaway toilet roll. Despite a sore throat, sniffles and body ache, I felt pretty content. It was Saturday morning and I had woken up naturally, rather than by the usual alarm, shivered through the arctic air-conditioned apartment to the kitchen, fed a meowing Tippy, coughed and blew my nose through breakfast then dawdled in the shower as the hot water soothed away my cold. How was this a recipe for happiness?

Surrounded by staff members at work, in the car and at home, each of whom knew my movements and habits, I felt, in low moments, like a rare animal species watched by David Attenborough and a BBC film crew. It was a feeling more intense now that Alec was gone and all attention was on me. Briefly, each Saturday, I savoured the little freedom of being in charge of my own departure time and having no staff in my life.

I knew it was a fleeting break.

Ekologika Papers, perpetually short-changed of my time because of my weekday focus on consulting clients, was calling. As the paper staff – like so many others in manufacturing in Lagos – worked Saturdays, this was the perfect day to give its business my attention.

I pulled my front door shut and heard another door bang closed in the flat below me on the ground floor. It was my thirty-something neighbour, also on his way to work. I took the stairs and emerged from the stairwell into the parking area to see him pass his bag to his driver. We exchanged greetings. Through irregular exchanges, I'd learned his name was Jean. He was Lebanese and in the printing business, too. I also knew that, like me, he left early and arrived home late six days a week.

'Come and see my factory one day, if you like,' he offered. It seemed a kind invitation and could provide useful ideas for Ekologika Papers.

'Sure,' I replied and climbed behind the wheel of my car. I sketched a friendly wave then pulled a tissue from my bag. As I attended to my dripping nose, I doubted I would take up his offer. There were not enough hours in the day or days in the week to follow up every nice idea.

As I drove through the relatively empty streets, only a few potholes rattled my progress, the chill of the car air-conditioner dried my nose and my mind wandered. I had managed a brief trip to see Alec a few weeks back but now he suggested joining him in London for tennis – he had a corporate invitation to the Wimbledon men's final in late June. It would mean dappled sunshine, strawberries and cream, and constant electricity. Although a delightful break to contemplate and the timing matched our commitment to see each other every six weeks, I didn't see how I could afford more time away from the demands of two businesses.

I passed the signboard for La Pointe, a small French supermarket whose main appeal was a weekly delivery of exotic produce, imported by air, which expatriate women and their stewards scrambled for on a Friday. Shopping trolleys were used both to block sideways tackles by bejewelled Natashas and to make a forward-breakthrough by home county Penelopes to the refrigerated cabinet. I rarely joined in this frantic gold rush but suddenly I decided to stop.

Food bills in Lagos had the capacity to make one gasp. Any foreign food was outrageously expensive due to a combination of import duties (or bribes to avoid paying them), the use of air transport and a relatively small market. Like other expatriates working for large international companies, Alec had received a monthly allowance, which made it easier to cover the cost of these imported items. Now I had them only as occasional treats. The exception was on my return from a trip to London. Like Nigerians on trips overseas, I left with an empty suitcase. When I came back, after a last-minute trip to Marks & Spencer, it was heavy with groceries.

I went to the refrigerated cabinet. My prize looked a little wilted, and some outer leaves were bruised and brown, but I knew they would be sweeter and crisper than the local equivalent's dark green and bitter leaves. I triumphantly grabbed it, took my delicacy to the checkout and handed over 1500 naira – at that time about twelve US dollars. Yes, twelve dollars for an iceberg lettuce.

Madness. How could I justify it with so much poverty around me? A rare purchase, and today it was a treat to compensate for my cold. Savouring small gratifications was becoming my strategy for dealing with stress. Better than whisky, I supposed.

O

Having arrived at my office and stored the precious lettuce in the shared refrigerator in the staff kitchen, I went around the back of the compound. To secure my tenancy, Philippe had permitted me the use of this space for Ekologika Papers. One room of the rear staff quarters was its storeroom and I'd built a workshop – a tin-roofed, open-sided shed – for papermaking. As I turned the corner to greet my staff, I was assaulted by a noise loud enough to scrape the wax off the inside of my eardrums. It was the electric-powered grinder, used intermittently to pulp batches of sodden and shredded office paper, the principal ingredient in our handmade paper. The grinder was actually for groundnuts (peanuts) – for making large batches of peanut butter – but it worked well for pulping paper. The other noisy piece of equipment in our workshop was the New Zealand-made Hollander beater. Today it was not working and fortunately, as this pulp batch was done, all the noise suddenly ceased.

Remi had started moulding and I went to watch. I loved this process.

A large plastic bowl filled with water rested on a table. Prepared paper pulp was in a smaller bowl. Additional ingredients were also assembled in other bowls nearby. On another table was a pile of mesh moulds (wooden frames to which mesh had been stapled) and loose wooden-framed deckles (matching frames without the mesh that acted as a 'fence' to the paper pulp) and a stack of pressing cloths. We created paper in a variety of sizes, dictated by the size of the mould. Mainly we used what we called an A4-plus-sized mould, which was slightly larger than A4 so we could trim it to regular A4 dimensions once the sheet was dry. Behind Remi was a pressing table on which rested a foam cushion covered in a blanket.

Remi picked up a wet cotton cloth and laid it carefully onto the pressing table. He then picked up a mould and deckle and fitted them together. With his free hand, he used a small container to scoop up some wet paper pulp, which he released into the basin of water. He did the same with a measure of dried dung, then stirred the mixture into a whirling and evenly distributed suspension. With a swift and well-practised movement, he dipped the mould and deckle into the suspension and quickly lifted them. A thin film of pulp now rested on the mesh (and on his arms, like lumpy white freckles). He gently rocked the mould back and forth in his outstretched hands to ensure that the pulp stayed evenly distributed as water drained through the mesh. Satisfied, he turned to the pressing table, lifted off the deckle and pressed out the mould and its contents onto the cloth. He held it for a few seconds, firmly see-sawed the mould back and forth to ensure the pulp was densely deposited, then lifted it away in a quick movement.

Voila. On the cloth lay a sheet of wet paper.

Even though I had seen it often and was a master of the process myself, I remained captivated by the apparent magic of the pulp's transformation into paper.

'It's Fulani paper,' said Remi as he pinched the laden cloth at two corners, carefully lifted it from its foam bed then laid it on a pile of cloths already stacked behind him.

Fulani paper was the name we gave to our paper made with processed cow dung. Cow dung, even washed, sounded pretty gross. Was I turning out to be more like Fagin rather than the enlightened social enterprise owner, job creator and, environmental recycler I was trying to be? Cow-dung paper was a bit of a con – a marketing ploy, but very popular.

Fulani, one of the major tribal groups of northern Nigeria, had traditionally been nomadic. Herdsmen drove their distinctive white longhorn cattle from the north to the abattoirs of Lagos. We bought the cow dung from one of these abattoirs in the outer Lagos suburbs and paid for it to be processed offsite. First it was soaked in bleach, then rinsed and rinsed again. All that was left were the millet seeds and hay that had not been digested in the cow's four stomach chambers – and that lovely organic residue was what went into our Fulani paper. It could sound repulsive, but our customers loved the rough and earthy texture of the finished sheets. It was one of our best sellers.

Remi began moulding a second sheet. This was relentless physical labour that strong Remi seemed to relish. He was as wet as a fisherman and looked the part with rolled-up jeans and a way of grabbing moulds like lobster pots that he was about to sling in the sea. Once he had a pile of about fifty pulp-laden cloths, he would take them for a first pressing. This was done in a hydraulic press we had built using car jacks from directions found in a book. Leaving wet papers in this press as long as possible – up to two days – helped produce a flatter sheet once it was dried.

Peter emerged from the storeroom and walked over to join me. His smile was more guarded than Remi's jolly grin and his smooth movements and actions matched his habitual neatness of dress. I still knew little of his background. His natural reserve did not encourage personal questions and I did not like to pry for more information than he offered.

Our biggest production headache in a humid tropical climate was drying the paper. At Peter's recommendation, we had informally rented the floor of an unfinished building nearby by 'dashing' the security guards, and he employed a couple of other casual workers to lay out the paper and gather it up again once it was dry. Now that the wet season had started, sudden downpours spoilt some batches unless the laid-out papers were gathered up quickly whenever a storm threatened. Laying out and gathering up each batch several times was inefficient, and one of my priorities was to work with Peter to develop a less costly approach, possibly using a dryer. I needed to look at options with him, but the current humidity was bringing out my cold again and my eyes were streaming so I suggested we meet upstairs later.

Peter was happy to delay as he had other priorities. 'Before we meet, I'll sort the papers by type and grade and pack them,' he told me as he showed me the storeroom. We held our inventory in blocks of 200 sheets wrapped in brown paper until needed for conversion into finished products. Towers of these 'wraps' as we called them stood in one corner and the other was piled with unsorted paper.

The hard-working casual worker James walked into the store carrying a new batch of dried papers to add to the unsorted pile. He was shabbily dressed but I now knew he was a graduate. He seemed over-qualified for this role, but I guessed it was a sign of the lack of work in Lagos that graduates took up labouring jobs.

'I want to be a papermaker,' he beamed at me. His enthusiasm was infectious, and I liked him but, when he left, I tackled Peter.

'Still no women on the team, Peter?' This was a bone of contention between us.

'They are too weak, Madam,' he said with his careful smile. 'They do not like the work.'

I snorted at this comment. Was it my cold or my disbelief?

I remembered a woman named Caroline in the Republic of Congo. I had stayed overnight at her village in 1993 during my bicycle journey. Having done her family's washing in the river by hand, she washed my filthy, road-stained T-shirt with such vigour it regained an 'Omo' brightness not seen for at least 2000 kilometres. I also remembered Marie Carmen, who gathered firewood in the deep forest surrounding her tiny village in Equatorial Guinea. She carried the wood back on her head then worked into the night cooking bush meat and roasting groundnuts to sell the next day to passing travellers. I thought of Lydia in northern Ghana, who worked her own plot of land to grow onions at four in the morning and then tended her husband's land during the day. She added this gruelling extra labour in order to sell the onions and pay for her children's education.

She had said to me, 'If you are after something, you must grab it. Otherwise, you cannot say you are too tired.'

These women were memorable only because I got to know them. I observed so many women just like them in every African country through which I travelled – women who could not rely on welfare or council housing or a national health scheme to look after their children's health, and so they worked instead, relentlessly and honestly.

I remembered the man I challenged when I stopped under a shady tree at midday in Burkina Faso. The sun was hot and overbearing, yet out in the fields I could see the bent backs of women harvesting yams. The man was spread-eagled in the shade with his friends, and already drunk on palm wine.

'What do the men do here?' I had asked, but not as genuinely as I once had. I had observed too many scenes like this already.

He sat up. 'We make decisions.'

Experiences like these had made me want to run a social enterprise and to employ women, but I was finding Peter intransigent on the issue.

'I had two girls come last week, but when they saw the work they ran away,' he said.

I found that hard to believe. How could chopping some pandanus leaf and moulding paper be too difficult for a strong but unskilled and unemployed young woman? I figured Peter only employed young men from his own area of Ajegunle. But with little time for Ekologika Papers, I was dependent on Peter's leadership and good judgement. I needed him to take responsibility for his team and so, for now (again), I did not insist.

O

The financial situation at Ekologika Papers kept me awake for many nights. I priced products from rough calculations based on our production trials, and I invested without knowing the break-even volumes. I didn't even know which products would become bestsellers. Would this be how I advised my consulting clients to enter new businesses?

I went back up to the office and made myself a Lemsip. Patience, my no-nonsense accountant, was waiting for me. Ekologika Papers had expanded from producing handmade paper to converting it into products such as cards, table calendars and notebooks of different sizes. Patience had prioritised developing the cost management system, but she needed my help to develop and agree on the revised cost categories to be used in our accounts – our cost centres.

I could hear a group of voices from the Ekologika Papers room so, before settling down to work with Patience, I went to greet them.

Sonny sat on a stool at a high table. He was one of my founding trio and our craftsman and artist. His tie-dyed T-shirt today was pink and blue, probably his own work. He also wore low-slung jeans and leather sandals; a twenty-first century beatnik. He had a pair of scissors in one hand, coloured paper in the other and about 500 crafted Christmas trees in a plastic container.

500? It might have been twice that.

A completed Christmas tree comprised a piece of wire bent into the familiar outline of a pine tree, which was glued to a similarly shaped hand-cut piece of our decorative paper. This in turn was glued to a small square of full-fibre backing paper. I had asked him to create a stock of this design to use on customised business Christmas cards, and to help with the workload during our peak season.

During the first half of the year Ekologika Papers sales slowed to a trickle but, because he was salaried staff, I needed to keep him busy. Financially, it would have been better to employ him as a casual staff member brought in for the busy Christmas season, but—I was fond of Sonny.

I wanted to say, 'Stop. We'll never sell that many Christmas tree cards.' What came out was, 'Great work'.

After all, it was clever work and I needed to motivate him. I tried to gather my thoughts. 'Maybe you could develop another design – say the Three Kings or a camel or something.' That was the extent of my management guidance. Patience was waiting.

'Welcome, Madam,' said Chuks as I entered the main office. He was an engineer by training and inquisitive, cheerful and resourceful by nature. He was probably the oldest of my Ekologika Papers employees – still in his early thirties. Ekologika Papers was a young organisation in all senses. The conversion processes Chuks managed included in-house printing and production as well as outsourced services. As we didn't have the equipment for some of the processes involved, he dealt with printers and other suppliers who helped us to fashion the finished products.

He handed over a notebook. 'I just got back from Mushin and these are the new samples.'

At my suggestion, we were developing a new product – a hardcover wire-bound notebook that I hoped could be sold year-round to reduce our dependence on end-of-year sales. The hard covers were made from our paper (custom-printed with a corporate logo), laminated for longevity and glued to strawboard before binding. We made the covers entirely in-house but did not have equipment to print the lined pages or to do the final punching and binding. If the product proved itself with sales, I would approve investment in the equipment but for now we outsourced these services to printers in Mushin.

Mushin, a rough and tumble suburb on the mainland, was a mecca for printers, and the team often went there to source supplies and services. It also made sense that one day we would relocate the business there.

I excitedly examined the samples. They were pretty and of a quality unavailable in Lagos but, as I opened and compared them, I discovered numerous faults. The back and front covers were different sizes, the binding holes of the covers and inners were misaligned, and the inners had been bound upside down.

'Didn't you notice any of this?' I asked Chuks.

'Sorry, Madam,' he murmured, looking crestfallen at my criticism. I didn't want to deflate his enthusiasm by being negative, but he was, after all, a university graduate.

'We can't do this in production,' I said, trying to be patient. 'The cost of rework would be horrendous.'

I had already asked him to develop 'standards' for a notebook – the size of each component, the size of the finished product and the issues to look out for. Nothing had been delivered and I was not sure if he understood what I meant.

Patience called to me, 'Mr Haresh is on the phone for you'.

Haresh was an Indian family business owner and entrepreneur. The assignment that Strategyworks was engaged to conduct for his chemicals trading business had been delayed since April.

As I blew my nose and sat down in front of my computer, I noticed a new email from Alec. Subject: Wimbledon? I knew he wanted an answer. A London break was very tempting. My mind saw an image of a lithe Rafael Nadal, bronzed arm upstretched to smash a ball across the court.

I picked up the phone to speak to my consulting client. Bad news. Haresh's assignment would be delayed again.

'My general manager has resigned,' he said. 'I cannot start until I replace him.' Nadal's image was swiftly erased. Kevin, the banking client I had taken over the wall at the beachside workshop, had commissioned further consulting work that was starting next week, but without Haresh's assignment how would I make up the income? The monthly pressure to pay salaries was like a bad rash – red, itchy and always coming back.

O

It had been a long Saturday but, as I was driving home just before sunset, I did feel better. The worst of my cold seemed to be over and I'd made progress on the cost centres (although made no progress yet on paper-drying). But with the pressing need to crack on and find new consulting work and to deal with so many issues in Ekologika Papers, I'd emailed my reply to Alec. I would not be going to Wimbledon. Both my teams needed me to guide them just as I needed them to improve their game. I found I was cheered by having made a decision – and also by a suggestion from Patience.

'Peter won't employ women in papermaking,' she observed when I had told her about my frustration. 'He wants his boys.' Patience might be new to the team, but she was an astute observer.

'But why not employ women in sales and graphic design?' she added.

We were already advertising for those positions so I could get more involved in who was recruited. It was a great idea. As I arrived and saw Jean's car already parked in his spot, my thoughts turned to my now quiet, staff-free evening in and Tippy, who would be hungry for her dinner.

Dinner. My nascent optimism was deflated. I remembered I had left my lettuce in the office fridge.

CHAPTER FIVE

Long Rains

Loneliness is good, but only sometimes.

– Nigerian proverb

Most Sundays I went to Agaja Beach, one of a string of village beach havens along Badagry Creek that flowed westwards towards the border with Benin. Between the creek and the sea was an island breakwater to the Atlantic Ocean, and the beaches along the island were Lagos's secret hideaway for its Nigerian and expatriate elite.

It was still odd to think of myself as a member of an elite section of society. I associated the elite with thirty-metre super-yacht-owning Greek billionaires, American trust fund progeny on five-star-hotel gap-year jaunts and Nigerian criminals and politicians (made of the same stuff) quaffing Cristal champagne. I did not associate the term with simple management consultants. My 'super-yacht' was a five-metre Glastron motorboat with a 'fairly used' (a Nigerian term for second-hand) 120-horsepower outboard motor – both dating from the early seventies – which was parked on a rusty trailer in a dilapidated boat pen. But I had to admit to myself, compared to the crushing poverty of most Nigerians, I definitely was in this society's elite.

Alec and I had even built our own hideaway – a simple wood and thatch beach hut – in Agaja in 2002. For me, the forty-five-minute boat ride from frenetic Lagos offered the welcome opportunity to sink into a mellower mood before arrival into another world of bucolic village life.

Was this a Marie Antoinette-like example of the elite emulating the impoverished life for escapism? Possibly and sometimes this bothered me a great deal, but mostly I simply enjoyed my Agaja escape.

It was early July and that Sunday morning I'd had a welcome lie-in but now I stretched in my bed and looked forward to the Agaja escape I had planned. Getting up, I pulled back my blackout curtains. My windowpanes were wet with internal condensation and I rubbed a section clear to gaze outside.

My plans were in tatters.

The atmosphere was funereal – the sky was a heavy shroud that smothered any hint of sunlight, and heavy rain fell like the inconsolable tears of a mourning mother. A white egret, a migratory bird from Siberia, sat in a tree across the carpark. Its wings drooped with the weight of the wet day on its ruffled feathers and its forlorn expression matched. I tapped at the window to attract its attention, but it didn't notice.

Then I thought, 'It's a water bird—what has it got to be depressed about?'

I looked at my phone. Nothing yesterday and still no text message, no missed call. Where was Alec? I felt as glum as the egret. Perhaps he was waiting for his mate to call from Russia? Today was the Wimbledon men's final, the invitation I had turned down. Somehow, the rain would have been easier to accept if my imagination did not conjure up Alec enjoying champers, canapés and a day of tennis.

May to July was known for the 'long rains' in Lagos. The term seemed to refer both to the persistence of the showers and their frequency. Now, in early July, I longed for the month to pass. Next month we could expect a drier month called 'the August break' before the 'short rains' – more intermittent but often more violent storms – in September and October. The long rains seemed to be accompanied by postponed plans, time passing slowly and waiting for conditions to change.

Shaking myself from my self-pity, I picked up the handset – but not to call Alec.

'Luke. Can you hear me?' The sound through the phone was distorted, like someone speaking underwater. 'Luke, if you can hear me, I wanted to let you know I won't be coming to the beach today.'

I hung up with no idea if Luke, the caretaker of my beach hut at Agaja, had heard me – or understood. He had been expecting me with a large party, but this weather could only mean cancellation.

During the wet season when there were poor connections, I sent him the same message by text, which often proved more reliable.

'OK, Madam, come next Sunday,' he texted back. 'The hut needs repair due to a bad storm.'

More expenditure. I frowned.

I then started to text my guests, a mixture of friends and – as Agaja was a good place to cement business relationships – a few pro-spective Strategyworks clients. Cancellation wouldn't be surprising to anyone given the weather, but it was disappointing, especially as I'd hoped to lay bricks around a badly needed new assignment with a multinational soft-drink company whose Australian managing director, Aaron, I knew.

I opened the fridge door and saw containers of fishcakes, potatoes in foil and two salads – a small quantity of beach food that I had asked my steward Edward to prepare. Everyone brought food when we went to the beach yet Edward's notion of 'a small quantity' seemed somewhat inflated. There was enough for Nadal and Federer and the entire contingent of Wimbledon umpires, ball boys and ball girls. Even the BBC broadcasting crew would not go hungry. I didn't

mind the over-catering when the excess fed Agaja villagers, but now
I wrapped fishcakes in foil and placed them in the freezer. Perhaps
it shouldn't be re-frozen but food in Lagos was far too expensive to
waste. As they could not be frozen, variants of jacket potatoes would
be on the menu for the next week.

'Meow.'

Tippy reminded me of her presence. I unwrapped one of the
fishcakes and added it to the two I had left out; we would both enjoy
fishcakes for lunch. She was in the Nigerian cat elite.

Tippy was a nervous cat. Dennis, her brother from the same litter,
was a lively and brave ginger tom who Tippy adored and followed
everywhere. Just the year before, Dennis had died dreadfully, having
eaten fish laced with rat poison and left in our garden. As I had heard
some Nigerians believed cats were evil spirits, I wondered if someone
laid the bait out of fear of a cat roaming freely in a lush garden? Or,
as I believed, was the perpetrator one of our security guards, jealous
of our pampered lives?

It was the downside of being relatively wealthy amongst such
poverty. It was a consequence that some members of the Nigerian
elite and even modest middle-class professional families suffered.
Kidnappings of family members and demands for ransom were on
the rise, often perpetrated by poorer relatives or neighbours from the
victim's village. In a society with better leaders, such events would be
met with outrage and action to redress the lack of equality that was
destabilising society. Instead, without leadership action and trusted
law enforcement agencies, it spurred families to build higher, barbed-
wire-topped walls and live with an embattled mentality. I no longer
trusted anyone other than Edward near Tippy.

Shaking away the bad memories, I focused on what was now
a late breakfast and sat at my kitchen table to eat a modest bowl of
bran flakes. Between mouthfuls, I checked my phone again. There
was still no message from Alec, although there were some messages from my guests acknowledging the cancellation. I re-planned

my day. I could use the time to reassess my financial projections for the year. Project delays in Strategyworks and overspending in Ekologika Papers meant my annual projected expenditure in both companies was, at this stage, higher than income. I did not need Charles Dickens's Mr Micawber to remind me this was a recipe for misery. I wished I could have been at Agaja instead, engaged in action to bring in revenue rather than only making plans on an electronic spreadsheet.

Lacking energy for such a dispiriting exercise, I sipped at my coffee and let my imagination take over.

The roar of the engine. My hair blown tight against my skull by the rush of wind and fresh air tingling on skin damp and oily in the heavy humidity. Sweet chlorophyll in the air, delivered straight from the palm trees and mangroves lining the coiled lagoon. I imagined another Sunday journey begun, the motorboat ride taking me from the grime and graft of Lagos and restoring my soul along the way.

We arrive at my rickety jetty protruding into the lagoon. I jump over the side with my light trousers rolled up and my toes sink into the soft mud as I wade through the brown water, rich in organic matter but clean and mildly saline, to the shore. Children come running, with women and men following at a more sedate pace, creating a greeting party of up to twenty villagers to help us unload. There's a shy wave from a familiar youngster hiding behind his mother's faded wrap. The light is bright and the hot sand burns my bare soles, so it is a relief to walk into the shade of the primitive open-sided hut. The morning passes in animated conversation about the state of the nation and business and continues as my guests and I move upstairs for lunch. My village steward brings dishes cooked on the charcoal barbecue and salads and drinks emerge from the scattered cool boxes we have brought. The views from the table – out towards the lagoon on one side and the ocean on the other through gracefully swaying palms – are stunning. As plates are cleared and serving dishes still laden with leftovers are taken to be shared amongst the villagers, we continue talking and laughing, and maybe finally one or two of us go for a swim in the thrashing Atlantic Ocean surf while others sleep in hammocks strung between palms. Late in the afternoon we are sad to leave. I pay my caretaker for the villagers who have helped, my guests dash them and they appear happy with their earnings. The sun glows orange, low in a hazy sky, as we re-board the boat for the journey back to our more stressed workday lives in Lagos.

O

What a paradise, I mused. But I shook my head, releasing myself from my delusional wonderland. I knew not everything was right with Agaja and my relationship with the villagers was complicated.

O

Agaja was a microcosm of Nigeria: alluring but broken, with corrupt leaders, suffering amongst the downtrodden who struggled for survival and a blurred perception of good and bad.

The villagers were poor, really poor – sidelined and forgotten by their own government.

For the most part they were fishermen who eked a precarious and dangerous living launching heavy dugout canoes and wooden boats through the surf. Despite living close to the ocean, many did not know how to swim and regularly drowned as they tried to navigate the vicious breaks. As in so many parts of the world, the size of catches from these traditional methods and the fish themselves were getting smaller due to the trawlers operated offshore by Taiwanese and other nationalities, including wealthier Nigerians.

The fishermen, originally from Ghana, belonged to the Ga-Adangbe ethnic group as did many of the other nearby coastal communities. Prevailing currents travelled eastwards along the West African coast so, in previous generations, fisherman had drifted and put down roots where they landed. The land on which they lived was rented from the traditional Yoruba owners and their tenure was insecure.

State and local governments neglected these communities and public services were limited. There was no power, the only water supply was of dubious quality from public wells, there was no health centre and the only primary school was underfunded, understaffed and overcrowded with up to sixty children in each class. Many children and adults were illiterate and unable to speak any English, the official language of Nigeria. Most shocking to me was that some children had withered limbs – evidence of polio. All of this within about thirty-five kilometres of Lagos.

The Agajans, like all Nigerians, worked hard, and their underdog status made me impulsively want to help them. But there was another side to my relationship with them that made me more wary.

Luke was the caretaker of our hut and the person I knew the best, especially as he was one of the few villagers who was literate and spoke English. He made his living out of the construction of new huts at Agaja and their maintenance. I was dismayed when he built our hut twice as big as planned, using twice as many materials as planned, and hence, it was twice as expensive as planned, but thought these errors were the honest mistakes of a naïve villager. Over the years, I learned he was neither naïve, nor that honest. He monitored the hut for maintenance, and Alec and I had started to believe that 'storm damage' was sometimes given a helping hand and his quotes included healthy mark-ups way beyond the going market rates. We paid an annual rent for our plot to a Yoruba landlord, and paid villagers a good monthly salary for security and a daily rate for cleaning and preparing lunch. Luke insisted he distributed all salaries to avoid 'bad feelings' and because this was 'traditional'. Despite this, a few years back there had been discontent among the young boys who helped out, and we suspected he took a cut on the salaries. His name should have been Luciano and this a Sicilian village.

The inequality in our relationship – Alec's and my privilege and his and his villagers' poverty – made me want to be generous and forgiving of this extortion. Could I say that in Luke's circumstances I would not do similar? Perhaps or perhaps not, but the fleecing took its toll on our relationship to the point that sometimes his antics made us want to leave and never come back.

Now the hut was mine and I faced his voracious demands alone. But there was an added dimension to our relationship – I was also indebted to Luke.

○

The Atlantic Ocean along the West African coast is deadly, and not only to fishermen. Except during the dry season, the beach profile is steep and the heavy swells break close to shore. The swirling backwash can flip the unwary visitor paddling by the shore onto her bum, sweep her seaward and leave her flailing in deep water. Sometimes the prevailing current creates strong offshore rips – with only a line of white water and bubbles travelling back out to sea to identify them.

One year, our new neighbour, the incoming expatriate managing director for a shipyard, had gone for a solo swim, been missed and was found floating face-down and drowned, a victim of a rip tide.

One should treat such coastal waters with respect. As a qualified surf survival instructor – the best job ever, done under electric-blue West Australian skies cruising on a surfboard and teaching teenagers to read and navigate waves, retiring to the pub for a beer and being paid for my 'work' – I normally checked conditions prior to entering the water. On one long Easter weekend, I did not.

Alec and I had been cleaning out the water tank at our hideaway – something we'd long ago asked Luke to do but he'd demurred. We had refused to pay an exorbitant sum for this tank cleaning that we thought should be covered by his salary and indignantly decided to do the work ourselves. Alec stood high on the tank stand and reached in to fill buckets with the stagnant, smelly water and decayed organic detritus. I was the crew – climbing up and down, taking full buckets for emptying and clambering back up with the empty buckets. A crowd of village children looked on, bemused by these *oyibo* antics. After an hour of this labour, desperate for a wash and a cooling break, we'd run straight into the ocean.

Having swum for a while inside the break, I saw Alec striking for the shore, and turned to follow him. I made no progress; I was going backwards. Focused on getting his attention as soon as he got to shore, and not realising he was also in trouble, I failed to notice where I was in the water.

Wham. I was hit by the break, swept into a whirlpool and pulled metres below the surface. The water was a beautiful aqua aerated by the pounding waves above. I surfaced for air but was hit again by a new wave and submerged into the ethereal but lethal world below. I was being churned like a ragdoll, drowning and panicking. I surfaced a third time then immediately cast into the depths with little air in my lungs.

'Stop panicking,' came a command in my mind. 'Save yourself.'

I was shaken by the voice of my surf survival training, but it made me think. I twisted in the water and when I surfaced the third time, I was facing the oncoming wave and dived under it. It was a weak kick but enough that when I surfaced for the fourth time, I was beyond the break and was safe.

Well, safe enough to float on my back and get my breath and strength back in calm water. How would I get to shore? I was caught in a rip that was taking me further out to sea and I'd have to swim sideways to get out of it. Later, I'd discover that Alec and I had entered the water just as the tide changed and, being an Easter full moon, this was a powerful tide.

I became aware of villagers swimming toward me. One of them was Luke swimming rather inexpertly on my boogie board. He was tossed in the break and I watched nervously to see him emerge. By the time he'd reached me he was exhausted while I'd recovered my strength. I insisted he hold on to the board while he recovered, then side by side holding the board we kicked alongshore to get out of the rip. By now the shoreline was busy with villagers watching the unfolding drama. I was pleased to see Alec was amongst them. Clear of the rip, I turned my head to see the oncoming wave.

'Hold on,' I shouted to Luke. 'We'll catch this wave.'

But Luke didn't hold on. Instead, he'd given me a shove on the bum and I had the ride of my life 300 metres in to the shore. Luke followed, flapping his arms ineffectually in an imitation crawl and body surfing to shore, but he had put my safety before his own. No matter how much of an Agaja Don he was, it was hard to begrudge him any extra money after that.

O

I got up from my breakfast table.

Yes, my relationship with Luke and Agaja was complicated. Something like love and hate? But despite these reflections, I got up with a new energy and resolve about what I would do with my Sunday gone astray. I would work on trying to repay my debt to Luke and the Agajan villagers.

Agaja faced a threat. It was under attack from the sea. The waves that were so dangerous for swimming were also eroding the beach. In 1998, an old freighter being towed to Ghana for salvage had broken its towing line (local gossip held that it was done on purpose) and been wrecked. Its rusting hulk had come to rest on the sandy bottom close to shore about three kilometres further west. With the owners having long ago collected their insurance, it sat there as nobody's problem – except, as we discovered, ours.

The prevailing current on the coast went alongshore, moving eastward in a swirling cycle. In equilibrium, as much sand as the swirl picked up at the front of the current, it later deposited behind it. The presence of the wreck had disturbed this equilibrium and just as Bar Beach on VI had been eroded when the harbour defences had been built to the west, so Agaja beach was disappearing – at an alarming rate.

I didn't want my hut to fall into the sea but there were two much greater concerns. A combination of high tide and sea surge could break through the narrow point between the creek and the ocean. The narrow point, now down to a couple of hundred metres (half what it had been a few years before), was where my hut was located. A tsunami-like wave could rip through and continue without obstruction to submerge the very busy town directly inland. Once penetrated, the break would widen and destroy the fragile mangrove ecosystem of the creek.

These were risks in the future, but village families, who invested their savings in building cement block homes with galvanised roofs, were suffering now. It was heart-breaking for them to see their homes collapse as they were devoured by the invading sea. The cement column remnants of water wells, formerly at the back of their compounds, stood bizarrely above the eroded sand, straight and tall as horse guards on parade. As complicated as my relationship with Luke was, I could not stand by while his home and those of other Agaja villagers fell into the sea.

Perhaps I was more bothered about having my elitist escape in the middle of their impoverished village than I let on to myself.

Surely, I reasoned, someone could do something.

The Yoruba man from whom I leased my plot of land on the island, Wale, was an elderly Nigerian with a colonial-era education and a patrician manner to match. Wale was not from Agaja, and only had the head lease of the land from another traditional ruler, but he shared my concern to help and touchingly still believed the government would take responsibility. I might be naïve on some things, but I had no faith in local, state or federal politicians and civil servants acting in time – or at all – and had more faith in the private sector, especially those companies with huts at Agaja and a vested interest in saving the beach.

Just last week I had suggested to Wale that he focus on the government connections while I contacted the tenants and their companies.

I had a role model in mind – Toks.

Toks was a new friend who loved coming with me to the beach. She was a Nigerian property developer with a major investment in an office block on Lagos Island. In her late fifties, but with a smooth, flawless complexion and a funky fashion sense, she sometimes looked like a glamorous starlet, despite being a serious businesswoman. Last Sunday, under dry skies, she had accompanied me to Agaja. As we sped in my boat across the harbour, we had a terrific view of Lagos Island, and one that hid all the dilapidation, dirt and slums through which I had driven some months before.

'It's not as bad as it was,' said Toks after I told her about my escapade earlier in the year driving through Lagos Island's chaotic Balogun market without a driver. She looked as though she had come straight from St Tropez in white shorts, chiffon top, large designer sunglasses and a wide-brimmed straw hat. 'A few years ago there were cows grazing on Broad Street. When I saw them, I knew I couldn't wait for our useless government – I had to act. I heard about the rejuvenation of a rundown American city using a participatory process, so I called in the consultants who had worked there and brought them to Lagos.'

Bringing together property and business owners in 2003, Toks formed an action and lobby group that created a rejuvenated vision for Lagos Island and a plan to reverse the dilapidation of this once-vibrant financial district. The plan included fund-raising, lobbying the government, community mobilisation and direct action for clean-up. Although investment still seemed to be heading mostly for VI, at least there were no longer cows on Broad Street.

Toks was a serial activist. When the schooling system fell apart under the weight of corruption and unpaid teachers in the eighties, she got a group of like-minded mothers together and founded her own secondary school. When her only daughter tragically died in a car accident, she created an innovative charity to offer grief and trauma counselling to other Nigerians suffering loss. When the government failed to act on its responsibilities, Toks simply got organised to make things happen.

I hoped to follow her lead with an action group to save Agaja. Surely other business people with huts there would want to help.

O

It was now Sunday evening, the end of this slow, wet day that led to so much introspection. I had spent the afternoon drafting a letter to send to the corporate tenants of Agaja and designing a poster I would print and attach to palm trees. 'Save Agaja Now!' was its emphatic demand. I'd see whether I could get a response.

The rain and thunderstorms meant there was no television signal and so I was listening to some moody Malian string music accompanied by a beautiful voice crooning as if under a star-studded sky.

I pondered what to do about Strategyworks. The business really needed to win a new assignment. Was the Australian managing director of the soft-drink company serious about his project? Or would it go the way of other once-promising leads during the last few months? Many senior directors and managers had escaped this bleak Lagos 'winter' of heavy rains and left Lagos for their summer holiday in Europe – probably some were at Wimbledon. There had been further developments in Strategyworks's problems on Friday.

Both Feyi and Deola had resigned, each with good reason. Feyi was pregnant with her second child and wanted to stay at home, and Deola had been offered a better job. I was disappointed as I had put time into training them and I had hoped in future to get more help from them. Now I would again have to put time into recruiting and training. But in a way I was also relieved – I would have some respite from paying their salaries.

It was now four months since this independent life began but everything was taking so long to get going. Two steps forward and one or three steps backwards. A conversation during the last week with the new Australian High Commissioner in Abuja came to mind.

'Good news,' he said when I called him for an update. 'The Nigerians have signed off your appointment as Honorary Consul. Now we must wait for our minister of foreign affairs to sign it off.'

That sounded soon, I thought, until he continued. 'Yes, it should come through in the next three months.'

O

Alec finally called.

I gathered he had had a good time at the tennis. We could not hear each other well on the poor connection but he was buoyant and cheerful. I was introspective and in need of an empathetic ear for my professional worries and domestic woes.

More than anything else, I wanted Alec to say, 'I'm sorry to hear that' or 'Don't worry—it'll be all right'. I wanted encouragement from my partner and a sense that he thought what I was doing had worth.

Instead, relating my worries brought only silence in return. Hadn't he heard me?

I shouted more loudly to be heard above the crackling line, but it was the wrong tone to invite sympathy or to sound loving. Our call ended abruptly. Was it a dropped line? Or did he end it, frustrated by the line or by my mood?

Having looked forward to his call all day, it left me without the sense of shared camaraderie and support I craved. Long distance relationships were hard. I wondered where ours was going.

CHAPTER SIX

What Have You Got for Me?

One of the truest tests of integrity is its blunt refusal to be compromised.
– Chinua Achebe, Nigerian novelist and poet

Two months later, in September, the slow wet season was a thing of the past and the business year was finally accelerating. Two new consultants, Zainab and John, had joined and I was back to my professional staffing starting point. Executives, returned from their European vacations, had their sights on winning year-end bonuses by reaching goals set optimistically in January. Consultants were suddenly popular – to start assignments that would help deliver goals, or to shoulder the blame when they didn't.

Ekologika Papers's business customers were also awakening from the wet-season hibernation as managers turned their thoughts to spending budget allocations on Christmas cards, calendars and other year-end gifts. We had recruited an experienced corporate gift sales leader and a wonderfully talented graphic designer to target this important market. Kola, a man, had won the sales role but the new graphic designer was a woman, Yinka. I was happy that Ekologika Papers was fully manned and jollier still that it was partly 'womanned'.

It should all have been hectic, hurried and exciting. Instead, it was as quiet as a British pub after last orders. I had not reckoned with the trade unions.

The government had announced it was removing the contentious fuel subsidy, which would lead to a doubling in retail fuel prices and the National Labour Congress had followed this proclamation with a general strike. Don't get me wrong – I appreciated (and indeed shared) the workers' mistrust that the removal of this benefit would result in a flow of cash and benefits elsewhere. But for my small businesses, which simply wanted to earn some cash so we could pay our workers' salaries, a strike was deeply unwelcome.

O

I drove down Adeola Odeku Street, a main thoroughfare on VI, without Tayo, and marvelled at how quiet it was: mid-week and hardly any traffic. The government stand-off with the unions showed no sign of breaking and we were in the third day of the strike. I saw a blue-uniformed policeman stopping a brief line of cars. What did he want?

When it was my turn, I rolled my window down. Did he want to see my papers? Was my driver's licence in my wallet?

'Good morning, Madam,' said the grim officer. 'What do you have for me?' he asked carefully.

Without dropping a beat, I gave the practised answer.

'I give you God's blessings.' I said. Although smiling, my jaw clenched, undoubtedly giving my face a slightly offbeat look. Would he notice?

He held my gaze, probably assessing that smile, then took a step backwards and waved me on. I put my car into gear and let a relieved puff of carbon dioxide out of my lungs. I had won that encounter.

My policy on demands for bribes was to refuse – an emphatic, no exceptions, time-constraints-no-problem, mess-me-about-I-don't-care 'no'. I might temper the delivery with a bit of humanity and humour, but the answer was still no.

I had discovered on my African bicycle journey in the early nineties that demands for cash by underpaid policemen could usually be side-tracked with time and a bit of relaxed chat. Verbal pleasantries such as 'Happy Friday' or 'May your family prosper' delivered me safe passage – most of the time.

The white men with whom I discussed this issue did not have the same experience. An *oyibo* man trying to offer 'Have a lovely life' instead of passing over a wad of hard cash might end up with a punch on the nose. But I was not convinced the success of saying 'no' was gender specific. I believed my male friends' shakedowns happened also because once someone paid, word got around and he became a target for hucksters in Lagos.

Arriving at the office, I noticed it was as quiet as the roads. Both my consultancy and papermaking staff – none of whom were unionised, and were paid well for their jobs – had promised to try and make it in. I switched on the air-conditioners, as much for a reassuring hum as necessity, watered the potted plant in reception and went into the kitchen to make myself a coffee.

Coffee would sharpen me up for a long session analysing Nigeria's economic and political outlook for Kevin, my Australian banking client, who needed it as input for a board investment decision. My work would involve crunching unreliable statistics and reviewing international reports and government policies. I knew one key to Nigeria's future prospects was how successfully the present government tackled the cancerous corruption that had long derailed spending on infrastructure and services. If I relied on the speculations of my boat club friends the night before, I'd be pretty pessimistic. It had been a sobering discussion.

O

Dapo, well-oiled on Gulder beer, was perched on 'his' bar stool when I arrived near sunset. Toks arrived shortly after me. In a dark blue outfit, she looked the part of a businesswoman – though one adorned, as was obligatory for Lagos women of her generation and class, with ornate chunks of gold at her ears and a large diamond on her finger. Like businesswomen anywhere, she also carried a large statement handbag. She should have appeared smart and sophisticated, but instead seemed tired and dishevelled. Toks worked hard for her success and that night it showed. I knew I too presented a creased and rumpled look after my long working day grappling with ongoing financial worries.

Despite the strike, the club bar was open and many members were in. The kitchen staff had not arrived, so food was limited to groundnuts. We grazed and chatted about the state of things. The strike had principally affected government services such as schools and hospitals and unionised workers. Lawyers, managers and business owners, frustrated like me by this stop-start year, had not downed tools.

But Dapo was in jubilant form. Maybe, with a corrupt and criminal political history and ruling class, in the face of a system that one was powerless to change, the only reasonable thing to do was drink beer, tell stories, and laugh. 'Let me tell you the story about the Nigerian and the Indonesian who went to university together,' said Dapo. 'After graduating, each went home to join the government. Several years later, the Nigerian visited his friend in Jakarta and found him living in a big, luxurious house with a Mercedes parked outside. "How do you afford all this on a politician's salary?" asked the Nigerian.'

'"Do you see that road?" replied his Indonesian friend, pointing to a four-lane highway outside. "Ten per cent."'

Dapo convulsed with laughter and Toks smiled but I was confused and must have shown it.

'Ten per cent' exclaimed Dapo, lighting up a cigarette. 'The Indonesian had taken ten per cent of the highway's contract value. That's how he could afford the house and car.'

I got the joke. I knew people often compared Indonesia and Nigeria's economies – both had large, young populations of a similar size, both had the curse of oil-based economies, and both had suffered thirty years of military dictatorships (with the first coups launched at similar times: 1965 in Indonesia and 1966 in Nigeria) prior to both democratising at the end of the twentieth century.

I called David over for another round of drinks. He was dapper in his club uniform but seemed weary, too. This strike was taking its toll on all of us.

But Dapo's tale was not finished. 'Several years went by and the Indonesian travelled to Nigeria to see his friend. Behind the gates of a large compound was a marble-clad mansion. There were two Mercedes and three Toyota LandCruisers outside. The Indonesian was amazed and asked where the money had come from. "Do you see that road?" said the Nigerian pointing to the rain forest and dusty track outside. "100 per cent."'

Dapo chortled with his smoker's raspy laugh and Toks and I joined in, but really it was no laughing matter.

In recent comparisons between Indonesia and Nigeria the similarities were clear but so were the differences.[1] In the intervening years of military and democratic rule, Indonesia's corrupt but less greedy leaders had invested more in productive assets. The life expectancy of an Indonesian child at birth was around sixty-seven years in 2005, but Nigeria's was stuck at an appalling forty-eight years. What happened to the proportion of people living in poverty? All was much improved in Indonesia so that now four per cent were estimated at living in extreme poverty versus forty-six per cent in Nigeria.[2]

Another way to look at it was through a truly productive asset ripe for government investment – mothers. In Indonesia in 2005 there were an estimated 212 maternal deaths per 100,000 live births (nine per cent). In Nigeria, having a baby still caused a chilling 946 deaths per 100,000, or twenty-three per cent – more than double the rate.[3]

We laughed at Dapo's tall tale because that was what one did in Lagos. It was one of the endearing but perplexing aspects of the Nigerian (or was it Lagosian?) character – the capacity to dissect truly depressing facts about their country and its awful leadership and to laugh at them.

But Toks was serious in her reaction. 'That must have been after Babangida took over,' she observed contemptuously. I knew she described herself as a 'student of history' and saw no joke in her country's post-colonial leadership. 'Siphoning off so much, I mean.' She was outraged by how her country had changed in her lifetime.

'Once upon a time, when we showed the green passport at immigration in Britain, they'd be falling over themselves to let us in,' she had told me. Nigerians were then big spenders in the United Kingdom; many of the elite were educated at private school in the United Kingdom, and before the failure of the domestic education system had been valued as highly skilled immigrants. Since the upsurge of corruption, theft and fraud, the green passport was treated with suspicion. 'They think you're a crook until proven innocent.'

Toks explained the various views behind Nigeria's descent into corruption.[4] Some maintained that patronage culture, where traditional leaders looked after their kinsmen, was a contributor. To this day, poorer villagers approached their urban Nigerian relatives who had (even modestly) paid jobs for help with school fees and medical bills. They asked their better-off kin to use their influence to get youngsters into work. And wouldn't you, if you earned less than five dollars a day like ninety-eight per cent of the population?

But the pressure on the relatively well-off earners was also real. For some, the constant petitions for support created a powerful excuse for succumbing to petty (and not so petty) corruption and nepotism. For other Nigerian professionals, escape from familial demands came through an eagerly anticipated overseas posting.

The discovery and exploitation of oil in the early sixties was also considered a major cause for government exploitation. As in many oil-rich countries (Indonesia, Venezuela, Russia and Kazakhstan to name a few), high exchange rates – artificially inflated due to the strength of dollar-based oil sales (the 'Dutch Disease') – led to a collapse of agriculture and manufacturing. In Nigeria, older folk still grew misty-eyed describing northern Nigeria's formerly vibrant economy.

'There were mountains of groundnuts,' I heard on more than one occasion as people spoke of the massive harvests of this 'before-oil' export earner.

'People were employed in the leather tanneries, lace and textile factories, palm-oil production and car plants.'

All that economy was now dead. The northern states were barren of education and employment, with poverty, anger, depression and extremist Islamism the only crops.

Toks went on to describe how the civil war between July 1967 and January 1970 was another explosive contributor to corrupt society. I remembered the moving images of stick-thin Biafran children with malnourished potbellies, their skin curling off in tatters and their dark eyes moons of pain and despondency. In the 1980s, images of starving African children became distressingly common enough – currency for an international aid business seeking to alleviate suffering from several famines and wars on the continent – but the first images remained seared in my young brain.

Toks told me the ethnic divisions and tensions behind the civil war had a long simmering history but the powder was lit by a coup staged in 1966, six years after Nigeria gained its independence. Igbo soldiers ousted the government of Sir Abubakar Tafawa Balewa, a northerner, killing him in the process. The ousting of Tafawa Balewa by Igbo soldiers, and the emergence of Johnson Aguyi-Ironsi in the wake of this coup led to a retaliation coup by northern elements in the military six months later and the emergence of General Yakubu Gowon, a northerner. Before and after the counter-coup, an estimated 30,000 Igbos living in the north of the country were the victims of mob and racially targeted killings.

In response, the Igbo-dominated southeastern states took control of the oil-producing delta region, seceded from the federation and announced the formation of their own nation, Biafra. This action sparked the vicious two-and-a-half-year war with the federal military government in which possibly as many as two million people died.

The legacy of that dreadful war lives with Nigeria today. Toks described how distrust between ethnic, religious and regional groups deepened after the war and had never really been resolved.[5]

Following the war there had been a succession of military governments, some stained by growing corruption. General Gowon's military government was succeeded by that of the generally considered honest but brief rule of General Murtala Mohammed (1975–76) and that of Major General Olusegun Obasanjo (1976–79).[6] A civilian government led by President Shehu Shagari, returned in 1979, oversaw a new and reputedly greater explosion in corruption and a decline in public services and infrastructure. The military government of Major General Muhammadu Buhari (1983–85) briefly checked the corruption. Then, in 1985, along came the allegedly corrupt military regime of General Ibrahim Babangida.

Toks was intensely frustrated by the apparent extent of such wide-scale vice and the impunity of its perpetrators.

'Under IBB,' she continued, referring to the former military head of state by his initials (Ibrahim Badamasi Babangida), 'corruption seemed to grow rampant again. It is disgusting that so many people have enriched themselves on our country's wealth and taken it offshore.'

General Babangida was known in Nigerian media as the 'Evil Genius', a reference to his political adroitness during his time as dictator, and there were allegations that corruption became endemic under his rule.[7]

Toks's passion for her country and frustration at the path it had been taken on by its leaders was clear. The conversation would stay with me for a long time.

O

Thinking over our discussion the next day, I sat in my silent office in a reflective mood and traced the line of recent history further to see where it led. After eight years in power, General Babangida aborted a first attempt at bringing democracy back to Nigeria in 1993. He installed an interim and reportedly 'puppet' government under Ernest Shonekan. Less than three months later, General Sani Abacha grabbed power in a coup and began a four-year kleptocracy and reign of fear until his death, rumoured to be by poison, in 1998. It was not until the return of democracy in 1999, and the election of former military ruler Olusegun Obasanjo as President, that any meaningful reform could begin. I believed in the efforts of this reformist government, now in its second term of office, and some of its key ministers. They had notched up some victories, such as new telecommunications licences, which had led to a mobile phone revolution. Recapitalising the banks (such as Kevin's) had improved their stability and capacity to lend. But power reform was slow and creating an improved power ecosystem across all the supply chain was proving complex; it was clear it would be many years before Nigeria's power delivery capabilities would promote rather than hinder economic development.[8]

Another major source of concern was that the South-South oil-producing region, a 70,000 square kilometre delta of the Niger River – an area the size of Ireland – had become ever more politically unstable. It was a fragile environment of creeks, swamps and mangroves, and yet more than thirty million people lived there, making it one of the most densely populated parts of Africa. It was also criss-crossed by pipelines and oil wells producing two million barrels of oil per day. Since the Civil War and under successive northern-led military regimes, the region suffered from a lack of investment in infrastructure (roads, schools, medical facilities and more) and widespread environmental degradation from oil spillages.

During the mid-nineties while General Abacha was head of state, Ken Saro-Wiwa had emerged as a leader of the Ogoni people, one of the many tribes living on oil-producing lands and pressured for environmental and social justice. He mobilised the support of many Ogoni but also alienated many others. When four Ogoni chiefs who resisted his movement were brutally killed, he was arrested for allegedly inciting their murders. Many thought his trial was rigged by the government of General Abacha but, despite intense international lobbying, he was summarily executed in 1995.[9]

The return to democracy in 1999 saw governors, local politicians and leaders in oil-producing states arm youth (a term which could cover any male under fifty) groups to engage in attacks on oil installations and increase pressure on the federal government for an increased proportion of oil revenues and other demands. In 2003, needing more money and arms to ensure their re-election, these same people turned their thugs to kidnapping for ransom and oil theft. At first the oil theft was small scale and amateurish involving thieves using hacksaws to tap into pipelines, some international sales and the production of kerosene and petrol in illegal local refineries. But now, with complicity at different levels of government, the armed forces and business, the experienced youths, flush with arms and cash, had become entrepreneurial criminals and the scale and sophistication of the theft seemed inexorably on the rise.[10]

I sighed. While the president and some government ministers meant well, there was a long way to go to stabilise this situation and even longer before any real reform of such a deeply corrupt government would take hold.

I would do my analyses as objectively as I could for Kevin, but I knew I saw Nigeria's prospects as a glass half-full. I refused to believe that such dynamic, educated people could let their country continue to sink under the criminally vested interested actions of the few.

Despite my sadness, I chuckled to myself at another memory from last night.

O

'Let me tell you another story,' Dapo had said, late into the moonlit evening.

I looked out to the lagoon and the silhouettes of the luxurious boats docked there. A waxing gibbous moon shone clearly in the cloudless sky. I was surprised to see another gaunt fisherman passing by in his dugout canoe. He'd certainly be earning less than five dollars a day.

'It's about the Englishman, the American and the Nigerian who died and went to Hell.'

Toks and I picked up our glasses and listened.

'The Devil allowed them each a phone call,' he continued. 'The Englishman called his local pub to hear the football results. He talked for five minutes and when he'd hung up the Devil presented him with a bill for 500 pounds. The American called his bank to hear about his investments. He talked for ten minutes and when he'd hung up the Devil presented him with a bill for 10,000 dollars.

'The Nigerian called his wife and talked for an hour and a half.'

That *would* be the Nigerian, I thought. They could certainly talk.

'When he'd hung up,' Dapo continued, 'the Devil presented him with a bill for thirty naira—the price of a bag of groundnuts. Surprised, the Nigerian asked the Devil why the call was so cheap.'

Dapo paused, took a drag on his cigarette and exhaled a thin stream of smoke. 'The Devil replied, "You're calling from Hell. A call to Nigeria is a local call".'

We laughed some more – what else could we do?

As I emerged on this quiet day of the general strike from the office kitchen with my welcome cup of coffee in my hand, Remi and Chuks burst through the office front door, chatting loudly. They broke my reverie about last night's boat club encounters and reflections on Nigeria's past and I greeted them.

'It was very expensive to come in,' Remi announced. 'The *okadas* are charging too much.'

Now the sun was out, we were under pressure to build up paper stocks. I had asked Remi and some of the papermaking casual workers to come in on this mid-week strike day. I wanted them to mould paper and had told the team I would pay their transport fares (in addition to their daily rate), which would be inflated due to the strike.

'My Molue was held up by the police,' said Chuks.

Like me, he had experienced a shake-down. 'The driver eventually paid, but he collected the money from the passengers before he'd travel further.'

I had come to appreciate that my approach of saying 'no' did not work for my Nigerian employees. They were hassled at road checks and asked for documents that were hard to come by or which did not exist. On many occasions, I'd receive a call from a stressed employee telling me he was 'settling' a policeman who had held him up for half an hour and that he would be late. As it was on an official assignment or coming in to work, I reimbursed him for his dash.

I did not see then that I was setting up the same kind of expectation in my employees that I had so carefully avoided with the public officials.

At last this difficult day seemed to be coming together. Peter and Sonny were already downstairs in the workshop and Remi went to join them. Chuks went to his desk in the Ekologika Papers craft room to develop mock-ups of table calendars. Zainab, the new senior consultant, then rang to let me know that she was on her way and I saw a text from John, the other new consultant, with the same message. I had asked them to start planning for Haresh's long-delayed assignment, which was finally due to start after the strike. It felt great to be able to hand over some of the workload to experienced consultants (and I was particularly hopeful that the mature Zainab might be partner material).

I was still standing in reception with my empty coffee cup when Yinka and Kola arrived. Yinka was doing great work developing original graphic designs for our calendars and Christmas cards, and Kola had prospected amongst his former corporate customers to gauge interest in our products. Despite the setback of the strike, I was grateful to have this show of commitment from both my teams.

'Madam, can I speak with you?' asked Kola, who seemed agitated.

I ushered him into my office.

'Madam, I know you have said we must not pay kick-back ...' I had given Kola a lecture about this before he joined.

'But we need to give them something to win the order.' He named a manager in an international firm's corporate gifts department. I was shocked at the blatant request.

'I'm sorry, Kola,' I said. He was persistent.

'Can we at least give them a Christmas hamper?'

Learning to say no was going to be difficult for my staff, I thought and that day I stuck to my guns.

What I did not realise was that, for me, learning the consequences of refusal was to be even harder.

CHAPTER SEVEN

Our Woman in Lagos

The earth moves at different speeds depending on who you are.
— Nigerian proverb

Sometimes it does not pay to advertise.

'Don't put a signboard outside your office,' my auditor had advised me. 'Once they know an *oyibo* is working in an establishment, the tax authorities will swoop and make up reasons for you to pay enormous fines or exorbitant back taxes, and then suggest a smaller sum to "settle them".' He was describing their demands for a bribe to make the tax demands disappear.

Businesses (especially small ones) in Nigeria, even when not evading tax, learned to avoid rapacious, blackmailing tax officers. My landlord Philippe had no signboards outside the building and had also asked me to keep a low profile.

'They want you to pay them—personally,' continued my auditor. 'So they use their power to make you weep.'

Because of this I stood outside the door of my office on the dimly lit second floor, late on a Thursday evening in early October, now seven months into my independent life, admiring my brass plaque, which was seen only by those who already knew it was there. After two and a half years of impatient waiting and with my security clearance completed, the McKinsey & Company strategy recommendations had been accepted and the Australian Foreign Minister found time to sign me into existence. I was appointed Honorary Consul for Australia in Lagos. My brass plaque bore the engraving 'Australian Consulate'.

I was excited.

I moved through the front door into the brightly lit reception, which was now adorned with an Australian flag on a wooden pole and stand. My handyman, Thomas, had made it for me – this time without too much *wahala*. Alone in the office, I looked proudly at the carefully arranged brochures about Australia and the somewhat out-of-date Australian yearbook. These items, together with some business cards embossed in gold with the Australian coat of arms, comprised what was grandly called my Establishment Kit.

It seemed these bits and pieces were all I was going to get from this appointment – apart from a small honorarium that did not seem much at all in Lagos where rents and salaries rivalled New York's. I thought back to my recent phone conversation with the High Commissioner in Abuja.

'The cable just arrived from Canberra,' he said. There was never any small talk from this High Commissioner. 'Your appointment is official. Congratulations. You are now our woman in Lagos.'

I felt more kindly towards him.

'And there is more good news,' he said. I imagined a diplomatic bag bringing some Australian delicacy (contraband Vegemite?) or a diplomatic number plate to foil the dash-hungry policemen. Maybe even a stamp in my passport to speed me through immigration. But these benefits remained in my imagination.

'Canberra has expanded your remit,' said the High Commissioner triumphantly. 'You are responsible for Lagos and the eighteen southern states of the Federation.'

Lagos *and* the eighteen southern states of the Federation. There were thirty-six states in total so now my remit included half the country, including the oil-producing states that generated ninety per cent of Nigeria's government revenue. Was this part of McKinsey's cunning strategy to save Australian taxpayer's money?

'Will I have trade responsibilities?' I asked.

That would have made sense to me – after all, I was in the commercial capital of this emerging giant. Britain had a huge trade and cultural representation in Lagos and Abuja, matching the importance of Nigeria as a trade partner and destination of United Kingdom foreign aid. The level of investment in the relationship also reflected the numbers of Nigerians in the diaspora in the UK – said to be up to one million. In comparison with this, Australia's interests in Nigeria (and vice versa) were minuscule. But I felt the British had proven that, despite its complexity and difficulties, profitable trade and investment could be made in Nigeria. So I anticipated using my role to encourage Australian business people, and especially the significant education sector, to look more closely at this part of the world. I hoped the payoff for my consulting firm would be advising Australian investors and universities on the opportunities and facilitating connections between Nigerians needing goods and services with Australian providers.

'No,' said the High Commissioner, disappointingly. 'There is an Austrade commissioner in Pretoria.'

Austrade was the Australian government's trade and development agency, but Pretoria was 4500 kilometres away to the south. In my now nearly six years in Lagos, I was yet to see a representative from Austrade.

'The McKinsey study recommended a focus on southern Africa,' continued the High Commissioner by way of explanation. It felt like a self-fulfilling prophecy to me – Australia's interests in Nigeria, except for a few intrepid investors, would remain small with this level of investment by our government in the relationship. I figured I'd continue to wait for Austrade.

'How many Australians will I be responsible for?' I asked, wondering what this expanded remit might entail.

'We don't know,' he replied. 'Actually, that's what we hope you'll help us find out. We only know about those who register on our website, but we think there are a lot of Australians who don't register—they don't think they need to or else they don't want to.' He laughed uneasily. 'You know—unpaid alimony, running from the law. They don't like to be on the record.'

Australians as convicts. Our diplomatic service clearly thought highly of the citizens they served.

O

My musings were interrupted by a knock at the door. It was Dapo. He had promised to come to admire my new plaque and was grasping a bottle.

'This is Number One Prayer Libation Drink,' he said as he waved it in front of me. I was pleased to have his boisterous presence but wondered what on earth he was talking about. I read the label – Seaman's Aromatic Schnapps.

'This schnapps is used to call the spirits of the ancestors,' Dapo clarified. I wondered if he'd been drinking it.

'That's how it's advertised. Number One Prayer Libation Drink,' he repeated.

I later found out it was true. The aromatic schnapps was the best-selling liquor for traditional libations where the ancestors and spirits are called upon to help the living, such as the annual Yoruba festival at Osogbo Forest in Osun State, north of Lagos. Around 600 years ago, a river god startled villagers who were felling nearby trees, telling them to stop because the *orishas* (spirits) lived there.

Nowadays, partly thanks to Suzanne Wenger, an Austrian woman who devoted her life to saving the forest and its traditional culture, Osun-Osogbo is a sacred grove and UNESCO World Heritage site. Each year priests and devotees of these traditional beliefs arrive with sacrifices of chickens or rams, or offerings of kola nuts or gin, to implore the spirits' assistance and blessings. Seaman's Schnapps (amongst others), now sponsored the annual festival and even sold schnapps in handy single libation-size sachets.

'What are you going to do with that?' I asked Dapo, but before he could reply Toks put her head around the office door.

'Good evening, Consul General.' She gave me an enthusiastic hug, side to side in the Nigerian way.

'It's time to get the support of the ancestors,' said Dapo and with a magician's flourish, tossed a sizeable dollop of liquor on the clean, tiled floor by the entrance and began to speak in pidgin. 'As schnapps no dey expire, the good work wey you wan do wan do no go spoil.'

His rough translation was: 'Just as liquor grows better with age, may your work continue to bloom and grow'. But he did not stop there and added a second dollop. 'Make we ancestors dey helep you well well and ya mama/papa spirit go day protect you,' he said.

He asked that the ancestors' light shine upon me, and that the spirit of my mother and father protect me all the days of my life.

Very nice, I thought. I could do with some help from the spirits, but one problem remained – my parents were still alive.

I was still surprised that traditional beliefs sat alongside organised religious practices. I often saw groups of women wearing white prayer gowns and hats – old-fashioned, floppy housemaid's head-coverings – entering the sea or lagoon to pray, possibly to God or possibly to Mami Wata, the mermaid spirit of the ocean. Dapo's ceremony, however, had no mystique as it was a bit like going to a Scottish Burns Night supper and hearing the toast to the haggis in an equally incomprehensible tongue. I was touched by his theatrics and the effort he had gone to – and took it as an expression of goodwill and friendship.

But Toks was unimpressed by Dapo's performance. From her capacious handbag she produced another glistening bottle. 'Get some glasses Pamela. I think we'd all prefer some champagne.'

O

Mike was the incoming second secretary of the High Commission in Abuja, which I gathered was also the Deputy High Commissioner role. He seemed more real and unpretentious than any of the other diplomatic staff I had dealt with to date. He was knowledgeable about the system within which he operated – the Australian diplomatic world and associated public service – and was cynical about it. In that, he reminded me of Dapo and I liked him.

'You probably won't have much to do really,' he told me when I first met him and asked about my nebulous-seeming role. 'The busiest honorary consuls are in places like Milan where Aussie mums and dads come over for their first trip away and mum gets her handbag pinched by a bloke on a motorbike. In Lagos, the Aussies working here are likely to be streetwise, and you don't get any tourists.'

This first meeting with Mike was only three weeks after my appointment and was in Greece, courtesy of the Australian taxpayer. My appointment had come through in time for me to be invited to a regional management conference of consular staff from the Middle East and Africa. I turned out to be the only Honorary Consul amongst the old hands.

In the run-up to my departure, I was fully briefed about my predetermined travelling allowance. There was a five-page document on how I could save money on incidentals such as local transport and drinks and which meals were to be paid from the fixed daily allowance. On arrival at Athens airport, I followed instructions and economically caught a train into the city only to find I was being lodged at an opulent five-star hotel on Syntagma Square. The incongruity between the frugality encouraged of an individual on their fixed allowance and extravagance for the group paid for by the departmental budget, seemed lost on my new colleagues. Public servants and I came from different worlds.

I had also been perturbed that with all this attention to my purse, there had been nothing about the agenda or objectives of the conference. On arrival I discovered that it was focused on serving consular customers and dealing with emergencies. The underlying assumptions about customers seemed to be that most visa applicants were up to no good and that most Australians who sought help at far-flung diplomatic posts were dim-witted fools who lost their passports or got unreasonably angry with bureaucratic delays. As a result, the customer service training given to consular staff advised us to call security and eject these suspicious and bothersome individuals.

Developing an emergency evacuation plan to ensure the welfare of all affected Australians was also an essential responsibility for any mission, I learned.

'Do not make your evacuation plans top secret,' said the trainer.

Apparently, one country's mission had made their evacuation plans classified, and when there was a major terrorist bombing, the consular staff found they were not allowed to tell anyone what to do, thus proving that idiots inhabit all walks of life.

Now that I was in a position to do something about such matters, I wanted to find out from Mike what I was expected to do in the case of an emergency.

'What if there was a plane crash at Murtala Muhammed Airport in Lagos?' I speculated as I drank a beer with him in Athens. This was not a very far-fetched scenario. Airlines had a very poor safety record in Nigeria and deadly accidents were an almost annual occurrence. 'What should I do?'

I envisaged finding out if any Australians were on board, discovering who they worked for, liaising with their company, possibly facilitating medical treatment or evacuations, and providing information to family members.

'Just sit tight and wait for the head of the mission to tell you what to do,' said Mike. 'And if you don't hear from him, you could head out to the airport to see what you can find out.'

Well, it was a plan – of sorts.

O

Following my return from Athens in early November, I organised an introductory drinks evening at a small restaurant with all the Australians I could locate through my own networks.

'We can't give you the names of those Aussies who register with DFAT,' Mike had told me and went on to explain why. 'It's the Freedom of Information Act. We can only use data for the purpose intended and when they register it's for emergencies, not parties.'

Champagne was not on offer but there were copious quantities of Australian wine. One of my connections was an Australian wine distributor, Bruce, who flew in from time to time to do his West African market rounds. At my request, he'd kindly donated some bottles to my group of twenty grateful consumers.

It took a surprising amount of time to arrange the event. The High Commissioner was no help.

'There's no budget left this year for a trip to Lagos,' he told me. 'And no budget left for events.'

The McKinsey strategy for Australia to focus on southern Africa meant a shoestring representation in Nigeria.

It was all very frustrating; and it made me feel that in this role I was on my own too.

A friend kindly offered the private room and Yinka designed an invitation. Kunle, a young analyst who had just joined Strategyworks, was given the task of compiling records for all the Australians, and Gloria rang them up to invite them. I, of course, paid for the canapés.

Planning all this required time I did not really have. Strategyworks was now swamped with work – Haresh's strategy assignment needed a final push for completion, there was further work for Kevin's bank, and various workshops to design and deliver. At Ekologika Papers, the team was busy (although the big sales Kola had been promising for months were slow to close).

'Clients send Christmas orders just before Christmas,' Dapo had told me, scoffing that I might think they'd make their minds up any sooner. 'Of course, you could speed things up with a brown envelope.'

So I could have done without organising this consular event. But I wanted to make progress on the one goal I'd been set – to build the Australian community in Lagos – and I hoped to begin relationships that might lead to consulting work. Some of my guests, such as Kevin, were familiar to me but most were barely known or completely new acquaintances. Having last worked in Australia in the mid-nineties, I found it odd to be amongst Australian voices and characters. After mixing with hugely ambitious, risk-taking, exuberant Nigerians they all seemed a little quiet and restrained, like warm milk compared to a shot of tequila.

I chatted with Father Jim, a Catholic priest I'd met a few times, who had been posted to Lagos over thirty years ago. With a large, beer-fed tummy, tufts of thinning hair and a thriving white beard, he had a kindly Father Christmas air about him. He was attached to the Lagos University Teaching Hospital (LUTH) and did valuable work counselling young people. But once conversation turned to the nature of Catholicism after Vatican Council II and how it had changed under the last two popes, I looked around the room for rescue.

Making my excuses to Father Jim, I moved away to introduce myself to a woman nearby. She had a hearty laugh and seemed to be attracting glances from around the room. Striking, with enviably sleek dark brown hair framing her long oval-shaped face and rather lovely amber skin and dark brown eyes, she looked as though she had an Asian background. Her name was Michelle and she told me about how she ended up in Lagos.

'I'm from Kuching in Malaysia,' she said. Later I discovered her Chinese–Malay mother met her Anglo–Australian father when he worked for a palm oil company in Sarawak in the seventies. From her story I gathered she was in her mid-thirties but she looked about twenty-five. 'I grew up in Kuching and only came to Perth on holidays until I studied software engineering at UWA.' This was my alma mater – the University of Western Australia. 'I was an environmental activist too, but when I finished, I took up teaching, married too young and became a Cottesloe wife, until my marriage fell apart.' She grimaced, possibly from a memory of her failed marriage, and I matched her facial expression – her comment reminded me of a fate that could easily have been mine if I hadn't been determined to find my destiny elsewhere. 'It was devastating— then I realised I was still young and free to see the world. A job in international software sales for a company that sells into the mining industry came up,' she said. 'And I grabbed it.'

She was an animated storyteller and seemed ambitious. Was there more hidden dynamism in this roomful of Aussies than I'd given them credit for?

Michelle continued, 'I lived out of a suitcase for five years, but I've discovered I'm not really into the corporate gig so was wondering what next. Last year in London I met a Nigerian guy, he told me about Lagos, and I thought it sounded wild, so I came on spec—the rest is history,' she said.

What was she doing now, a year later? She had an IT role with an American NGO that built schools around Africa. She seemed passionate to be back in education – 'helping deprived kids instead of working to help mining companies improve their profits' and her NGO work – 'We build schools and give the kids a chance in life'. It sounded vague and rather clichéd. Why did no one ever get excited about opportunities to help children's mothers? They were the ones who suffered and scraped to give their children the best chance in life. I also thought her story rather unlikely. How had she found this role and changed track so quickly? And as she described her trips to different African countries, I wondered why a school-building NGO would base her in expensive Lagos. Was it an excuse for travelling around Africa undetected? Was she a drug runner or an arms dealer? I thought about the High Commissioner's comments about Australians lying low and running from the law.

At least, she was a vibrant character who, like me, seemed to have exchanged business certainty for a more adventurous life.

Was she a kindred soul? I figured I'd enjoy learning more about her later.

I ambled over to Kevin and Aaron, the Australian soft-drink managing director (who had communicated to me that the time was not right for his consulting work), and a third person – a tall but overweight man in suit trousers and a crumpled shirt that strained around his middle. He had his back to me but guffawed at something Kevin said as I approached. As he turned I saw a loudly patterned tie that matched his booming laugh, strangled his throat and scrunched his unbuttoned collar. Who was this dishevelled guy?

'Let me introduce you to Steve,' said Kevin.

Steve? Was this Stephen, the Australian head of petroleum engineering for a major United States oil company? I knew he was on the invitation list and had planned to introduce myself. The company had two beach huts at Agaja that were threatened by erosion. I'd written asking for support to save the island but had never got a reply.

'G'day mate,' said Steve and extended a fleshy hand while he disconcertingly looked at the wall above my head. While I thought about how to make my play for support for Agaja, Kevin told him about the work I was doing for his bank – good old Kevin helping market Strategyworks's services.

'Sounds beaut,' said Steve in such a strong Australian accent that I wondered if he was putting it on.

'You know what they say about consultants,' said Aaron. 'It's someone who borrows your watch to tell you the time.'

So original, Aaron, I thought and brought my glass to my lips to hide a grimace. Thanks for the soft drinks. I thought it unlikely I'd ever get any work from him.

But the laughs were not over.

'Have you blokes heard about the man who went to the pet store looking for a monkey?' asked Steve. He paused to toss back some red wine like it was a thirst-quenching beer. 'Three monkeys sat in separate cages and the salesman showed him the first one. "This one costs $500," said the salesman. "It can sing Happy Birthday.'"

"'How much is this one?" asked the man, pointing to the second monkey.'

"'That one costs $1500", said the salesman. "He can speak three languages.'"

Kevin and Aaron listened intently – after all, Steve seemed to be speaking to them, rather than me.

'The astonished man then asked about the third monkey,' Steve continued loudly. Was he telling the whole room?

"'That one costs $5000," said the salesman.'

"'Hell, what can it do?" asked the man.'

"'I've never seen it do anything mate," said the salesman, "but it calls itself a consultant"'.

Funny, I thought. Australian men could be relied on to start a conversation with a put down but I was so long out of the country that I wasn't sure how to respond. I considered telling them the one about the priest, the lawyer and the engineer who were to be executed during the French Revolution. After all, I bet Steve had originally been an engineer. But I decided on diplomacy by silence instead.

I picked up a knife from the bar and tapped it against my glass to gain the room's attention.

'Welcome and thank you for coming,' I said as a circle of liquor-brightened faces looked towards me. I had prepared a brief speech to describe my new role and plans. Lacking much direction from the High Commission, it was all a bit vague, but there was something the High Commissioner had asked me to say.

'We'd like you all to register on the DFAT website,' I said. It was the same register that I was not allowed to access for names. 'In the event of an emergency or something happening to any of you, it can speed up the High Commission and me being able to provide support and to make contact with your family.'

'With all due respect,' came a loud voice interrupting me. I looked around. It was Steve, who moved into the centre of the room. 'I think my company, with all its resources, will be more help to you in the case of an emergency than our Hon Con.'

He was right – after all, he was part of a multinational organisation, and quite a number of the Australians present lived behind his company's compound walls. Mike's suggestion that I sit tight to wait for instructions was, after all, pretty passive and vague and the High Commission could not even provide me with funds for a party so what hope was there for an emergency?

Steve flourished a refilled glass of red wine – the wine I had provided – and held centre stage. I disliked this boorish move as much as him calling me 'Hon Con' and I brooded over my joke about the execution of the priest, lawyer and engineer.

The executioner asked the priest if he wanted to face up or down beneath the guillotine.

'I want to see my maker,' declared the priest. The blade went down but stopped inches above his neck.

'It is divine intervention,' declared the priest, and was released.

The lawyer was next for execution and he too chose to lie face-up. The knife came down and stopped inches above his neck.

'It's a precedent,' he said. 'You must let me go too.' So they did.

Now it was the engineer's turn. He decided what was good for the others, was good for him too and lay facing up. The executioner was getting the blade ready when the engineer looked up and pointed.

'Hey!' he said. 'I see what the problem is.'

I imagined Steve lying under the repaired guillotine. Whoosh!

'Thanks Steve,' I said, interrupting him. 'Maybe we can talk further about the help you can provide for our Australian community.'

Then I thought again of Agaja. 'And how you can help our host communities, too.'

Perhaps I could make use of his ego and resources after all.

CHAPTER EIGHT

Black Goats

Black goats must be caught early, before it gets dark.

– Nigerian proverb

At the end of November Alec was finally in Lagos again, his first visit since leaving last year. In brief flying visits to London, we had seen each other every eight to ten weeks – not the six we'd planned, due to our work demands. But during the past couple of days, I had heard Alec explain he was in Lagos to transact some gas business. Wasn't I the primary reason for his visit?

For me, it felt unsettling, being a couple again – in my town.

'Has she left Alec?' people wanted to know. 'What is she up to?'

A Nigerian friend told me that I was a topic of conversation amongst the Ikoyi set, both expatriate and Nigerian. Despite my own work, when Alec was in Lagos it was his status as a gas executive that apparently defined me. To others, I was an accompanying spouse (or spouse equivalent). In the past ten months, people we knew had reportedly speculated about why I stayed on in Lagos without him.

Was my motivation still unclear to them? Was running two businesses and being Honorary Consul insufficient motivation? Or was the most interesting thing about me my relationship with Alec?

Now that Alec was back in Lagos, I assumed these folks would realise we were still together. But given how hard it seemed for people to 'see' me, I hoped his presence did not muddy the waters again.

Alec's visit coincided with an event that, as a Scot, was quintessentially his – the St Andrew's Day Ball. St Andrew is the patron saint of Scotland and 30 November was his feast day, Scotland's national day and a day of celebration for the Scottish community everywhere. Scots took their celebrations seriously and here in Lagos their ball – on the nearest Saturday evening – was a highlight of the expatriate social calendar. Alec had got tickets.

He looked fabulous – resplendent in a green and blue kilt made from his clan's tartan, white dress shirt, bow tie and short black Highland jacket made from thick wool. The ensemble was very hot for tropical Lagos, but Scottish men were ever slaves to fashion. Completing the traditional outfit was a leather sporran hung from a decorative belt and a *sgian dubh* (a small knife) tucked into one of his knee-high socks. Good legs and a macho swagger fluttered his kilt with every step. Mel Gibson certainly had competition.

Scots men in Highland garb also easily rivalled Nigerians for sartorial impact. But tonight, not many Nigerians were coming, at least not in their dazzling traditional outfits. At other events I was used to the impressive display of acres of brocade and rich lace fabric worn with a flourish in bat-winged *agbadas* – and that was the men.

Women's traditional outfits involved as much gold jewellery as a Spanish conquistador could wish to plunder, colourful wrappers and enormous headdresses. If I wanted to see anything at an event, I'd learned to avoid being seated behind one of these flamboyant fabric crowns.

I'd also observed that, excluding the eternally (and enviably) elegant French or Lebanese women, white women in the tropics struggled to look anything but as wilted and pale as week-old leeks. Some tried imitation but the bright colours of African wax-print fabrics made white skin look a seasick green. I'd long since stopped competing. I admired the splendid display but wore a little black dress.

Tonight, the other women, like me, looked like dully-plumaged peahens. But there was one item that diminished the romantic, swashbuckling, devil-may-care appearance of the glamourous peacocks. Most of them carried jauntily coloured plastic cool boxes in which they stored the evening's supply of booze. After all, true to the Scots' thrifty reputation, it was cheaper than paying at the bar.

'Alec!' a familiar voice called out.

Dapo and his wife Esther, and Toks and her husband Ayo, entered. I rarely saw their hard-working partners, so this would be a welcome opportunity to enjoy their company. They were our guests, joining us at our table, and looked extremely smart in formal western dress.

'Welcome to Lagos,' said Dapo to Alec, using a common local greeting for a new arrival.

We hugged then paused to have our photos taken – part of the evening's festivities – before joining another queue to enter the hall. The members of the organising committee were lined up like a firing squad on the other side of the entrance to greet arrivals. The last to greet guests was the President of the Lagos Caledonian Society. With a reference to Scottish clans, and not to Nigerian chieftaincies, he was called their Chieftain.

'I hope we're not at the high table,' I whispered to Alec.

'No problem about that,' said Alec. 'I'm not in favour after my email.'

In our first year in Lagos the organising committee had warmly received the authentically Scottish Alec and we were seated at the high table. Being a spectacle was not my scene and after that we had scrambled for the 'low tables' – if we could get the sought-after tickets. This time, on being told tickets were sold out within a day of their release (giving rise to the suspicion they were pre-allocated to friends) – Alec sent a strongly worded email to the organising committee. We got our tickets, but I wondered how we'd be greeted.

As we waited in the slow-moving queue, I discussed with Dapo the disappointing results from offset printing on our paper. Chuks had recently shown me papers printed on Dapo's machines – the designs didn't print sharply and the colours were muddy.

'I don't think your friend's machines do high-quality colour work,' Chuks told me.

It was disappointing but also surprising, as I knew Dapo was very busy near to Christmas with printing corporate calendars. 'His workers aren't very careful,' Chuks continued. 'But this printing method doesn't work on our paper. There are four-colour runs to build up the final picture and because our paper's surface texture is uneven the image gets blurred.'

I understood the problem, knowing handmade paper was not smooth.

'And our paper has a high moisture content, so it absorbs too much ink and the colours become muddy,' Chuks finished.

I wished I could have visited Dapo's printing works myself but with the end of the year looming, my time was dedicated to completing the consulting assignments that paid our bills. I increasingly relied on the most senior Ekologika Papers team members – Peter and Remi in papermaking, Kola in sales, Yinka and Sonny in design and Chuks in conversion – to run the business. Frustratingly slow production rates, mainly due to waste and rework, combined with the high cost of ink and printing, meant I wasn't sure we'd make a profit on the orders we had taken.

'Chuks recommended we keep using desktop printing,' I said to Dapo.

'You can't afford it, Pamela,' he said, with strong emphasis on each word. 'Your staff is being mischievous. They do not want it to work.'

'What do you mean?' I had seen the printed papers and the quality *was* poor. How should I tell Dapo I thought the fault was at his end?

'Your Chuks—you trust him, but he is playing tricks. They all play tricks.'

'If you don't trust people, they live up to your expectations, Dapo,' I thought but did not say. His printers might play tricks, but I was building a different kind of team. While they frustrated me with mistakes, I believed they were dedicated. I changed the subject.

'It looks like we're not going to make our sales target,' I confided. Kola's promised corporate sales had failed to materialise and, with less than four weeks to Christmas, the sales now looked very unlikely. 'Anyway, if we'd won all the orders he'd prospected, we might have run out of paper.'

'Cards or calendars?' Dapo asked.

'Quite a few of each. It's amazing the way companies here want Christmas card orders of 5000 and 10,000 cards.'

Dapo guffawed.

'You'll never win those, Pamela,' he said. 'UNICEF have killed the Christmas card market for Nigerian suppliers.'

I knew UNICEF was a tough competitor. Each Christmas we received a lot of corporate Christmas cards, mostly from the UNICEF range.

'What do you mean, killed the market?' I asked.

'Their annual collection is created by international designers— so no work for Nigerian graphic designers. They print the cards in China—so no work for Nigerian printers. I used to print tens of thousands of cards each Christmas,' Dapo said. 'Now, nothing. It's the same for all printers here. UNICEF!'

'But can't you compete?' I asked.

'Mass production in Asia means cost per card is low, and they use independent sales agents. The agents are given high commissions. It gives them room to manoeuvre, Pamela. Do you understand me?'

I did. I had heard that independent sales agents were known to make illicit payments, and sometimes this was a method by which companies kept bribery at arm's length in corrupt environments.

I felt sad. Africa had industries and business people who could look after their families if they were given the chance of fair competition and access to markets. Unfortunately, this sort of dubious and hyper-competitive behaviour by outsiders, which pushed out local suppliers, was not new.

For example, if Africa should be successful in anything surely it should be as farmers feeding themselves – but not with the world's largest agricultural trading bloc as a competitor. The European Union's (EU) iniquitous common agricultural policy (CAP) had stunted the development of local agri-processing industries and damaged the livelihoods of Africa's poorest farmers – most of whom were women – for decades.[1]

Established post-war as the EU mechanism to ensure the EU's farmers a fair livelihood and to guarantee food security, the CAP had instead become an instrument of oppression against the same achievement by the farmers of developing countries. Since the seventies, surplus dairy, beef, sugar and wheat – unfairly and massively subsidised and protected in the EU – were dumped in Africa at prices below the local costs of production. In the nineties, the story came out that EU-subsidised beef was damaging the same West African cattle farmers that EU aid supported.[2] It was a scandal then, so it should be old news by now. But despite some reforms, the damage and distortion to aid recipient economies and food security remained.[3] The seemingly benevolent EU provided aid to build rural schools and start programmes to send girls to school. But, at the same time, it engaged in practices that stole the income from agriculture, which would allow poor people and developing country governments to build rural schools and hospitals for themselves. What double standards.[4]

'Buy a UNICEF card to save the life of a child,' quoted Dapo, breaking into my thoughts. 'Huh! What Nigerian child? The child of the UNICEF bureaucrat living in Geneva?'

I'd never feel the same way about receiving a UNICEF Christmas card again.

Would our premium-priced cards be chosen for smaller orders, as they were local and handmade? I hoped so, but that would be a strategy for next year.

The queue moved forward and it was time to greet the Chieftain. To my relief, the large, red-faced Monarch of the Glen joked with Alec and patted him on the back as though nothing had happened. We moved into the tartan-decorated hall full of excited voices and the live band was playing ceilidh music. I took a glass of champagne from a hovering waiter and, while Alec chatted with friends, I looked for the board displaying seating arrangements. The number of tables dismayed me; it would take a while to scan them all.

Glamorous, shape-shifting Toks came to my side, her own glass of champagne in hand. Tonight her hair fell in long glossy tresses. She'd probably spent at least a whole day (or two) having real Indian hair woven into her own to achieve the look. It was one beauty treatment white women did not have to endure (and pay big bucks for), although I might have swapped my wild and curly Caucasian hair for her wrinkle- and cellulite-free skin. Wearing a sheath dress, she looked very different from her Agaja self, and her dainty, strappy and tottery high-heeled golden sandals did not look suitable for the night's ceilidh.

'Scots' idea of dancing can involve a lot of foot stamping,' I said. 'Stamping *on* women's feet.' I pointed out the sensible flat and closed footwear worn by women who came each year – some even wore boots.

'They'll feel my knee if they do,' said Toks laughingly, although I was not sure she was joking.

I turned back to the seating list and told her about Alec's email and my trepidation at reprisals. She looked at the board with me then suddenly shot her painted fingernail towards our table.

'The Chieftain *has* got his revenge,' she said.

Indeed. Our table was in the farthest corner of the room.

O

Alec had left and it was mid-December, the busy run-up to Christmas and year-end and the culmination of all my, and my teams', planning, work and focus.

There was a knock at my office door and Zainab walked in. Both teams had been working the Saturday before Christmas, striving to deliver clients' urgent deadlines. I could not fault anyone's commitment.

'Can I talk to you?' she asked.

Immediately I worried what was to come.

'Of course, sit down,' I said.

'I felt I had to tell you straight away ...'

'Yes?'

'You know that my husband has had difficulty finding work?'

Yes, I knew. He was younger than her, an IT consultant, and I privately thought he seemed rather feckless.

'I have a British passport and he feels he will get work if we move to the UK. We have decided to go ... and so I am resigning.'

'That's disappointing,' I said, my heart pounding. With Feyi it was a baby, with Deola it was a better job offer, and now with Zainab, her husband – all going when I needed them. Zainab had maturity that the other consultant John, and Kunle, the relatively new analyst, lacked. We had already spoken about her becoming a partner and I had felt that with her support we could build up the consulting practice.

'Don't worry about this assignment, Pamela,' she continued, referring to the work we were doing for Haresh. 'I'll stay committed and I won't leave until February when it's done. But I wanted to tell you so you could start recruiting for someone to replace me.'

I knew she was sincere, but my eyes were moist and my chest tight. I felt on my own again.

There was uproar outside. It must have been serious to travel up two storeys and through glass windows. I jumped up, as much for a distraction as to check out what was going on.

Downstairs, I saw a large black goat running loose in the car park with three of my team members chasing noisily after it. The lithe animal jumped nimbly onto the bumper of my CRV, then the bonnet, then up the windscreen onto the roof, as easily as if it were a pile of rocks in a Malian village. Though Peter, Sonny and Remi seemed to have him covered, my money was on the goat's ability to slip through their clumsy dragnet. I went to join them.

'Why is a goat on my car?' I called to the perspiring team.

'It's the goat for Agaja, Madam,' said Remi, whose sweat made him look as though he'd been swimming. 'You said to get them food for the feast. We have a bag of rice as well.'

Tomorrow was the last Sunday before Christmas and I'd decided I'd like to provide a special meal for the villagers at Agaja. It was my gift to them, as well as the 'thirteenth month' salary payment – a bonus that was traditionally expected. I'd spoken to my caretaker, Luke, who had suggested rice and meat and I had given money to Peter to get supplies. I'd expected something frozen and in pieces. Now dinner was looking straight at me with appealing, doe-like eyes. I had a soft spot for goats. Could I send him to the cooking pot?

'Madam!' shouted a voice from on high. I looked up and saw Gloria on the office balcony. 'Madam—you have an international call,' she said. 'From London.'

'Catch the goat, guys,' I instructed and dashed back to the stairs. I'd think about his fate later.

James, the casual trainee papermaker I liked was waiting for me in the stairwell.

'Madam, can I talk to you?' he said with a shy smile.

Although I knew Remi was teaching James to be a papermaker and I had seen him wet and grinning at a papermaking station from time to time, I still really did not know him. However, experience with others meant I guessed what was to come.

I had received many requests for financial support from the Ekologika Papers casual workers. Each request had merit as the poorest in society struggled to find savings to pay lump-sum expenses such as paying two years' rent in advance, school fees, medical expenses and funeral bills. Without credit available from banks, it was expenses like these that drove people to commit fraud or theft. I helped my staff as much as I could, but their demands seemed to be getting higher and more frequent. The last time I paid a mother's funeral bill, an unworthy inner voice had wondered if she'd died twice.

'Can you talk to Peter?' I asked.

Although James seemed better educated than most of the casual workers and trustworthy, listening to the stories accompanying each request was draining. I now relied on Peter's judgement as to which were valid. James looked worried.

'I'll help if I can,' I added, still assuming this was what he wanted to speak to me about – and hurried up the stairs.

O

I returned to my office, and Gloria put the call through to me.

'Is that Pamela Watson?' said the voice. 'Are you free to talk?'

Now I was really worried.

'It is about a payment on your credit card,' continued the voice. She mentioned a sum of 2000 pounds and a payment to an online consumer electronics firm in the UK, a firm I had never heard of. I was confused and a bit slow on the uptake. She repeated the details. 'We wanted to check the transaction,' she said. 'It was flagged as potentially fraudulent.'

It was. I could hear rising, energy-filled voices and laughter coming from the offices outside. My teams were like my family. Had someone here done this to me? Was it an outsider? Like a virus being coughed into the air, spiralling up, waiting to be inhaled and to start its damage, her message brought terrible doubts.

Was this attempted fraud perpetrated by one of my team?

PART TWO

Palus (2006)

Palus is a topographical term applied to dark plains on the moon's surface; in Latin it means swamp, marsh or bog.[1]

CHAPTER NINE

Red Bull

If you want to go quickly, go alone. If you want to go far, go together.
— African proverb

It was a new year and I was dozing lightly in my seat on the overnight flight from London to Lagos. I was awoken by the clattering arrival of the trolley and a perky offer of breakfast. My sprawling seat companion, with a mask shielding his eyes and a seatbelt restraining his generous paunch, did not respond. Shaking off sleep and struggling to get an arm free from my blanket, I set my seat upright and groggily accepted a black coffee, just the stimulation needed to deal with an early morning arrival.

Our current position, overhead of Mali and the Niger River, was displayed on the flickering screen in front of me. The names alone conjured romance and mystery and in my dreaming mind's eye I could see the spreading inland delta of the Niger River, its waters slow-moving through a shadowy, sandy landscape. In my mental otherworld, the river was enveloped in a perpetual harmattan haze. I pictured the tightly packed mud-brick buildings, the sand-filled streets and the shuffling dun-coloured camels and donkeys of ancient Timbuktu 10,000 metres below me.

A memory flickered like the flight screen in my half-slumbering mind – Alec and I driving from Lagos to Timbuktu several years ago. We'd gone without a driver, not wanting to repeat the experience of travelling out of Nigeria with an English-speaking driver into nearby Francophone Togo. The man had needed help to order *poulet et frites* for his dinner, and – more worryingly – had not known what to do at a sign proclaiming *Arrêt*! This second time we'd gone in my lightweight, four-wheel-drive Honda CRV rather than Alec's heavy Toyota LandCruiser, which I had heard was a favoured target of the armed bandits said to be at large on the roads of Mali.

We spent one night in the remote trading town of Gao, beside the wide and milky Niger River. The manager of the *campement* asked us to leave our vehicle overnight at the police station.

'Why?' I'd asked.

'People have never seen such a beautiful small four-wheel-drive before,' he said. 'There are rumours that tonight it will be stolen by bandits.'

I reflected that the best laid plans of mice and women often go awry; not so different a conclusion drawn from last year. That thought and the caffeine jolted me into the present.

With Christmas in Australia passed, I was now back to Lagos for the start of a new business year. Three weeks in Perth with Alec was rejuvenating for our relationship, but in time spent with my parents I had been disconcerted by my father's short-term memory loss. I had also spent hours online and on the phone directing my teams from the other side of the world, so the break was less worry-free than I'd hoped. My plans for the previous year had not been entirely fulfilled, I knew. Running two businesses had proved a major source of stress and much harder than I had anticipated during the rosy optimism of early last year – especially as staff retention had proved so difficult.

But more fundamentally, the attempted fraud on my credit card (for the purchase of hi-fi equipment) lay heavily on my mind. The perpetrator was probably a member of my team.

Before my Christmas trip, I had tried to establish the guilty party. As an aspiring Hercule Poirot, I concluded the most likely culprit was a better-educated and more computer-literate member of my staff. My need to discover the offender outweighed any ethical doubts and I stayed behind at the office several evenings to search through employees' desks and read their emails. Chuks in Ekologika Papers and Kunle, my Strategyworks analyst, had vast collections of illegally downloaded music files, which may have demonstrated a possible interest in hi-fi equipment, but nothing directly implicated them.

With the chain of clues at an end, I gave up.

'Worry about what you can change, and not about what you cannot,' Toks had advised when I consulted her.

It was easier said than done. Our IT and credit card security systems could be improved, but this would not allay my suspicions. Before the holiday, I found myself still watching Chuks and Kunle, still looking for signals about their characters and loyalties.

As I gazed out the plane window at the red spear of dawn piercing the billowing dark clouds, another memory from the journey to Timbuktu with Alec arose in my mind.

We'd been driving for some hours through soft sand towards the crossing point in the Niger River that would take us to Timbuktu. I was behind the wheel and Alec was navigating. The landscape had changed; there were more bushes now and ahead, down a slight ridge, the ground seemed firmer and a deeper brown.

'The river is over there,' I cried, spying a sliver of silver glistening in the distance beyond the dark plain and I drove directly towards it.

Thunk.

Seat belts arrested our forward movement as we crunched firmly to a halt. What had happened? Had I hit something? I leapt out of the car and fell straight into mud. Black, sticky, gooey mud.

We had arrived on the floodplain of the Niger River and were bogged to our axles.

Alec swore while rummaging in the back for a spade. I looked around, stunned by our change of fortune and by my mud-splattered body. Then, as if by magic, a red fire engine appeared on the ridge above us.

'My name is Helmut,' announced a large ginger-haired German as he walked to our stranded vehicle. 'We have a 1972 Munich fire truck. We can rescue you—we have a 100-metre fire hose and can pull you out with that.' He waved back towards the truck and his companions.

Why were four German couples travelling across the Sahara in an old fire engine christened Red Bull? There was no time to ask questions and the local village was gathering to watch the spectacle. Within a half hour we were pulled free.

A turbaned Tuareg arrived on a camel and gesticulated wildly, indicating another vehicle in trouble further downstream. Helmut and the Red Bull crew sped off to perform another international rescue. We could only scratch our heads in wonder at the strangeness and serendipity of it all.

That was the Africa and the adventures I loved – a place where things had an unexpected way of turning out well, where people looked after each other, regardless of their backgrounds. It had been a happy trip, in simpler times.

Returning to the present, I wondered where Helmut and Red Bull were now – I felt in need of another rescue. I had two employees whose honesty I doubted, and my most reliable and smartest lieutenant, Zainab, was leaving. Her departure still felt a huge blow. I'd placed recruitment ads before the Christmas break and now had a shortlist of candidates. Yet on paper none was as experienced as Zainab and I wondered if I'd ever find a partner who would help share the burden of running the consulting business. Meanwhile my papermaking team's lack of attention to detail seemed incurable and the costs of rework were steadily rising. The team needed tight supervision, something I could not provide stretched between two businesses.

I glanced out my window again to watch the dawn's approach. The dense forest canopy was giving way to a mosaic of rusty roofs, unpaved tracks and patchy areas of sparkling light where NEPA was available. The red glow of taillights bobbed as cars and vans wove their way forward carrying early workers. We had begun our descent into Lagos.

I reached into my bag for my passport. Each Nigerian visa was valid for twelve months, so my years of residence had resulted in many pages covered in its familiar green sticker. I found the last one, renewed last April. Instead of twelve months I had been granted only nine months – something to do with the separate renewal date for the expatriate quota granted to my companies.

My mouth dropped open. Nine months had passed and my visa was several days out of date.

O

I left the aircraft in a dither, thoughts fluttering in my brain like a caged butterfly. Would I be put back on the next flight? Would I be arrested? This was my own fault, yet more plans gone awry. When Alec had been here, his company's protocol officers met him before the immigration counter. They took care of any pending issues and ushered him through. But I was on my own.

Well, not entirely.

My hands shook as I pulled out my phone and put a call through to my lawyer, Mr Atta. It was barely 6am.

'Wait, I'll call you back,' said Mr Atta, unperturbed by an early call but equally agitated at my situation. 'This is serious.'

Excruciating minutes passed as I fretted. I looked around the dilapidated airport. Air-conditioning outlets and a moving walkway promised a modern experience but neither had worked during my many years of arrivals. A ceiling tile hung down precariously above my head and I thought I'd better move. Then, my phone rang.

'I have a policeman on the way to help straighten things out,' said Mr Atta. He still sounded worried.

Would this involve payments to extricate myself? My scruples were about to be seriously challenged.

Having entered the immigration hall, I dawdled near the back of the very long queue of Nigerians, but my pale skin made lurking rather obvious.

'Foreigners to that queue.' A stern official pointed to a short line.

I excused myself to the toilet to buy some time but minutes later there was nowhere else to hide. It was time to face the music.

I was the last expatriate and held my breath as I handed my arrivals form and passport to an immigration officer. He peered at my form and laboriously transcribed the information to his own list. I tried to look nonchalant, deciding to feign surprise when he discovered my illegal alien status. I glanced towards the baggage and customs hall to see if any policeman might be making his way towards me. There was no friendly face and the man flicked through the pages of my passport until he got to my last visa page.

He copied details of my visa and looked up.

'Welcome, Pamela Jane,' he said with a broad smile.

He had either not noticed the unusual nine months' validity or was confounded by the maths of adding nine months to an April date. Whatever the reason, I was through.

For once, I was grateful for a lack of attention to detail.

Despite the muggy humidity, wafting body odours and the failure of the bags to arrive into the baggage hall, I could not wipe a smile off my face – it might have been relief, but I also enjoyed the dynamic spectacle. Relatives or friends spied one another, and joyous reunions followed. Two middle-aged men took exception with each other. Their argument was loud and fierce, with insults exchanged in Yoruba, words pelted like shotgun blasts into each other's face – just millimetres separating their noses. Surely fisticuffs would follow,

I thought, but minutes later I saw them burst into laughter and give each other an unrestrained hug.

A carousel finally lumbered into life – but not the one around which we were gathered. Passengers rushed to surround the active one. But no sooner had its stuttered movement commenced than it died. We collectively sighed and tittered disappointment.

After another fruitless and sweaty half hour, an official called us over to a hatch that opened to the tarmac. Through a murky window, we could see a baggage handler tug a heavily laden trolley into view and then start to offload bags, singly, through the hatch. It seemed that the luggage of more than 300 passengers was to be offloaded manually, one by one, through this small door.

'This is my country,' sighed the young man next to me. 'And I don't like it.'

The chaotic baggage hall had always aggravated Alec too, but to me this was Nigeria in miniature – exuberant, unruly, unexpected, alive.

I watched a small, determined woman gather six teetering cases onto her trolley. These were not the modest bags that would meet any twenty-three-kilogram limit. These massive cases could hold a smuggled stowaway, and possibly their family. Airlines had given up trying to limit Nigerians' luggage by weight; on this route, the limit was on the number of bags. The bags likely contained trading goods and the customs officials knew it. They had a brisk trade stopping passengers hoping to make it into the arrivals hall without payment of duties or bribes. Finally, after more than an hour and a half, my modestly sized case came out and I shoved through jostling passengers to grab it.

I thought I'd pass customs unmolested, but a flinty-voiced officer called out to me.

'*Oyibo*! What is in your luggage?'

No matter how innocent the contents of my bags, a demand like this made my stomach lurch.

'I have a box of Lego,' I replied evenly. Clothes and sweets were of no interest, but I thought I should declare the present I had bought for my driver's youngest child. 'It is a gift for a small boy,' I explained.

'What gift do you have for a big boy like me?' he asked, his demand tempered by the twinkle in his eye.

'I have plenty of gifts—but they are for my friends,' I said, amused now.

'Am I not your friend?' he asked in a mock-serious tone as he waved me through.

Perhaps everything would be all right after all, I thought as I emerged into the arrivals hall. I was due some luck with sales. I pushed my trolley and bags towards the exit. The heady scent of Lagos filled the hall and I wiped sweat from my brow. This was not Australia or Britain. It was a beautiful New Year in Nigeria, my team was willing and in the main, trustworthy. They were my Helmut and Red Bull. I was back and together we'd muddle through.

Touts at the exit barriers, standing alongside armed security guards, tried to offer 'help'.

'We have to eat, Madam,' one dubious-looking fellow called as I passed. 'I will push your trolley. It is my job.'

I spied Tayo, my driver, outside. His clothes were rumpled and he had probably slept at the airport in the car overnight to be here to meet me at daybreak. He stepped forward beaming and we shook hands. I was contributing to this pulsating nation through my businesses, energised to do battle again.

'No,' I said to the tout as I passed the trolley to Tayo. 'It is his job.'

CHAPTER TEN

The Warrior Pose

Trouble awakens the warrior within you.
— Nigerian proverb

Worries — mainly financial — now surrounded me. The new year had barely started but was already turning into a cashflow skirmish. After the Christmas rush, I expected a slow season but both businesses had virtually no new income.

'You won't get any new work until after the census,' Dapo had told me in early February over a beer at our watering hole. The nationwide census involved the country coming to a halt for five days as people stayed indoors to enable one of the one million enumerators to call and count them. That loss of time was bad enough to contemplate, but Dapo's prediction was especially discouraging as the census was to be held in late March.

Nigeria, although long regarded as Africa's most populous nation, had never actually succeeded in credibly counting all its inhabitants. The first census in 1952 was considered a serious undercount and subsequent polls had been abandoned due to ethnic tensions and rivalries that turned violent and made the numbers more unreliable. The last census data to be used was from 1991 and even that was thought to have underestimated the population by as much as twenty million. The urbanised and mainly Christian south had long accused the mainly Muslim north of inflating population numbers to ensure higher allocations of federal revenues (especially those from oil) and to legitimise their control of the federal government. Also encouraging rigging was the fact that relative population percentages of ethnic and religious groups were used to share out all federal appointments, including the civil service and the armed forces.[1]

I suspected the controversy would continue with this census and that Nigeria's population would remain an estimate. But I had more pressing concerns.

I went to meet Haresh, a former client now with a new project, at his factory in a grimy Lagos suburb. His boardroom was a functional space befitting a serious, no-frills operation. My chair wobbled and only had one arm and Haresh propped his short, muscular arms on the conference table to steady his own precarious chair.

Haresh was an Oxford-educated economist who had left his glittering British career when his father unexpectedly died a few years previously. He and his brother were called back to Africa to run the family businesses. Haresh had embraced the entrepreneurial Nigerian life with gusto. I later learned that his family, originally from India, had lost significant business assets when Idi Amin expelled Asians from Uganda in the late seventies. But unlike many other Asian families who fled to Britain, Haresh's father had decided that Africa would remain their home.

'My father taught us to be grateful to Nigerians for taking us in,' Haresh told me several times over the years I knew him. This was not superficial sentiment – his desire for expansion into areas such as health and education seemed fuelled as much by a genuine desire to give back to his host country, as it was by ambition.

Having completed a first strategy assignment on his chemicals trading business, we were lined up to develop plans for new investments.

'Let's wait until after the census,' he cautioned, echoing Dapo's dire predictions.

While this delay was not unexpected, it was unhappily familiar to me. Clients delaying work until after the fuel strikes of last year had been a source of sleepless nights. How would I pay everybody's salaries?

I normally enjoyed Haresh's company as he kept me on my toes. His brain's quick wiring enabled thought processing and verbal delivery as fast as a belt-fed machine gun. Yet a downside of this startling rate of fire was his mercurial temperament and I never knew from which direction the next pull of his thought trigger would come. As I pondered my business predicament, he now caught me off guard.

'You must choose between Strategyworks and Ekologika Papers,' he told me firmly. 'Strategy is about choice—you taught me that—and now you need to make a choice.'

Haresh was right. I would ponder his words and the advice of my friends in the slow weeks to come.

'Ekologika Papers is wearing you down,' said Toks.

She was right. Ekologika Papers was a major source of stress and it was showing in streaks of grey hair and a semi-permanent worried frown.

'Your team is fooling you,' said Dapo. He advised sacking all my Ekologika Papers staff, which seemed a bit extreme. He really was a cynical fellow, I concluded.

Only Alec didn't have any advice; he had long advocated I focus on consulting or leave Nigeria and now seemed fatigued. He was very busy with his own job and its demanding travel schedule. We had now lived apart for a year and although we spoke almost daily, he didn't seem that interested in my business concerns. Perhaps not too surprising as they were becoming a bit repetitive, even to me.

Seasoned businessman that he was, Haresh further surprised me. He was positive about Ekologika Papers, a precarious micro-business.

'It is your passion,' he said. 'And it has long-term promise.'

Haresh understood – I was not yet ready to give up on 'my baby', the business closest to my heart. The more obvious decision was to close Ekologika Papers and focus on Strategyworks. After all, my consulting business already had a good local reputation, made a profit and paid my and Ekologika Papers's way. Instead, I decided to use this lull in sales through February and March to see if I could make Ekologika Papers work – I would look for ways to bring down costs and to secure growth. Only then would I make my choice.

O

In search of cost savings, I went to Mushin, a huge and densely populated local government area on the mainland of Lagos. Birds and trees were scarce, and buildings jostled together like massed herds of wildebeest on the Serengeti plains. Cheap single-storey, low-rise housing, once painted in jolly blues, pinks and greens was now faded and overlaid with florets of the black mildew of rising damp. Thick NEPA power cables festooned the streets like black bunting for some sombre festival, while tangled coils decorated each electricity pole. Multiple illegal wiretaps ran from transformers into each building. '419—This House Is Not for Sale' was painted on various compound walls and gates. 419 was the number in the Nigerian penal code for fraud. This was an effective warning to prospective buyers that they might be dealing with a charlatan.

In reality, Mushin was a gritty slum that surely could serve as a set for an African Ken Loach-type film aimed at pricking viewers' social consciences. But Mushin was also a slum focused on commerce, and there were no signs of helplessness or hopelessness. Without the government providing any kind of social safety net, people in Mushin (as elsewhere in Nigeria) had no time to protest; they had to work.

Multiple businesses were housed within each small compound and every inch was deployed to productive use. Each business required its own signboard, workspace and storage space and, despite the duplicitous NEPA wires, its own generator. Cars, Danfo and Indonesian *tuk tuks* carried people and their crammed goods. The various vehicles clanged, smoked and wound their way along narrow roads, sharing them with men and women carrying goods on their heads or in wooden barrows – all watched by slinking, hollow-sided yellow dogs and frisky goats.

Mushin was also home for much of the Lagos printing business. Chuks, in his role as chief conversion officer, and I had come to meet existing suppliers to negotiate better rates, check out new suppliers for better deals, and consider investment in conversion equipment.

'By purchasing our own punching and binding equipment, we can save money,' Chuks had confidently told me. He had printed the spreadsheet that supported his case and pointed at the investments and resulting costs. His idea also meant the team could finish our notebooks and calendars in-house, possibly taking more control over quality. Some of my doubts about him were mollified by his initiative – he certainly seemed to be putting the company's interests first. But I thought some of his assumptions were optimistic and I wanted to first try to negotiate rates with our current supplier.

'It's that compound,' Chuks directed Tayo to park. I had only previously met the ebullient Mr Babatunde in my office. As he was said to run the largest punching and binding service in Lagos, I was interested to see his place of operation.

We drew up outside a dilapidated house. It would definitely *not* qualify to be part of an international business printing franchise.

There was no signboard and outside the compound was a public tap where young girls chatted as they filled buckets of water. Next to the tap was a fast food outlet – a table, chairs and two blackened cauldrons on a charcoal fire. A laughing woman joshed with her customers and served Kilimanjaro-shaped platefuls of spiced jollof rice and chicken, a favourite Nigerian food.

'Mama Put's food is ready,' said Chuks, hungrily eying the platefuls being consumed by seated customers as we got out of the car.

'Mama Puts?' I queried not having heard this expression before.

'Put your money here, she'll put your food there,' he explained, pointing to his stomach. He laughed at his own joke. 'It's what we call street food vendors!'

I turned back to Mr Babatunde's premises.

The building was set back from the entrance, and young men – and it was entirely men – toiled individually at rickety tables set up in rows inside. Each had piles of papers and covers in front of them and a punching or binding machine. They barely looked up to see an *oyibo* walking through their midst, a rare reaction that suggested equally unusual focus. The front compound had been partially filled with crude wooden huts, which housed finished goods or printing machinery. On entering the main building, we walked down a corridor cluttered with trimming tables and offcuts. Here more workers were collating documents in dimly lit rooms.

Mr Babatunde bustled into view. After greeting him, I exclaimed at the enterprise and diligence of his team.

'This is the off-season,' he declared. 'You should see the factory in December. More workstations, more boys—and we work all night, seven days a week. We have to get your job finished for you and your clients, Madam.'

Mr Babatunde looked as dishevelled as his compound – trousers slung below a pot belly (perhaps too much of Mama Put's chicken and rice) and an un-ironed shirt, buttoned askew. But he was affable and charming, and he signalled for Chuks and me to come into his office.

We had not yet started negotiating prices, but as we followed him my brain diverted down a different path.

Could I imagine imperious Peter, assertive Chuks or any member of my team working under the same conditions as Mr Babatunde's staff? Could I imagine asking them to work under those conditions? Mr Babatunde's employees would be on a piece rate, probably with no base salary, and with no guarantee of work – he would employ them as he needed them. These were 'normal' conditions in the Lagos printing industry. Yet my salaried team probably earned three or four times as much as Mr Babatunde's team and my casual staff earned a base and overtime rate, which meant their earnings were much more than Mr Babatunde's piece rate. I wanted my team to be paid fairly but it meant our papermaking costs were very high. If I brought these conversion processes in-house, our finished goods would be totally uncompetitive.

Would it be hypocritical to keep purchasing services from a supplier whose salaries and working conditions were worse than those I offered, even though they matched the Lagos labour market? Possibly, but I reasoned that I couldn't hope to be a one-woman reformer for every printing industry worker, and if we couldn't sell our calendars, cards and notebooks, then everyone would be out of a job.

'I am sure I can give you a good price, Madam,' said Mr Babatunde as I pondered my dilemma. 'You should keep your work with me.'

Despite Chuks's analysis, I concluded Mr Babatunde was right.

O

Another priority for Ekologika Papers was to find a new paper-drying method. I'd recognised the issue last year, but my attention had turned to more pressing issues.

In the dry season we could make paper economically by laying out the cotton cloths on which each piece of paper was moulded and pressed and drying the new sheets of paper in the sun, but soon the long rains would be upon us. If I produced a full inventory now, I'd spend scarce cash on stock that would lie idle until the last quarter sales rush – and anyway, it was hard to predict how many sheets of paper I'd need for year-end. Last year we had produced during the wet season and, at Peter's suggestion, I had employed casual labour to pick up the drying sheets of paper whenever the rain threatened. What had started with James and two other casuals assisting had turned into a small army of casuals as the rainy season coincided with our heaviest production period. It was a slow and labour-intensive approach, doubling our unit paper costs. The ideal process would be to spread production through the first three quarters of the year then make up the finished products during the seasonal rush. But how could I dry papers more efficiently during the rainy months?

The simplest solution seemed to be line-drying under cover. We could peg the wet cotton sheets laid with moulded paper pulp on lines stretched under the veranda and wait for them to dry. It might take days in the high humidity, but lines could be added and fitted in a relatively small space.

Peter, in charge of the papermaking section, was adamantly against it.

I insisted he try.

On my way to see the results of his experiments, I greeted Remi who was busy moulding papers and noticed a new casual worker moulding papers at the second station.

'Where's James?' I asked, realising I had not seen him for a while.

'Peter sacked him,' said Remi. 'His papers were too bad.' I was sorry that James had left and puzzled that Peter had not brought the matter to me. But it seemed a good sign that he was such a stickler for quality.

The dried papers were as disappointing as Peter had warned. Paper pulp gathered in ridges along the bottoms of the sheets. Gravity, it seemed, was our biggest enemy. The corners were buckled and cracked, and the wind, it appeared, was our second enemy.

'We cannot achieve the paper quality we need.' Peter had become more assertive at voicing his opinions now that he was no longer my boat mechanic, and it was something I encouraged. After all, I wanted him to take charge.

My next idea was a two-pronged attack to get technical support. Peter's favoured solution was a paper dryer, so I set him the task of finding a local engineer to design something simple and energy-efficient. After all, he had done well to harness a groundnut grinder to mash our paper pulp.

Meanwhile, I researched the support available from various international aid agencies for social enterprises. Some provided technical support by matching social enterprises with suitable retired engineers, while others provided donor funding for research and development. Throughout February and March I spent a lot of time reading agency profiles and submitting applications for support to UK, Dutch and German agencies.

One by one, we were turned down. As responses came in I heard a common theme: Ekologika Papers was ruled ineligible because legally it was incorporated as a 'for profit' company.

'We only support social enterprises that are NGOs,' I was told.

This fact was not in their profiles.

I explained that, unlike in Europe, I had been advised there was no simple social enterprise incorporation model available in Nigerian law. I pointed out that profits, when and if we made them, would not be redistributed as dividends but would be reinvested for growth with a portion given to a local charity. But my protests cut no ice. They did not appreciate that reinvested profit was the only way in which any social enterprise could be self-sustaining, able to grow and do further good. Despite trumpeting social enterprise, their monotonous refrain was that they only helped NGOs – entities dependent on philanthropic funding for their survival.

There seemed a huge lack of clarity and fuzzy thinking about social enterprises, which did not take into account circumstances faced by those of us trying to make a difference in a challenging environment.

Peter announced he had received a proposal for a paper dryer from an engineer in Ibadan, a university city north of Lagos.

It was from someone associated with an institution dedicated to appropriate technology. Peter showed me diagrams and declared that it would be very efficient and could dry many papers in a single batch. I checked the engineer's calculations on energy use, drying rates and batch sizes. It looked good on paper so I asked for a trial model to be developed. Peter travelled to Ibadan to pay the deposit and I got on with my long to-do list.

O

Time had flown by since I had signed the two leases with my landlord and they would soon be up for renewal. Where could I house my businesses and myself more economically for the longer term?

I looked at suburbs adjoining Mushin, in the more salubrious Yaba and Surelere, but it was difficult to find a property that had the right caché for a consulting business yet was cheap enough for manufacturing paper.

Then Toks introduced me to Theodora.

Theodora was a lawyer who offered legal advice to women abused by their husbands and also ran a shelter for those who decided to leave (or were forced out of) violent relationships. Toks thought Theodora might have space for an Ekologika Papers workshop near her shelter and would be keen on the work opportunities for women. It sounded like an interesting idea to me, too.

I first met Theodora at a restaurant. She was a tall and dignified woman with thoughtful, intelligent eyes and a sharply chiselled face. Her skin was the colour of charcoal, reminding me that there were so many shades of black skin in Africa. Her beauty was tempered by a sad aura. Toks had earlier told me that although Theodora came from a privileged, well-educated background and had married another lawyer, she found herself and her child abandoned by her husband once he learned their child was disabled.

'Young women come to Lagos from their villages, meet a man, live with him in a traditional marriage, and maybe children are born. Money is short, palm wine is cheap and before long the husbands are beating their wives. It is a common situation,' Theodora said.

'I have other lawyers on our board and together we offer the women legal advice,' she continued. 'When they come to us in a distressed state, we first enquire about their marriage. Most have only had a traditional ceremony that offers them no legal protection. Our first advice is to get married in a civil ceremony or at a church, but with a marriage recognised by the state.'

She went on to tell me how difficult it was for the women to convince their partner to do this. Although their 'husbands' might be poor and unable to support them, without legal rights the women could lose their children to the father's relatives who, under traditional arrangements, might claim them. Many of the women were young, illiterate and had no relatives nearby to support them. 'Once the women are abandoned, they sleep on the streets with their children and become victims of further violence or turn to prostitution to support themselves.'

Theodora's NGO offered emergency shelter for the women. 'I only know of one other shelter for women in Lagos and nothing else in this area,' she said. 'So I started my shelter to offer them some practical protection.' She told me that her NGO received about fifteen new cases each month and always had 100 active cases on their list. They tried to help the women to earn by giving them micro-financing and providing childcare services after school hours. Their resources were limited so they helped women to get their own livelihoods and accommodation as quickly as possible.

'We advise many of the women to return to their villages,' she admitted. 'They may not want to for many reasons but, for uneducated women with young children, city life is simply too tough. At least in the villages they have support networks.'

A few days later Peter and I visited the shelter. Seeing the simple but neat shelter and the women gathered for a monthly session to share problems and discuss solutions, underlined to me the value of Theodora's work. I understood how important it was to help women rather than solely focusing on their children. If these poor women were given resources, the ability to earn and be safe from abuse, and could make informed choices, their children would automatically benefit. The aid industry in Africa, in my opinion, was bloated and often self-serving and there were still under-addressed needs. Women had long been neglected, even though their role in African households as breadwinners and responsible decision-makers was more widely understood than when I had cycled across Africa in the early nineties. It was as astonishing as it was discouraging.

But could the work of Ekologika Papers be integrated with Theodora's?

In the car after our visit, Peter expressed his opinion. 'The women will be unreliable and they won't work hard.'

Still a chauvinist, I thought, although I too was uneasy. Toks had told us that most of the women came to the centre for just one or two months and then left Lagos for their villages or moved to wherever they could get a room, or went back to their husbands. They would not be worth training if they did not stick around. Also, the reality was these women had little or no formal education. They did not speak English and Peter was not familiar with their tribal languages, mainly from southeast Nigeria. Would they really be employable in papermaking where precision and taking direction was required?

'The location won't work either,' Peter added as we drove away.

The shelter was in Lekki, on the eastern side of Lagos. 'It is too far away from where the team live and from Mushin. Transport costs will be too high.'

All these concerns put an end to the idea. But our meeting with Theodora was productive in another way. I decided to make her

NGO the recipient of Ekologika Papers's social funding – once we made a profit – which currently seemed a long way off.

While my efforts created significant production cost-savings for Ekologika Papers, it was not enough to give me confidence in the business. Kola, our irrepressibly optimistic salesman, had been promising big orders for some time without them materialising. How could I choose to focus on Ekologika Papers when I might be dealing with a fictional sales forecast?

Once again, Dapo had some relevant experience. His credo for deciding whether an order was real or merely fiction was quite simple.

'Show me the money,' he said.

I was learning the truth of this and repeated it to Kola. 'Show me the money.'

Then one day in mid-March, Kola appeared wearing creased suit trousers, his lunch splattered on his shirtfront, his hair in need of a comb and a smile that stretched as wide as his ears.

'Madam, I have news. I have made a sale of 1000 notebooks.' He named the client – an evangelical church – and better, he handed me the cheque for advance payment. It was our largest single order yet.

We high-fived and cheered.

'What's the occasion?' I asked. 'Are they for a wedding or their ministry?'

'No, their senior pastor has died,' cried Kola gleefully. 'It is for his funeral.'

Oh. Cheering did not seem the appropriate response.

But we cheered anyway.

O

Just before the census I met Haresh again to finalise preparations for his forthcoming assignment, to start in April. I found him in a hyperactive frame of mind over a new acquisition opportunity – in an entirely new industry that he wanted to discuss.

'What about choice and focus?' I asked him. I knew him well enough now to point out his inconsistencies. For an hour, we explored the merits of the acquisition, but I concluded it was overpriced and would distract him from the opportunities in his other businesses.

'Enough,' he said suddenly, eyes gleaming with intelligent fervour. 'You may be right. Now tell me—what have you decided about your own business choice?'

I was nervous. Would Haresh think I was inconsistent? It was so much easier to give advice than to receive it.

'I have decided that Ekologika Papers *is* my passion and the business I want to grow,' I said, 'but I need to continue with Strategyworks for at least one more year'.

I explained that the Strategyworks outlook was strong; not only was I committed to his own assignment but also had a team-building workshop booked for a major hotel and some other promising proposals in the pipeline. I felt my commitments to my staff and clients were not ones I could walk away from immediately. In addition, I needed the consultancy work's cashflow.

I also told him how, after the aborted attempts to find new accommodation for my businesses and myself, my terrier-like PA Gloria had found a newly built townhouse for lease. It was bright and light, a cat was permitted, and it was cheaper than Philippe's apartment. To take the pressure off moving my businesses, I had negotiated a twelve-month lease extension for my office and workshop space. For now, I needed the cash and income from Strategyworks to pay for this and work towards managing only Ekologika Papers within a year or two.

'I can appreciate your dilemma,' said Haresh. 'It sounds like a good plan.'

I was relieved to have his approval, but the fact remained that the consultancy workload meant I could not give enough attention to Ekologika Papers.

'I've also decided to hire a GM for Ekologika Papers,' I continued. My plan was to hire one with sales experience to support Kola and to set higher growth targets for the year that would pay back the salary investment. The only problem was I had short-term cash shortfall – I needed money to fund the new lease, but I would not start getting the necessary funds until the second half of the year when work picked up again. How would I finance the gap?

'You can borrow money from me,' he said without pause.

I was stunned. It felt like a vote of confidence in my potential for success. Finally, this year felt back on track and I could raise a hope that everything would turn out right after all.

CHAPTER ELEVEN

Never a Dull Day

However long the night, the dawn will break.

— African proverb

'My people will talk to your people,' said the irate man, his voice raging through my office telephone. I half-expected the handset to glow red – I think my ear did. Certainly, I was flushed with the way this conversation had progressed.

A half-hour earlier, I had been congratulating myself on my new Strategyworks team. I had carved out time over the past month to train Sophie, my new consultant. Although relatively inexperienced, she seemed switched on and able to work well with John, who now had four months under his belt. Inevitably, during the first months, the burden was on my time to train and coach new recruits, but both were quick learners. I still felt the loss of Zainab but at least I had the makings of a team who could add more value than they took away – if they stayed long enough.

That morning I had briefed John and analyst Kunle on Haresh's new assignment and their roles, and Sophie and I were preparing materials for the hotel management team workshop due to run later that week.

I had interviewed some candidates for the GM role at Ekologika Papers but no one suitable had emerged. In the meantime, anxious to capitalise on the interest shown in our notebooks, I had encouraged the team to develop some sample notebooks we could use in a marketing campaign that would target wedding and other event organisers and professional service firms. These groups had shown the most interest in high-quality, custom-made products. Over the weekend I had written a letter of introduction to prospective clients and, following our Monday morning meeting, Kola had started distributing them. As always, he was positive this would be a terrific sales success.

Then came the call.

'There is an angry man, a Mr Olumide, on the phone for you, Madam,' Gloria announced.

'Who is Mr Olumide?' I asked. His name meant nothing to me, but my PA was already gone.

'You have used a photo of my wife and I,' Mr Olumide boomed down the line. 'She is very distressed.' I didn't need to ask many questions as his accusations erupted. Apparently, last year his wife had ordered some Ekologika Papers notebooks to celebrate their wedding, but this morning she had seen a letter and notebook – our marketing campaign – arrive at her company with her own photo on the cover. He shouted about unauthorised use, that he would sue me, that we had no right and that his wife was weeping at our insolence. I made shocked apologies, but this did not satisfy him. Honour for his wife, it seemed, would only be served if his lawyer talked to my lawyer about a claim for damages.

I was shaking when I got off the phone and composed myself before going into the conversion team office to establish the facts on our side.

There were now two women in the conversion team – Yinka, the talented young graphic designer who had joined late last year, and Molly, a versatile young business graduate with creative flair. Molly had freelanced selling wedding souvenirs, seen our products and recently come to the office to ask if there was a vacancy. Liking her energy and initiative, I offered her a three-month trial. She was working with Kola on sales and with Chuks and Sonny learning to make notebooks, calendars and cards and working with the Mushin suppliers.

Now I asked to see the notebooks we were sending out in our marketing campaign.

Chuks brought the samples showing Mr and Mrs Olumide on the covers.

I was aghast. 'Didn't you think using real people's faces without their permission was wrong?'

'Oh no, Madam,' said Chuks, with Molly, Yinka and Sonny all nodding their agreement. 'You said to mock up wedding samples so what else would we use?'

They were right, in a way. I had gone to great lengths to teach them about copyright after a previous incident where the team used images taken from the web. Yinka was tasked with producing our own wedding designs. So why didn't they use those? But I had not specified what designs they should use, and I had not checked. I really had no one else to blame but myself.

For now, I needed to figure out what to do about Mr Olumide's threat. All thoughts about the upcoming workshop were put on hold.

Back in my office, I made a series of phone calls that were more like trembling wails for help.

My first call went to Mr Atta to explain the situation.

'This is serious,' he said, unnerving me just as he had over my visa expiry, but he was ready to deal with Mr Olumide's lawyers if they contacted him.

Next, I rang Dapo for advice.

'It is because you are an *oyibo*,' he guffawed. 'Going to court is too hard with an uncertain result,' he declared. 'He will be all bluster.'

Toks's view was more succinct. 'It's only grammar.' This was a Nigerian phrase meaning he was just talking – the same advice as Dapo had given.

I went home uneasy, waiting for the legal axe to fall and that night told Alec my tale of woe over a poor phone connection. His only observation after several seconds of crackle-filled silence was: 'Never a dull day in Nigeria'.

I slept restlessly but reached a decision. Next morning, I asked Kola to track down Mrs Olumide's order then asked Gloria to organise a large bunch of fresh flowers. Tayo delivered them and a grovelling note of apology to her workplace. Soon, her husband was again on the phone but on being put through, instead of yesterday's ogre I met a pussycat – until his final words.

'You will have learned your lesson,' he said rather sternly.

I certainly had. As my stomach calmed down for the first time in twenty-four hours, I reached into my drawer for my file on applicants for the GM role. One of them would have to do.

Anzac Day – the Australian commemoration of thousands of brave Australian and New Zealand men and women sacrificed at Gallipoli during World War Two – had arrived. In the horrific slaughter, the young Australia (only created as a Federation in 1901) lost more combatants as a proportion of its fighting strength than any of the other main warring nations.[1] The ill-fated campaign, a major source of this sobering Australian statistic, was thus both a collective trauma and source of pride, and it marked both the separation from our colonial past and a milestone in the creation of our national identity.

ANZAC stands for Australian and New Zealand Army Corps and while Anzac Day on 25 April was traditionally observed with a dawn service in Australia, in Lagos the service was held in the early evening, followed by a reception. To honour this year's day of remembrance, the Australian High Commissioner was coming to Lagos. He had a budget from Canberra and had asked me to help him organise the event. Would I finally have a meaningful consular role?

'It might be a way to flush out some Australians,' he said over the phone. Was he still hunting alimony evaders and crooks? And what help did he need from his consular representative?

'I find Lagos slightly daunting and whenever I've come it has all been a bit unpleasant,' he observed. 'Can you recommend a good hotel?'

The night before the Anzac service, I met the High Commissioner for dinner. He was a silver-haired and bespectacled man. He did not give the impression of being one of life's movers and shakers, but I wondered if his demeanour reflected the careful diplomatic culture he inhabited. I suggested a restaurant, but he preferred the security of the hotel. By the end of the evening I knew every option for the Anzac celebration's order of service as the High Commissioner dithered through the choices. I could appreciate his need to get it right, but he was not organising a multi-lateral summit.

I tried turning the conversation to things Nigerian, but he was focused on domestic issues. 'Some of the other countries' residences are much better than ours.' Towards the end of the evening, he finally admitted some personal details. 'I will retire after this posting. It's been long enough.'

The man had spent most of his professional life in South America. Having limited representation was one thing but why did Canberra send a diplomat with no interest in Africa who was on the verge of retirement?

The next day, as I was leaving my office to attend the service, the phone rang.

'Could you bring your Consular flag, Pamela?' asked the High Commissioner. 'It seems my girl forgot to pack it in our kit.' The ultra-efficient PA to the High Commissioner was someone I knew well. Unlike the diplomats whose postings were generally no longer than two years, she was a fixture and I knew her attention to detail. It was puzzling.

'Could you also bring some Blu Tack?' he added. 'We have some posters to put up on the wall.'

As I left, the phone went again.

'My girl forgot to pack the CD of the music,' he said. 'You wouldn't have *The Last Post* in your Consular kit?'

I did not.

The minute's silence during the service was entirely silent.

I had never actually been a fan of Anzac Day, being from an Australian generation that had rejected the occasion due to a different kind of symbolism. During the sixties, Australia had entered the Vietnam War to support America's fight against the communism spreading southwards through Asia, and potentially to Australia. 'All the way with LBJ' had been the refrain of our then-prime minister about a policy to support US President Lyndon Johnson. In the seventies the US and Australia were still fighting in Vietnam but by then the war's horrors, ruthlessness and fruitlessness had been exposed by war correspondents, photographers and activists. I was still a child at the time, but I remembered the anti-war demonstrations and condemnation of Anzac Day as a glorification of war and an acceptance of misguided leadership and pointless death. People saw a parallel between the excessive deaths at Gallipoli and the deaths of young Australian soldiers in Vietnam.

How times had changed; an upsurge in nationalism and a lack of exposure to the horrors, complex motivations and questionable integrity of a real war had given Anzac Day fresh popularity. I was still ambivalent – respectful of and humbled by the sacrifices made by the Armed Forces yet suspicious of traditional rituals and populist patriotism. But now that I was a representative of the Australian government, I supposed I had better embrace it.

After the mess of this particular service, however, I embraced the chance for a drink at the bar.

Steve, the boorish Australian head of petroleum engineering for an American oil and gas company (who also thought he could serve the Australian community better than me), was there first.

'No *Last Post*,' he said, looking as though it was my fault. 'That was a bit of a cock-up.'

'The High Commissioner forgot the CD,' I said, irritated that his dozy performance reflected badly on me. I'd take charge next year. 'Have you thought any more about helping out at Agaja?' I asked.

After meeting Steve last year, I had emailed him directly appealing for help to remove the wreck causing the erosion threatening Agaja but had been ignored.

'What can I do?' he said, shrugging his shoulders and taking a swig of beer.

'We could benefit from any influence you're able to exert,' I coaxed.

Wale, my landlord at Agaja, had had visits from government officials in response to his letters but there was a lot of buck-passing. The federal government said it was a Lagos state problem while Lagos state said the opposite. Steve's company had access to government at high levels so his people's lobbying might be more effective than ours.

But Steve was clapped on the shoulder by a friendly male paw – the High Commissioner doing his rounds – and turned to greet him with a vigorous handshake. My moment to discuss Agaja was gone.

There were several other familiar faces, Kevin and Aaron chatting to Father Jim, but there were new faces too. Some Australians had duly been 'flushed out', as well as some Nigerian business people I had invited. I saw Michelle chatting enthusiastically with an attentive, long-limbed man clad in a slick grey suit, who seemed as drawn to the slinky dress as her words. She didn't look like an aid worker, I thought. Like many of the men present, I was in a sober work suit with sensible shoes while Michelle looked ready to party. She beckoned me over, breezy and enthusiastic with her welcome. There was something very likeable about her, I had to admit.

'I'm considering setting up my own software consulting practice,' she said. 'Can I ask your advice?'

'Come to Agaja one weekend,' I suggested. 'Soon—before the rains start in earnest. I'd be happy to help.' I wondered what had happened to her NGO contract and passion for 'saving African children'. Then she introduced me to the lanky lounge lizard whose smile revealed rather unappealing teeth. He had to be British, I thought. I learned he was a newcomer to Lagos and, yes, with a vague role at the British Deputy High Commission.

'I met your High Commissioner on the golf course last month,' he told me, his clipped accent a little slurred. 'He invited me when we met again at dinner at the Turkish Ambassador's residence last week.'

Did these people ever socialise outside the diplomatic set?

The lizard air-kissed Michelle, squeezed her arm a little longer than necessary and, as he shimmied off to refill his glass said to her, 'See you at the Flamenco dancing'.

'The Spanish Ambassador is hosting the event,' Michelle explained. 'You must come.'

It seemed a genuine invitation, yet I was nonplussed. I had enough on my plate without spending evenings attending superficial functions. But why was Michelle being invited onto the diplomatic social circuit and not me?

O

Back in the office there was not a moment to lose. Not only was Haresh's project well underway but Kevin had also commissioned further work to diagnose the bank's customer service issues. I urgently needed to recruit the GM for Ekologika Papers. I had interviewed a handful of applicants hoping one would be better in person than on paper but had scratched them all – there was no one with the experience or capability to manage both the company's myriad production problems and sales target.

Then Kevin sent me an email with an attachment. 'You might be interested in Gail's resume.' Gail turned out to be a Canadian, the wife of an insurance executive transferred to Lagos, and experienced in corporate sales. I had not considered an expatriate. Could I afford her? Could I get her a work permit? Could she be *the one?*

O

During late April, while supervising the move of my boxes and furniture out of Philippe's apartment, my Lebanese neighbour Jean finally confirmed an invitation to dinner. In my year living at the apartment our paths had only crossed in the carpark.

'Next Saturday,' he said climbing into his vehicle. I signalled to the removals van to allow him space to reverse. 'I've a few friends coming over.' As a work singleton and busy entrepreneur, *not* on the diplomatic cocktail party round, and with most evenings spent in with the cat, I was pleased to have a social invitation.

The following Saturday, it felt strange to arrive as a guest in my old compound.

Although I had just moved in, I was very happy with my new home. It was the central townhouse in a terrace of three, newly built and filled with light – it had balconies at front and back, one over-looking a neighbouring mosque. Again my landlord was a neighbour and, as with Philippe's apartment, there were teething problems. My new landlord had a relaxed attitude to ordering the water truck and I had already washed from my reserve bucket of water a few times. His relaxed attitude extended to the generator changeover. Moustafa, the likeable gateman who my landlord had employed for years, slept peacefully through any loss of power; there were no clanging bells to wake him.

But I took these kinds of issues in my stride now, and I loved the building's open-plan layout and freshness.

I also arrived in high spirits as Gail had accepted my offer to become the GM of Ekologika Papers. She'd be starting in July, much later than I'd hoped, but she'd interviewed well and I felt I had little other choice. She was an extrovert with the right sales profile, seemed to understand the various cost and production quality issues, and Peter and the team liked her. Best of all, she was enthusiastic to work for my precious business. Tonight, I could celebrate.

Jean opened the door and greeted me enthusiastically. He was a muscular guy with long black hair, strong eyebrows and smiling eyes. He ushered me into his living room. Though identical in layout to my old apartment, the place felt entirely different – a functional, masculine space with plump sofas, a large sound system and an African mask for decoration but little else in the way of ornaments, photos or other things to personalise it.

The party atmosphere was provided by six young Lebanese men – all at least a decade younger than me – chatting in Arabic and French. They wore tight shirts and jeans, were all black-haired and some sported dark designer stubble. I gulped at the gold neck chains, chest hair, large watches and testosterone on display. Would I get on with these macho guys?

They kindly switched to English as I was introduced. One man, André, was familiar – we realised we had met during Kevin's recent banking customer interviews. I learned that Jean ran a printing firm and that the other guests were his business associates, cousins, colleagues and friends with other businesses (snack food manufacture, export import clearance and consumer appliances importation). It was hard to follow it all, but I was handed a glass of wine and peppered with questions about how I ended up in Lagos. It was noisy, welcoming and convivial, and I almost forgot all the chest hair and gold chains.

Out of the kitchen a beautiful young woman with long brown hair, kohl-lined eyes and plump red lips emerged. She was André's wife, Vanessa, recruited to cook us dinner, although her low-cut top and high heels made her look an unlikely chef. She brought out some nuts and olives, but before I could strike up a conversation she disappeared back into the kitchen.

Jean started telling us about his experiences as a young boy in Beirut, divided between the mainly Muslim factions in West Beirut and the mainly Christian Lebanese front in East Beirut during the long Lebanese civil war from 1975 to 1990. The Green Line separated urban destruction – rubble, resilient plant growth and tanks patrolling on either side.

'We went down to the Green Line and threw rocks at the soldiers on the other side,' Jean told us. He had been about ten towards the end of the war. 'It was just a game. Until there was an explosion—mortar fire nearby.'

I gasped.

'What happened?' It seemed the others had heard the story before but were equally enthralled.

'My friends died, I lost two fingers and my legs were pretty much a mess.' He lifted his right hand to show me – I hadn't noticed and felt very unobservant. 'I spent six months in hospital, and they did not think I would walk, but I have.' Jean's injuries were the legacy of this youth spent in the midst of war. 'I limp when I am tired.'

I was now somewhat in awe. He again lifted his right arm in the air; his hand open and his missing middle and fourth digit fully visible and he mimed throwing a rock. 'It really ruined my aim when I went back.'

Somehow Jean's delivery made us all laugh.

He asked about my business and I told them about consulting and Ekologika Papers.

'You should get into printing,' he advised. 'Get an offset printing machine—you can make plenty of money with that.'

I tried to explain that printing was secondary to selling paper and that the business was a social enterprise.

'Forget the paper, forget hiring a Canadian, and make some money,' he said. For him, and the others, business was about making money. They had a point.

I then told them about my rough encounter with Mr Olumide and was surprised I made it humorous in the retelling.

'Never go to court,' said Jean with new passion. 'Have you ever been to the High Court in Ikeja? It is like a "face-me-face-you".'

This was a reference to the poorest accommodation in Lagos, often run by unscrupulous landlords, where tenants rented rooms separated by a narrow concrete strip used for all communal washing and food preparation activities. It was typically overcrowded and squalid.

'My boss once needed to evict a tenant from our warehouse,' continued Jean. The tenant had ignored a notice to quit and a year later was still there, paying no rent. 'My boss's lawyer was old school—very proper.'

He sounded like Mr Atta.

'But he was getting nowhere and he came to my boss, embarrassed. "Your case is with corrupt judges," he told him. "I don't operate their way, but I will send you someone."'

Jean told us that a man named Ismail turned up at his boss's office one day while he was with him.

'The guy was in traditional dress with crocodile shoes and mirrored Ray-Bans. I never saw his eyes,' he said. His own brown eyes glittered with energy and he made it sound funny. But I knew the reality would have been unsettling.

'Ismail told my boss that on the day of the court hearing he should come with two envelopes each containing cash. Later after the hearing, I heard what happened. Ismail met my boss outside the court and took the envelopes—he didn't know for whom. When the hearing started, he discovered that Ismail was the sheriff of the court. "Do you want rent and arrears from your tenant?" he asked my boss. "If you do it will take longer."' Jean said his boss cut his losses and asked only for his delinquent tenant's eviction. Six months later police used a court order to evict the tenant. 'Ismail delivered on his promise and my boss had his warehouse back,' said Jean. 'That's how justice works here.'

Once again, we all laughed. I felt lucky that flowers had worked for Mrs Olumide. What else can one do in the face of this depth of corruption? I was still holding out against using brown envelopes and paying 'agents' but how much longer could I against an inescapable system?

I could not follow all the simultaneous conversations and arguments of this long evening. There was a mix of pidgin English, Arabic, French and English. It felt very cosmopolitan. The guys moved onto football and argued about whether France or Italy was the best team in the beautiful game. I had no comments to add to that conversation but, despite my earlier reservations, I was enjoying myself.

These young men were not mentors like Dapo and Toks. Welcome as their advice was, it sometimes made me feel like I was wearing trainer wheels. And hearing about my problems did not make them impatient like Alec. It felt great to be mixing with people who ran small businesses, shared the same pressures as me and needed to let go of stress at the end of a long day.

An hour before midnight – normal dining time for the night-owl Lebanese – André's wife signalled that food was ready. As we squeezed around the dinner table to feast on a massive array of delicious dishes, Jean told us about his three futile visits to activate a bank account the day before. He had been thwarted in the end.

'Network challenges.' He laughed at his wasted day and added, 'Never a dull day in Nigeria'.

Alec had used those same words, I thought as I ate. But his tone was very different.

CHAPTER TWELVE

Kick to Win!

Where a woman rules, streams run uphill.

– African proverb

It was late June and, following a ten-day business trip to Europe meeting suppliers and industry experts for Haresh's second assignment, I had returned to Lagos. On this Monday morning we assembled for our usual weekly meeting. My office looked lived-in now – a library of Strategyworks documents and reports filled the bookshelves and Ekologika Papers notebooks were piled on the floor ready for packing and delivery. There were pictures and the Australian consulate sign on the walls, a small forest of indoor plants at reception and a flipchart covered in a client's industry jargon and urgent arrows for action. But I was reminded the office lease would be up next year and we would have to move and create a new business home again.

I had been in touch with my teams throughout my trip, even on the three days I had taken to see Alec. I had learned that, for an entrepreneur, there was no such thing as uninterrupted leisure. Time was needed every day to direct activities at one's home base, and to deal with crises.

Ah, crises.

While I had been away, there had been a system crash and much of the Ekologika Papers's design archive was lost. An IT advisor reported that most of the system's memory had been taken up by downloaded music, resulting in insufficient capacity for the design archive backup. I planned to read my team the riot act.

But my return brought further unwelcome surprises.

Kunle, my analyst and John, my consultant, had left resignation letters on my desk. Given my lingering suspicion about Kunle's involvement in last year's attempted credit card fraud and the new suspicion that he might have been involved in the illegal music downloading, I was ambivalent about his resignation; about John's I was not. He had only worked for me for ten months. Before the morning's meeting I went to meet him.

John explained that he had received an offer from a large international oil company. It included premium medical cover, international training and a pension – things with which I could not compete, but I could understand them influencing his decision, especially as his wife was pregnant.

'I won't leave until Haresh's assignment is completed,' he said, then added, 'But I think I've contributed my quota'.

I had spent more than a month recruiting him to Strategyworks, two months training him and increasing his skills, and had coached him intensively throughout his two assignments, yet he thought his work was sufficient in return. Was he kidding?

A rather tense meeting with the team then began. No one would admit responsibility for downloading the music, but I fully believed some of them knew who was responsible.

'Whoever did this may not have foreseen that their actions would result in us losing the design archive, but the downloading was against company rules and done at the company's expense. I feel very let down.'

Unused to me being anything other than forgiving and supportive, the faces around the table looked sheepish.

'There will be checks going forward, and any future downloading of music will be considered cause for dismissal,' I told them.

Peter looked as glum as I felt. I think he felt let down too, but he had another reason to feel glum when I moved the meeting on to other business. The results of his paper-drying experiments were not good. His attempts to improve the heat output and air circulation and the new, rust-proof trays had taken precious company money plus his time but without the success we'd hoped.

'We can only dry twenty sheets at a time, Madam,' Peter reported.

Our paper dryer's capacity was five times that.

'And it takes twenty-four hours to dry.'

No wonder his face was glum – this was the last straw. I had relied on Peter's technical skills, but this design was beyond his ability, and mine. I really wished some of the agencies I had applied to earlier in the year had not turned us down due to our status as a limited liability company. Rain was pouring down outside with no sign of stopping. We would have to again rely on Remi's team of casually employed friends to lay out paper during dry interludes and pick it up again when storms threatened. With its approach utterly uneconomical, the dryer had become an expensive fiasco.

Jovial, optimistic Kola, however, was upbeat about his sales forecast. But where were our solid orders? Molly lifted a notebook from the pile I had seen on the floor. They were for one of Kola's customers who had 'shown us the money'.

She handed it to me. Its back and front covers were not the same size.

'Sorry, Madam,' she said lamely.

I rounded on my team. 'Chuks, Peter—hadn't you checked these?'

'Sorry, Madam.'

I got up to look at the entire batch, and my worst fears were confirmed. None of the covers was the same size. Each cover consisted of our handmade paper printed with the client's design, laminated then glued over cut strawboard. The materials and labour costs were about half the total cost of a notebook.

I looked at the team in disbelief.

'Peter—you're meant to supervise. Chuks—you're meant to quality-control the cover making. Sonny—you're meant to make sure the strawboard is cut to the right size. Molly—you've taken these covers to Mr Babatunde's and spent money having the notebooks assembled. Didn't any of you measure the covers?'

I pointed to a sign I had put up with the standard dimensions intended to stop these mistakes.

'Sorry, Madam,' all four employees chimed.

'Sorry doesn't cut it,' I snapped. Remaking covers would take all profit out of this order. 'Give me a ruler,' I said, intending to measure each to see if any could be saved.

'Mine's gone missing,' said Molly. I had bought a metal ruler for each team member and spent time coaching them about noticing and measuring cover size just a few weeks before. Now only Peter still had his ruler.

'How can you have lost three rulers?' I exclaimed. The rising pitch would soon be a kettle scream.

'Gail's joining next week,' I said under my breath. 'She'll deal with this.'

It was a calming mantra, and I could not wait.

◯

Standing in front of my Agaja beach hut, I was awed by the power and noise of the Atlantic Ocean. Waves rolled relentlessly forward in an invasion of the defenceless coast. Each struck the backwash of its predecessors and created a whirlpool of surf. Only the suicidal would try swimming in this deadly foaming rip. The sandy beach and pretty palm trees were now a clutter of beach debris. The unstable cliffs had retreated at least twenty metres since my last visit. The new coastline further narrowed the isthmus between the sea and lagoon.

'The storm last Monday did it,' said Luke, my caretaker, as he came to stand beside me. 'All the palm trees came down,' he said, pointing to the dense grove that was now village firewood. 'It took the thatch off my house and many huts collapsed in the sea.'

Luke and I picked our way over fallen fronds and boards, wary of nails and splintered wood, and headed towards the wreck that was responsible for the angry waves. Wind grabbed my hair and flung it into my eyes. I brushed it back again and again as we stumbled forward.

'Mr Steve's hut has gone,' Luke announced as we went. The plot was difficult to see. 'It was out there,' he said, gesturing to the surf. Not even the well remained. Agaja's soil and houses now churned in the waves in front of us. The ocean's advance was pitiless.

A thick grey sheet of rain plummeted earthward, its drops dancing on the sea nearby. At this, I had seen enough and we turned back towards my hut. Despite the weather, I still wanted a day at the beach to take proper note of the advancing erosion, get some money to Luke to help with his woes, and blow some business frustrations away. Few friends would venture onto water on a day such as this. Toks declined, saying she felt unwell, and Dapo accepted but had not arrived on time for our departure. To my surprise, Michelle proved brave company.

'Have a drink,' she advised when I arrived back at the hut. Her dark hair ruffled in the wind but, despite the dampness and humidity that turned my hair into an unattractive, woolly halo, remained remarkably sleek. She wore a colourful wrap over her bathing costume and seated herself on a stool behind my bar. She held out a glass of prosecco. In the wind and rain, mulled wine would have been more welcome. I took the glass and reached for a towel.

'Tell me what it's like to run a consulting business in Lagos,' my new friend asked.

Where to begin?

In the boat on the way down, Michelle had told me about the Flamenco evening and then about the time she spent at university protesting against new mining developments that threatened old-growth forests in southwest Australia. Given that her father was in the palm oil business, I asked if she had also protested against old-forest destruction in Malaysia. She seemed more sanguine about that. There were other contradictions, too – I wondered how she had ended up working for a mining company, but the noisy engine didn't make conversation easy. Still, I knew the mining development she had protested against and agreed with her, I admired, too, the fact that she had been willing to take action. That was how I was starting to think of her – decisive and action-oriented. Now she wanted to hear my story, or at least part of it.

Her IT contract with the American NGO had finished and she was again looking for a way to stay in Lagos.

I should be positive, I thought. Strategyworks was taking off. Kevin had been impressed by the results of our work on the bank's customer service issues and now wanted me to travel around Nigeria to run workshops. It might develop into a long-term programme to turn his company around. Haresh also had further work that would involve more international travel, and other clients were knocking at our door, but I had other concerns.

'It's depressing,' I said finally, and my vehemence surprised me. John's defection was still fresh. 'Staff aren't loyal and you can't build a business training young Nigerians for a better job elsewhere.'

'It must feel good to be contributing to their personal growth,' Michelle suggested. 'That's what I liked about teaching.'

'I'm not a teacher or running a social enterprise—not with my consulting business anyway.'

'That's Generation Y,' said Michelle with the jocularity of someone who did not pay salaries. 'Just not loyal, always looking out for themselves.'

'If you want to get into consulting, do it as a freelancer,' I summed up. 'Work out of your home and don't employ any consulting staff. Get a good PA, an accountant and a lawyer. They're the people who add value.'

If this was my advice to Michelle, why wasn't I following it?

I was not in a good mood and I sounded like Dapo. Was it John's disloyalty? Was it the incompetence of my Ekologika Papers staff who bungled things the moment my back was turned? Was it the distance I felt with Alec? On the surface, our three days together were loving and reassuring, but he did not once ask me about my life or businesses in Nigeria.

Not a single question. What message was there in that?

I still needed the wind to blow off some frustrations, but it could not chase them far enough away.

O

With just six months of the year remaining, my diary packed with Strategyworks-related travel and the arrival of a new GM this week, I decided to hold a workshop for the Ekologika Papers staff. I figured it would be a good time to hand over the paper business responsibilities and introduce Gail to the team. We could stir up motivation to meet the year's sales goals, strengthen commitments to each other and reinforce some shared priorities. I decided to open with a motivating speech based on a sports metaphor – just like Kevin had done.

With the World Cup underway in this football-obsessed nation, what other sport could I choose?

'Let's kick to win,' I said.

The future of the company and our jobs depended on us making this year's sales forecast and getting costs down, and that in turn depended on everyone working together and not letting the team down.

'Help sales sell.'

This message was for Yinka, Chuks and Molly to ensure mock-ups were made for Kola on time, something he had complained about. It was also a message for Gail. In briefing her, I had already emphasised that her priority was to meet Kola's clients so she could nudge them into being real buyers or cross them off his sales forecast, and then develop her own clients.

'No more rework.'

I showed them how our notebook costs had soared due to wastage and implored them to be more careful. The same old mistakes were no longer acceptable. This was a message for everybody, including Gail who I had asked to be a sharp pair of eyes at all times.

'Get costs down.'

I showed them how our paper costs doubled in the last wet season even when monthly production counts were very low. I explained that papermakers got bonuses for reaching daily targets yet the numbers were only achieved because the company also paid for wet-season runners. The targets and bonus scheme were set for dry-season work, but it was also a scheme I set up when I had less cost information and before I understood the unintended consequences of the daily bonus structure.

'If we have to use runners, the company is paying to meet a daily target twice. It is fairer to the whole team and to the company if we readjust it to a monthly target,' I reminded them.

There was a lot of nodding except from Remi and his fellow papermakers. They liked their bonuses. I suspected they manipulated production to have high counts exceeding targets several days a month, ensuring they won the bonuses, yet missed monthly production goals. It was killing the business's ability to compete.

'Peter—work with Gail so we can get a fairer bonus system put in place.'

'That's fine, eh?' said Gail to the team. 'We don't want this to be a gonger, eh?'

Canadians, I discovered, had as many curious expressions as Australians. At least she looked like she was taking charge.

We moved on to developing our company values, and the right behaviours to help us achieve our goals. We brainstormed individual ideas and then created a shortlist we discussed at length.

Ekologika Papers Values
- Honesty, integrity, transparency
- Teamwork and collaborative effort
- Dependability
- Realistic approach based on experience
- Fanatical about detail
- Creative and customised solutions
- Self-criticism for continuous improvement

By working full time, Gail could get the team to work this way, I was sure. Lacking my full attention, I felt the team had played games, done things that had lost the company growth and profitability, and cost me sleep. Gail's constant presence would stop such bad behaviour in its tracks and reignite my passion.

'Shouldn't we have a value about caring for our staff, eh?' Gail asked me privately.

I believed that actions spoke louder than words and that caring for staff meant providing jobs that paid well above market rate and were full-time. Their salaries were paid on time, even when revenue was not coming in. I had done that.

'If we include that value, won't we have to say we care for our customers too?' I asked. Caring should be mutual. I felt I had cared for the Ekologika Papers staff for a long time and now, by changing their bad behaviours, they would show they cared about the company too.

I felt bruised by this team's careless attitudes and self-interested behaviour and, in a way, I was happy to hand over my frustrations to Gail.

She would kick to win – and kick them into shape.

'Seven values are enough,' I said instead.

CHAPTER THIRTEEN

Shady People

The fish that can see that its water is getting shallower cannot get stranded.
– Nigerian proverb

In Gail, I hadn't wanted a clone of myself – and certainly had not got one.

With her sunny disposition, she quickly made her extroverted presence felt and with her lively energy and complexion freckled by years of outdoor activities in sunny places she seemed a jolly cheerleading squad captain. She dressed more casually than the consulting staff and me but smartly enough to meet Ekologika Papers's clients while still practical enough for hands-on reviews in the workshop. I put her desk in the main room of the office, shared with the consulting staff, and she was immediately popular with both teams.

Each morning, I heard her sharing stories about Canada, her sister in Montreal, her outings to the beach or whatever she had been up to the night before. When not chatting to colleagues, she was on her phone, talking and texting – bullying people into agreement, rather than basing solutions on numbers and analysis, which was more my style. I hoped her skills at networking and forming good relationships would bring in the avalanche of sales orders we desperately needed in the second half of the year.

But by her second week, in mid-July, Gail's focus was not yet on sales.

'We need to buy boots for the papermaking team,' she decided a few days after the kick to win workshop. 'It's a safety and health issue, eh?'

I explained that I had bought boots for the papermaking team – twice.

'They ask for them, then won't wear them because their feet get hot and then the boots are "lost".'

'But their feet are always wet,' she countered. 'I'll make sure they wear them.'

I wondered if Remi and his team were testing what they could get away with under the new regime, but I didn't want to undermine Gail so soon after her arrival. I also wanted to smooth the way for her renegotiations on the new bonus structure, so I agreed to buy a third set of boots.

The next morning I overheard another call at her desk. 'Sonny. You can download music from my iPod—I have over 1000 songs.'

I called her into my office and reminded her about the past incident and embargo on personal downloading.

'Sure thing,' she replied immediately. 'I had forgotten. You're right. Not a problem; I won't do it again, eh?'

She seemed contrite at her misstep, so I let it go and moved on.

'Can you help get the mock-up out for Kola's clients? I'd like you to be on the sales call so you can judge how likely they are to place an order.'

'Sure thing,' she said again. 'Don't worry, Pamela. I'll get on top of it all.'

◖

Although I was hopeful Gail's arrival would lighten my workload, my 'third role' as Honorary Consul exposed me to what was becoming a worryingly common concern: fraud.

Working at home one night, I received an email from a woman in Tasmania. 'My friend has been conned out of nearly 7000 dollars by a man calling himself Danny Conan who claimed to be an Australian working in Nigeria.'

With Tippy asleep by my side, I peered at the laptop's bright screen. I had a few consular emails to go through and answer tonight but this drew me up short.

'The man promised my friend so much, and said he loved her and would marry her. She is recently widowed and very gullible. On three occasions he asked for money. He wrote that he and his solicitor had been bashed up in an office break-in and he needed money for an airfare to come home. A week later he asked for more money to pay for hospital fees, and a week after that money for legal fees over a land dispute so that he could fly out again.'

I was sure this was another successfully perpetrated 419 scam; another case of money fraudulently taken through deception. I imagined a lonely matron in a cardigan, crying at her kitchen table.

'My friend is distraught to the stage of suicide,' the email went on. 'She needs an urgent hip operation but used her credit card to fund the last payment, and is now penniless, in debt and desperate. Can you help?'

Other than offer my sympathy and confirm the fraud, there was nothing I could do.

Responding to emails about these scams was taking time, and so many kept arriving. My contact details had been added to Australia's Department of Foreign Affairs and Trade website and distressed Australians were reaching out to me by the dozens.

Living in Lagos I was familiar with 419 scams, but the High Commission had also recently briefed me, and I remembered the comments by Mike, the Deputy High Commissioner.

'Sophisticated gangs run this business,' he confirmed. 'They run teams of young Nigerians in internet cafés, get them to send out tens of thousands of emails and create profiles on dating sites. They build relationships with suckers who they manipulate into sending money.' He also told me the gangs were ruthless and violent, the polar opposite of their online identities, and there were instances where victims who arrived in Lagos looking for their fiancés were murdered.

I opened another email from Colin, a farmer in the Victorian Mallee region. This time, I imagined a loose-limbed, bronzed cowboy astride a horse looking out to a vast horizon for his female companion.

'My fiancée Deirdre is an American aid worker in Nigeria. She was in a car accident and her boss contacted me. He told me that she needed money for an urgent operation to save her life. I sent the money, but can you help me locate her? I want to make sure she is all right.'

Naïve Colin attached a photograph of his 'fiancée', young, highly groomed and buxom. To me, she looked like Playmate of the Month.

My response to Colin was direct.

'If you have never met your fiancée in person, and if this relationship is one developed over the internet, I regret to inform you, in all likelihood, your fiancée does not exist and you have been scammed.'

I had learned that these lonely-heart victims lived in a make-believe world of love and hope, and their dreams had been cultivated for so long they found it difficult to let go of the fantasy and cut their losses. I felt I could only help if I made the truth plain to them. I outlined the common kinds of 419 scams so they might see the similarities in their own situations.

'Money should only be forwarded to people known to you personally,' I wrote again and again.

It was quite depressing.

Victims who believed their fiancés had been arrested or needed money for immigration clearance had contacted me. Some victims were not Australians but believed they were in relationships with Aussies. Others thought they had been offered well-paying jobs and had paid 'processing fees'.

I wondered how these victims had allowed themselves to be defrauded. Surely, I thought, some part of their brain must have been sceptical about the predicaments their lover or correspondent described. Or was it a positive testament to their belief in the common goodness of people and willingness to trust them?

I did not yet count myself as such a person.

'There must be so many victims,' I said to Mike. 'I have several emails a week, sometimes a day, and they must be the tip of the iceberg.'

'Well, Nigeria is a sunny place for shady people,' he answered, mimicking Somerset Maugham's description of Monaco.

'What is the Australian Government doing about it? There should be a public awareness campaign and coverage by the mainstream media. Couldn't the Australian Police get involved?'

'We've put a notice on the DFAT website,' Mike said dismissively.

Who would look there *before* they were defrauded? It was not really adequate – like his response to my request for an introduction to the Lagos diplomatic circuit.

'The list of consulate officials in Lagos is updated annually,' he had told me. 'Canberra will get you on the list when it's time.'

I had hoped that I might get business networking opportunities from my role in exchange for the extra workload, but no diplomatic party invitations had yet arrived for me.

I opened another email.

It was from Cliff, an Australian businessman from Melbourne, who claimed he had a contract to supply boats to the state security services for patrols in the Niger Delta. He was vague about details but nevertheless wanted my help to expedite the contract.

'Have you paid any money to your local partner or agent yet?' I replied tersely. His supposed contract smelt as high as a three-day-old red snapper from the Epe fish market. I suspected that Cliff was the victim of advanced fee fraud, but I had no sympathy.

Advanced fee fraudsters did not play on their target's loneliness; instead they focused on their greed. Victims were seduced into believing there was a big financial reward – sometimes millions of dollars – from a deal, but that a much smaller sum of a few thousand dollars was needed to facilitate the transaction. Often the deals were transparently dodgy and appealed to those who didn't mind engaging in slippery practices.

Why would a small businessman from Victoria be asked to supply boats for the Nigerian security service? Just as not every Nigerian was a shady person, I thought, not every shady person was a Nigerian.

O

'What do you want?' Steve demanded.

My answer might make him indignant, I thought.

I was in Steve's apartment inside the secure oil company's residential compound. I was in a living room filled with African art, likely decorated by Steve's French wife who seemed too pleasant and softly spoken to be mated with such a charmless, brusque man. She had just left us and I was tense, unsure how Steve would respond to what I had to say.

The week before Gail joined, I had been asked for a private word by Segun, the Nigerian managing director of an Australian–Nigerian joint venture that supplied safety services to oil and gas companies. As Honorary Consul, I had got to know the Australian investors and managers well enough to know this was an authentic venture struggling to establish a formal presence in Nigeria.

I told Steve what Segun had told me. 'We were notified we won the contract (both the technical and the financial submissions) but we've been waiting weeks now for our local purchase order to be issued.' The order was the instrument issued by the purchasing department of a company to confirm its intention to contract goods or services from a local supplier. Segun told me the company in question was Steve's.

'An expatriate manager from the purchasing department asked for a meeting, off-site, at a bar,' Segun had said. 'I thought it strange but met him. I was shocked; he was so upfront with his demands. He wanted us to agree to them awarding the contract to another supplier. I was confused because we knew their bid was higher than our own, so I asked him why.'

I began to suspect the story's punchline.

'We were told not to worry—that we would still get the business. If we agreed, they would sub-contract the work to us.'

Like Segun, I was shocked, but not by the scenario. I had heard of this kind of thing before. Local companies won work, sometimes based on rules supporting local content, but had neither the capacity to deliver nor the intention to invest to develop that capacity. They were fronts for taking ten per cent or more of the contract value before passing the contract on to a more authentic supplier. But I was perturbed that an expatriate manager, who must be accepting bribes too, made such a brazen approach.

'The thing is, Pamela, we know that supplier. It's owned by the daughter of a board director.'

I took a moment to clear my head. This was even more startling. Segun was telling me that a director of Steve's company was conniving with expatriate staff in his purchasing department to have his daughter awarded a supply contract that she could not deliver. Segun then named the director, a respected Nigerian and someone I had met and knew reasonably well.

'Can you help?' he finished.

Segun knew that I knew Steve and wanted me to use my connection to help get the local purchase order issued. I was happy to try but was also curious as to what Steve would say to this serious allegation.

'That's pretty commonplace,' he said coolly. 'We have cliques inside and outside the company—you know, groups of people who work together to win contracts and corrupt the processes. It is very hard to root out.'

I was surprised by his casualness. I was aware of individuals using their positions to extract bribes, but was less aware of people acting together, in cliques, as he called them. But it explained a great deal.

Just recently, I had been perplexed as to why we were not getting paid for consulting work completed for a multinational food company. Patience had gone several times to their finance department to enquire about our payment but returned empty-handed. Payment was overdue thirty days beyond our standard thirty days, and with Haresh's loan to repay, my staff's salaries due and business expenses to fund, it was beyond a time for insouciance.

'They want something,' said Patience after her last futile visit.

'Have they asked?' I said. This was a Financial Times Stock Exchange (FTSE) 100 company that prided itself on its corporate ethical conduct.

'They don't have to,' she said. 'The invoice is in their drawer—they have no excuses. Delay tells us what they want.'

Toks's observation had been similar. 'Of course, the bosses turn a blind eye. If suppliers don't get paid on time these big companies have more cash to fund their own business. So why should they fix it?' She laughed at my surprise. 'They only focus on corruption at the front end—when they don't win a contract. There is nothing in it for them to fix back-end corruption.'

I wondered what Dapo would say. I hadn't heard from him since he'd missed the Agaja trip, but he'd probably agree with Toks. Both seemed to view human behaviour as fundamentally selfish and ruthless, a view that I had not shared but appreciated was not without foundation.

Now it was my turn to challenge Steve on why he didn't do more to root out corruption when he found it.

'We try regular weekend and evening raids,' he said more defensively. 'Security and audit staff open drawers looking for overdue invoices or cash. We check their text messages and calls. If we find anything incriminating, they get sacked. But with people working together, and in collusion with relatives outside the company, it's very hard to get solid evidence.'

I was still sceptical. Why make evidence of corruption the acid test? Why not just sack people for repeatedly not issuing payments on time within company terms of business? Why not audit supply contracts to make sure tender conditions were met? It was difficult to know where to start with my questions; this time I was here to support Segun.

'What can you do in this case?' I asked.

'I'll sort it,' he said. That was an end to it.

His wife re-joined us with some drinks and *hors d'oeuvres* and I asked Steve whether he would be rebuilding his hut at Agaja.

'Not much point unless the erosion can be stopped.'

'We have so much fun there,' said his wife. 'It would be so sad not to be able to go anymore, Stephen.' Even with her beguiling accent working on her husband, I noticed she didn't say a word about the plight of the villagers.

'I've asked one of my engineers to look into it,' said Steve, as much to his wife as to me. This was cheering news; action at last. 'In fact, we'll form a working group to take it further. That landlord of yours could be useful, Pamela—he'll know the local *Oga*.' *Oga* was the term for the Big Man or leader, and encompassed the local *Baale* (local chief) and the traditional landowner from whom Wale leased his plots.

Wale was a highly educated, successful businessman. He was also Steve's landlord and I thought he could add more than local contacts.

'Oh, and you know the villagers. Perhaps you should be on it too,' Steve added as an afterthought.

I gave him a tight-lipped smile. Should I be grateful for this rather limited endorsement?

But at least he was doing something about Agaja.

O

The following Friday evening, I felt re-energised. Gail had completed her second week of induction and soon she'd more fully take charge. This was timely as, in August, I'd be travelling again on Haresh's third assignment. And while Steve really irritated me, his planned working party to tackle Agaja's erosion, even if driven by self-interest, had given me some hope.

At the moment, however, I wanted some company. I still hadn't heard from Dapo and wondered if work was keeping him busy. Business spilled into every minute of my life, so I assumed it was the same for him. I lifted the phone to find out.

'It's not work; it's the house,' he answered, sounding more subdued than his answer seemed to merit.

'Are you redecorating?'

'No—it burned down.'

I tried to take this in. He told me there had been a fire last Saturday. It explained why he hadn't come to Agaja. His wife Esther and he had an inviting, much-lived-in middle-class home, which was filled with family photographs, favourite books, gorgeous African masks and sculptures, and Dapo's prized Afrobeat music collection. Had all of that been damaged?

'We've nothing left,' he said at last.

'Nothing?'

'A spark in a socket in one of the bedrooms in the roof probably started it.'

Power surges, especially on a changeover from generator to NEPA electricity, often burned out electrical equipment. My most valuable IT equipment and television were guarded by surge protectors, but only after I had lost one TV to a surge.

'The fire started in the second-floor ceiling so it had hours to grow,' he continued. 'We only knew about 11pm when smoke came downstairs.'

Esther had driven to the local fire station to raise the alarm while Dapo tried to fight the fire with buckets of water. 'No fire engines were in working order, so she had to drive on to another,' he said. 'The second station had no fuel for their trucks. She had to drive to buy fuel in two jerry cans. The fire fighters only got to the house two hours after we'd first discovered the fire.'

An inadequate fire fighting service was another example of the meltdown in Lagos's public infrastructure and services after years of neglect. I remembered Dapo's joke about the lack of a road due to all public funds being diverted into a contractor's beautiful house and cars. Corruption was so much more insidious than I had thought a year ago.

'The firemen had trucks and hoses but no water. They eventually got a hose into the neighbour's swimming pool and pumped their water, but by then the whole house was ablaze.' He lapsed into silence and there seemed little I could say.

Dapo and Esther were safe, at least, but had lost all their possessions. I felt very sorry for my friends and helpless to do anything about it.

Deflated by this news, I felt even more strongly that it was time to reach out to some friends and send our troubles away, if only for a night. Toks was travelling overseas and Michelle was out on a date, so I decided to text Jean. His dry wit and black humour would have been a welcome tonic for all the bad news of late.

'I'm in Beirut,' he replied. 'But let's get together soon.'

Without a Friday night companion and the July weather too wet for a trip to Agaja, I had no choice but to have a quiet weekend of admin and prep work for my imminent travels. It was dull but at least by the time Monday arrived I was back in a buoyant mood at the thought of Gail's second pair of hands to rely on for help supervising the team and watching for incompetence or corruption.

I arrived early at the office almost whistling at the thought.

But where was my second pair of hands?

By 10am Gail had still not arrived. Concerned, I rang her number.

'I'm going back to Canada,' she sobbed. 'I've found out my husband is having an affair. I'm leaving him.'

My headache suddenly returned. Where would we go from here?

CHAPTER FOURTEEN

Friends and Brothers

All lizards lie on their bellies but nobody knows which of them suffers belly ache.

– Nigerian proverb

I met Gail at Splendido, a rather scruffy Italian bar and restaurant on VI, on Tuesday evening, almost two days after her bombshell. The place was packed with mainly white, male office workers, probably from the head office of Steve's oil company nearby, who were taking advantage of the cheap happy hour. We chose a dimly lit corner, seated ourselves on wobbly stools and tucked into glasses of red wine and an antipasto platter of cheese, black olives and pepperoni. It may have looked like a celebration but that was as far as the similarities went.

Gail's eyes were red-rimmed and she looked tense.

'I've decided to stay,' she said. I hoped staying with her husband meant staying in her job, but she was talking about her marriage.

'I know the marriage is over,' she continued. 'I can't forgive him again.'

I nibbled at some cheese and tried to make sense of her decision.

'He's committed to investing in some land in Ontario,' Gail continued, 'and I'm going to wait until that is settled'.

'Why is that?'

'I want it when we divorce.'

I was appalled at her mercenary approach. Gail went on to justify her outlook by telling me about her husband's previous affairs and broken promises, but my mind wandered to my own important relationship, suddenly aware that it had become perilously fragile of late. Perhaps I was sacrificing my focus and passion for a business that brought me so much stress. If I lost Alec, would that be all I had left? I would ring him tonight, I decided.

'I want to stay in Lagos,' said Gail, interrupting my thoughts. I turned my attention back to her plight.

'I like Lagos—there's so much more opportunity here than in Canada.' She gulped down her red wine and added, 'I'll stay on as GM of Ekologika Papers'.

The waiter arrived with our order of heavily cheese-laden pizzas – more comfort food.

I felt relieved and hoped Gail would stick with her decision. But it felt an addendum; I wished she seemed more committed to me and to her job with Ekologika Papers. I wanted commitment, stability, and her focused energy.

I returned home and dialled Alec's number, hoping to hear some comfort or wisdom. He listened to my news about Gail's crisis in silence.

'Aren't you going to say anything?' I challenged, very close to breaking point myself.

'What more can I say?' he said.

O

Later in August I travelled to Delhi to help Haresh assess candidates for several senior executive roles.

Wanting an update on how things were going, I rang the office.

'James came to the gate to see you, Madam,' said Patience. 'The papermaker who left,' she explained when she realised that I had forgotten James. It seemed odd, but former staff did sometimes seek financial assistance when things got tough.

'Get Gail to handle it if he calls again,' I said, and put James and his concerns to one side. I had bigger issues to discuss with my GM. Patience transferred me to Gail and she greeted me chirpily.

'Don't worry. I'm a bit stressed but everything's fine.'

What was causing the stress then?

'The papermaking team missed its monthly paper production targets, again,' she answered, a little more seriously. 'Remi says it's been wet, but I think it's because they are unhappy about the new bonus structure.'

Where was her plan to get production back on track? 'Did you take them through the detail of why the structure was changed?' I asked.

At the kick to win workshop I had painted the reasons for the change but subsequently also done a report comparing dry-season and wet-season costs to support Gail's further discussions with the team.

'Did you show them how the daily bonus system plus runners in the wet doubled paper cost? And how they could still make their bonus if they achieved the monthly target?'

Gail dismissed this. 'The team was spoilt by the old daily bonus scheme and they assumed it would carry on forever.'

I'd let Gail handle the sensitive bonus negotiation, hoping to empower her and – if I was honest – because I lacked the time to do it myself. Could I have done any better? She had seemed someone well-suited to managing relationships, but it was becoming clear that her style made her the team's 'friend' rather than a capable manager.

'They are now "going slow" on production and holding you to ransom,' continued Gail almost blithely.

Me to ransom. Not us, not the business.

I was more than annoyed about a 'go slow'. The team pulled a high basic salary, which had continued during past off-seasons.

Even with a botched introduction of the new scheme, I had given them months of warning that the daily bonus was not working and needed restructuring. We had discussed options and tinkered with the detail to make it fairer for everybody. Was a 'go slow' the reward for my tolerance and loyalty to them?

'Money is key here,' said Gail. 'I've always said if you want loyalty get a dog.'

'Work with Peter,' I told her firmly. 'He'll influence Remi, and Remi will influence the others.'

I realised I had to coach Gail on things I took for granted. It was taking much longer than I'd anticipated for her to become an effective leader. We were in the third quarter when companies were getting active with their Christmas orders and I wanted her out in the market helping Kola.

'But it won't matter that we haven't got paper if we haven't got any orders. Have you seen Kola's customers yet?' I prompted.

'Kola hasn't given me many appointments. He goes to see them and I only find out once he's come back,' she complained.

'It's pretty urgent,' I said and tried to think what else I could do to get her out into the market. Gail had been on board over a month but seemed preoccupied by production and staff issues. 'How about arranging a programme with him for next week?'

Kola's strengths were his contacts and his enthusiasm, but he was not very organised. 'You might have to call to fix the appointments yourself.'

I knew I was micro-managing from afar, but it was hard to let go of my precious endeavour when the new custodian had not yet proved herself. It was getting rather fraught.

☾

'Nothing leaves the office without me seeing it,' announced Gail, grabbing a handful of groundnuts from the bowl on the bar.

It seemed the paper team were back on track, but the conversion team were still getting things wrong. 'I said that to Molly and Chuks on Friday morning and they both nodded.'

Like me, Gail was frustrated that the front and back covers of notebooks had been made to different sizes and bound into notebooks without the team noticing.

'But by Friday afternoon I caught them leaving the office with badly trimmed covers,' she wailed. 'Less than eight hours later. I couldn't believe it.'

At last Gail was showing some emotional investment in Ekologika Papers – even if she was having no more success than me at getting high-quality work.

I had arrived back in Lagos from my Indian trip and invited Gail and Jean to Agaja. Poor Dapo was still distracted by the loss of his home. And I had finally learned, to my shock, that Toks's recent ill health was a serious heart problem and that she had undergone surgery abroad. I was relieved she was now recuperating in London, but I would not see her for some time. My new beach companions seemed to be enjoying their time on the island, much to my delight.

Although it was late August, and with more storms likely, my hut had so far survived. Today, was a topaz-blue day and a rare gem we exploited. The sea beckoned the local fishermen in their heavy dugout canoes and palm tree fronds waved in a south westerly zephyr. Behind it all, the muted crash of the waves created a soothing soundtrack.

I tried to let the beauty of my surroundings banish my business worries, but it was too tempting not to add my own gripe to the conversation.

'No leave without my approval,' I related to the others. 'How many times have I sent an email around about that? Fill in the application form.' My latest exasperation had been with Sophie, the remaining consultant, and Edith, a new analyst for Strategyworks. To my surprise, I had returned from India to find they were on leave.

Their unplanned absence was terrible timing as I had to travel again before they returned.

'Gloria knew they were going and didn't ask for their application forms or check with me,' I grumbled. 'I might as well write admin procedures only for myself.'

Jean started relating some of the shortcomings of his workers when Luke and his mother walked into the bar. Delighted to see them, I got up and went over to greet them. Luke's mother was a hard worker who cleaned my plot and hut at Agaja and always had a ready smile. Although she was my age, she looked decades older. I admired her strength and liked to help her out whenever I could.

'Here is a present for you and for Luke,' I said after we exchanged hugs. Through the years, I found people expected a gift and it had become my custom to bring presents for Luke, his mother and the other villagers who worked for me whenever I travelled. This time I'd bought a polo shirt for Luke and a carryall bag for his mother. They took my gifts wordlessly.

Luke's mother did not speak English, so I put her lack of thanks down to that – I didn't know why Luke did the same.

As he turned to leave, Luke said, 'Next time you travel, Madam, my mother would like a watch and I would like a new phone.'

It was my turn to be struck dumb.

Bringing gifts seemed a minefield for an *oyibo*. Did he think I was implying his shirt needed replacing? Had I brought things they didn't want?

But it was hard to feel generous when I got no thanks and nothing I gave seemed enough.

Gail and Jean were still chatting animatedly as I returned to my stool. Coming along the sand towards us was a group of traders bearing all sorts of eye-catching items such as tie-dyed tablecloths, silver swords in embossed leather sheaths and strings of glass beads. We knew each other by name as I often bought from them, but today

I shook my head to let them know I was not interested. My generosity felt at an ebb and I turned back to my companions.

'When I go back to Lebanon, I find myself speaking to people the way I do here,' said Jean. He looked cool in brightly patterned shorts and a white shirt. 'I break down the task into its separate components.'

'They say: "I understand". And I say, "What did you understand",' he chuckled. 'It gets me into trouble. There, they think I am being condescending. But here, when people get so many things wrong, you have to do it.'

Gail and I joined in the laughter, a little shamefacedly, as we were each guilty of speaking like this. We had learned that seemingly clever people could agree to instructions and then do the opposite, leaving you gasping at the result.

In Strategyworks, I ran workshops on building skills to run effective teams, yet all my earnest efforts with my own team – coaching and giving constructive feedback, appreciative listening, mutual respect, sharing goals, striving for clarity, creating empathy – had not delivered the right response.

'I get angrier with people here than I ever am in Lebanon,' Jean continued. 'I can simply explode and shout.'

Gail and I nodded agreement. I blushed to remember the formerly unknown 'ugly me' unleashing her red wrath like a sudden Saharan dust storm. It sometimes felt the team expected their repeated bad behaviour to brew a storm then simply endured the fuss to pass out the other side. Who, I wondered, was managing whom?

'There's usually something in it for them. It can be difficult to see what it is, but that's usually behind the situation,' Jean went on. He sounded like Dapo, I thought. But I was no longer incredulous about this cynicism. I felt as though I was taking a course in human nature but didn't have all the answers yet.

Out of thin air my landlord Wale appeared on the sands, coming from the other direction and his beach hut. I waved at him and he joined us at the bar, a little unsteady on his feet as he climbed the steep bank from the beach. I realised I was not really sure how old he was.

He leaned towards us over the table, fresh news on his lips. 'Engineers from Steve's company assessed the options for the wreck removal last week. They will be coming back to assess the situation further in October once the seas are lower.'

'That's great progress,' I exclaimed. It was more than we'd had in two years waiting for government intervention. I had to give Steve his due.

'I wonder how they will handle all the different Nigerian government agencies and tiers of government,' Wale mused. He had dealt with them and knew the issues. 'They will all be looking for their pound of flesh and can block action if they don't get it.'

'They're already thinking about how to fund the wreck's removal,' I said, relating my own news from the last Agaja working party meeting attended. 'Once the budget is developed, they will approach other oil companies and ask them to contribute.' I had provided the list of companies with huts at Agaja – companies I had already approached and who had ignored me. But I had high hopes things might be different when approached by a fellow business with a plan.

We drank to further success and then returned to our favourite subject: our staff.

'If the leakage is five per cent, that is expected and manageable,' said Jean. He meant if staff somehow stole up to five per cent of business proceeds. 'But if they win your trust the eventual loss can be so much more. It'll break the business.'

'I have suffered that,' said Wale, surprising me. He had a large, diversified family business, which included a farm, distribution business for auto parts and a construction firm. He was an experienced and thoughtful director and I could not imagine Wale either suffering fools or foolish behaviour.

'A man named Bola had worked at the farm for many years,' he told us. 'I recruited him as a manager. I had him as a guest at my home. He was a friend for over twenty years. When we decided to invest in the fish farm, I put him in charge.

'Bola lived at the fish farm and our accountant worked with him on the books. But one day Bola had an accident and was hospitalised. I went to the fish farm to help out and in a drawer discovered that Bola and the accountant kept separate sets of accounts. They were running a shadow company, and breeding and selling fish that were our own on the side.' Wale shook his head at the memory and slapped the bar surface. 'It really crushed me.'

I was stunned. If this fraud by a trusted employee could happen to Wale, it surely could happen to anyone.

'I had a similar experience in a food business,' said Jean. 'The factory manager and the accountant got kickback on everything. They were both from the same place, it turned out.'

'Don't let staff bring in their friends and brothers,' warned Wale. 'That's one of my rules, although it's hard to do in practice. You can't really ask what village someone is from during the recruitment process.'

Jean and Gail chuckled.

The traders had ignored my signal to pass us by and began to spread out their wares on the sand in front of the bar. The sword dealer Ibrahim unfolded a mat and I glimpsed a new design. Curiosity got the better of me. Perhaps I could find a gift for Alec. I came out from behind the bar to greet Ibrahim.

'Good afternoon, Madam,' cried Ibrahim. 'I will make you a good price.'

As I dug my bare toes into the warm sand, I thought of Ekologika Papers's staff. Remi was Peter's 'brother' and Sonny and Chuks were their friends. Wale's bit of wisdom might have come too late.

O

In September I took a two-week holiday to Australia, my first proper break since a visit home the previous Christmas, mainly to celebrate my father's eighty-fifth birthday. It seemed he had kangaroo-hopped a decade somewhere; he was distressingly old. At a family gathering, he disconnected from a conversation to search his mind for a memory or to process some words, then suddenly delivered a funny anecdote or a startling, pithy pun. Just like that Dad was back in the room, but it was a fleeting glimpse of his former brilliance.

Alec joined me there. Our reunion began warmly but then we seemed to get on each other's nerves.

'Running two companies is a bad business decision,' he said. While this was likely true, moral support would have gone down better.

My gift of a sword bought from Ibrahim had not gone down well either.

'Why waste money on another sword?'

Even his new shoes irritated me, loafers with dainty tassels so unlike the shoes he'd normally wear.

We felt estranged and, despite the stress my businesses were causing me, I longed to be back in Lagos.

Some excellent news arrived from Ekologika Papers. We were featured on the cover of an environmentally-focused magazine – applauded for our recycling efforts – and Kevin, my banking client, had ordered over 1000 table calendars for his customers. It was our most valuable order ever.

Kola and Gail had been instrumental in making smaller sales, but we were still falling short of our forecast. I decided to use our growing environmental credentials and spend some money on public relations to spruce up our sales. I was booked to give a press interview on my return.

Good news came in from Strategyworks too. Kevin's new manager of change had decided to roll out a customer service change programme and accepted our proposal for a year-long assignment commencing in January. That sale, plus one assignment for a chemicals company and another for a telecommunications company assured a full workload for the foreseeable future.

My consulting firm was bringing in the cashflow I'd hoped. But would my social enterprise ever reward me for my faith?

O

On my return to Lagos, Jean had someone for me to meet.

'Max is a good guy,' he had said.

Jean had quit the printing firm he'd worked for and Max was his new business partner. They were creating a new large-format printing business together.

I was envious. I had failed to find a partner in Strategyworks or retain consultants who I could grow into partners and my experience with a senior staff member for Ekologika Papers was disappointing. But it was tough to face the challenges of Nigerian business alone.

I wondered what Max would be like.

We met Friday evening at seedy Splendido, the Italian bar in which I had met Gail to hear her marital woes.

Max, I learned, was French on his mother's side. And in conservative chinos, long-sleeved shirt and tailored jacket, he looked a casually cool Parisian. There was something about him and the chemistry between the three of us that made the evening sizzle with good humour and rapport.

We exchanged personal histories, the way you do on meeting, and I learned how he grew up in France and rarely visited the Lagos businesses run by his Lebanese father.

'I had to take over the business when my father died,' Max said. Not such a different story from Haresh, I thought.

Like Jean, he was in his early thirties but his kind, courteous and serious demeanour made him seem more mature. He had arrived in Lagos at the same time as me, making us time twins and we were learning the ropes of doing business in Lagos simultaneously. His father had run various manufacturing businesses, but after taking over Max had closed them down as it had been too hard to compete against cheap and illegal Chinese imports. Now, with Jean, he was investing in large-format printing.

'Our equipment is arriving from China next week,' he said struggling to be heard over the piped music, which was especially loud tonight. 'I'm working on the visa for a technician who will come to help train us to use it.'

'And I'm working on the sales,' Jean said. 'We need it operational soon.'

They were both enthusiastic about their prospects.

'But what are we calling it?' asked Max. 'We need to register our business name.'

As they bantered around ideas for the proposed name for their business, I drifted back to my happy day at the beach doing the same thing with Peter, Remi and Sonny. It seemed a long time ago.

'Where will you work from?' I asked curiously.

'From the compound where my father's manufacturing businesses were located,' said Max. 'It's a big complex of warehouses and even apartments. It's where I live.'

'It's far,' said Jean. 'Try driving and it might take you one hour or four hours.'

'It's in Ikotun,' said Max.

'So where's Ikotun?' I asked, oblivious then to its place in my future.

○

The following Monday I was back supervising the Ekologika Papers team alone. Gail was in Canada.

'I need to fly out for a week. A financial transaction has gone wrong and I need to go and sort things out. It's bad timing, but I have to go,' she had said.

Before she left, however, she had made time to go to the interview I'd arranged – in my place.

The newspaper ran a full-page story about Ekologika Papers accompanied by a photograph of Gail. This was the public relations exercise I had organised, the interview I was to have done.

'The journalist rang up and asked to do the interview sooner as they wanted the article for this week's edition. As the year's running away, I thought I better do it,' Gail said.

It was strange as I had already agreed to the publication date and she had not asked my opinion about an earlier one. I scanned the article. Why was Gail described as MD rather than GM?

'You know journalists,' she laughed. 'They just get the wrong end of the stick. But we've had quite a few enquiries since it came out.'

That had been true enough. But it didn't seem right, any of it.

Now with Gail gone, my attention went to production. With drier weather, productivity from Remi and his papermaking team had increased and they seemed committed again to the success of the business. Peter was working long hours, helping to sort out issues in paper production and conversion. He was my right-hand man and, without Gail between us, it was just like old times.

The availability of paper was not now the problem. We still needed more sales and some were in the pipeline, but we had to produce Kevin's calendar job plus a few other smaller runs of calendars, notebooks and Christmas cards. The immediate challenge was to produce these orders to the right quality, on time and without breaking the bank.

Molly worked with Mr Babatunde on outsourced tasks such as binding and, as long as I kept a close eye on quality control, these tasks were being handled reasonably efficiently. During her induction, I had asked Gail to experiment again with offset printing. True, the results using Dapo's offset printers last year had been poor but both Jean and Max agreed better print quality should be possible. But she had failed to get on top of this task so jobs could still only be completed using costly desk jet printing. In-house we had six desk jet printers. Seasonal casual staff had joined the in-house conversion team, led by Chuks, and all were working overtime at night and on the weekends.

I had previously asked Gail to draw up an internal production schedule and to have the team keep records, especially for printing, but she hadn't seemed to understand what I wanted. So, although I had Strategyworks client work to attend to, that week I developed the production schedule, drew up production record templates and put together printing policies and procedures.

Why was our production of calendars and cards so slow and our ink cartridge usage rates so very high? I wondered. The business was rushing towards a large loss if we didn't get ink cartridge usage back under control.

'Chuks, why haven't your casual staff filled in the number of sheets printed on their shifts?'

'It's too hard, Madam. It slows them down.'

'But these numbers don't make sense—we cannot possibly have printed this many sheets on one cartridge.' The numbers from the next shift were unbelievably high.

'They probably forgot to mark up the sheets when they changed the cartridges, Madam.'

Then another shift and another set of unbelievable numbers, this time too low.

'It seems that some of the ink cartridges are only printing ten sheets,' Chuks claimed. 'It is because we used recycled cartridges, Madam.' We had switched from original cartridges to save money. 'Some of them are bad—they come to us nearly empty from the supplier.'

Another excuse, I thought. I had already instructed Chuks to keep all cartridges for counting and collect them for recycling.

'Chuks, make sure that any cartridge that is empty or does not print a normal quantity is marked up and put to one side. I want to see the supplier.'

A couple of days later, the supplier was due for a meeting.

'Chuks, I cannot reconcile the ink cartridge purchases against the empty ink cartridges in the store.'

'I think one of the casuals threw some out by mistake.'

Where would it end? Everything was happening so quickly and in such disarray.

O

Gail returned a week later with tiny stitches behind each of her ears. Financial transaction, my foot. She had had a facelift.

I tried to get her to take over the staff supervision, but all the mistakes seemed to either happen on night shift or at the weekends and Gail would not come in then. She either still didn't understand the way things worked or was putting together her exit plan.

Frustrated at her lack of progress on production and in making sales calls and closing the sales still in the pipeline, I provided her with a list of target firms.

'I called about half the people on your list,' said Gail a couple of weeks later. 'I was told some people were off sick, not on seat, or travelling from one firm after the other. I got one yes, but it was a "Call me back next week." Don't worry … I won't give up, eh?'

I had heard this before.

'But it reminded me how much I have always hated sales,' she added.

I couldn't believe it. Gail was now clearly a recruiting mistake.

'Sack her,' advised Toks, now recovered from her surgery and returned to Lagos.

'Sack her,' recommended Dapo, at last at the club again.

'Sack her,' said Jean, now a regular drinking companion.

At least the advice was consistent, and I was consistent in not following it. I had Strategyworks clients to serve and I needed her help to see through the peak season. After that I planned to let her go.

O

Early November, I had made several surprise visits to the workshop at night and at weekends and at last, there was steady progress towards acceptable ink cartridge usage rates. Around 10am one Friday I was in my office answering emails when my mobile rang.

'You do not know me, Madam,' said a female voice on the other end of the line. She had a Nigerian accent but otherwise I did not recognise her voice. 'I am calling to warn you about your staff.'

I listened, only later realising I had barely taken a breath.

'They are thieving from you, Madam. You trust them, but they are stealing and they are in it together.'

'Who?' I asked. 'What are they doing?' My mouth was dry and my heart pounded against my ribs. This was surreal; an anonymous tip-off about criminality among my own staff.

'Chuks is the ringleader. He has some of the casuals involved too. Chuks inflates the prices of the ink cartridges and keeps the money for himself. He also makes you think the ink cartridges are empty so he can keep the money. He has been taking money for other things too.'

The attempted fraud on my credit card?

'They are bleeding your company dry,' she finished.

I asked who she was, but she would not say anything more and hung up.

I felt gutted and I was shaking. Could the allegations be true? I was not sure. But immediately I knew that I had to decide what to do about it.

PART THREE

Dark of the Moon
(2006–2008)

Dark of the Moon is a phase when the moon lies directly between the Earth and the sun; the moon's sunlit side is no longer visible to us.[1]

CHAPTER FIFTEEN

Some Babies Have to Be Killed

When the roots of the tree begin to decay, it spreads death to the branches.
— Nigerian proverb

Reeling from the allegations of fraud committed by Chuks, in collusion with some casuals, I phoned Alec on his mobile. My mouth was dry and it was hard to get out the words as I related the anonymous call.

Alec was in a different time zone, far away physically and emotionally.

'Pack up and leave,' was his blunt assessment. 'Anyway, I can't talk now.' He was impatient to be away to a business meeting.

Wanting more advice than that, I rang Toks.

'Don't do or say anything,' she said. 'You don't have evidence, so it is important you don't make accusations yet.'

She insisted we meet in the early evening and cancelled her other plans. I met her at the Boat Club and, as it was a dry November evening, we were seated at a private table by the water. With diamond drops at her ears and an outfit glittering with sequins, she was dressed for a social event. I had spoiled an evening out for her, but she didn't seem to mind.

'I know this venture is your baby, your passion,' said Toks with quiet sympathy, beginning to address the crisis that Ekologika Papers and I faced.

My shoulders sagged in preparation for the bad news and I reached out to pour us a glass of wine.

'Did I ever tell you I also once had a business that was my passion too,' she mused. 'It was an interior design company. We made curtains and soft furnishings and imported furniture to decorate entire houses—some of the biggest homes in Lagos. I loved it. I felt I could express my creative side in this business, perhaps more than I could through property.'

It sounded exactly like how I felt about Ekologika Papers.

She paused then her tone became sombre. 'My staff cheated me, just like yours probably have, with inflated invoices. They colluded with suppliers and drove me crazy with rework and wastage. In the end I couldn't make any money.'

I was shocked that Toks had been cheated. Then I remembered the story Wale had told me only last month. Was it comforting to know that even people as business-savvy as Toks and Wale could experience thieving staff? If this is what mine were doing, then I was in good company and knowing this did alleviate my sense of humiliation.

Toks broke into my thoughts.

'I knew my interior design business was a passion I could not afford.'

Then she said what I'd been dreading from the first whispers of doubt that had reached me so many months ago.

'I closed it down, Pamela, despite it being painful,' she said. 'Some babies have to be killed.'

○

Two hours later I looked up to see grey clouds backlit by a rising moon scudding across a sky speckled with stars. They were sped along by a high-altitude wind that was insubstantial at ground level. The anxiety I felt was at last subsiding with the help of alcohol and an action plan. A waiter served Toks and I beef and chicken *suya*, a tasty Nigerian specialty. Thinly sliced beef or chicken was threaded onto skewers and coated in *suya* spice, a combination of herbs and spices as unique as Colonel Sanders's own secret recipe, before being grilled and served with chunks of onion, thinly sliced cabbage and more spice. The dish was delicious, although I barely appreciated it. We poured out another bottle of frosted Australian white wine and paused to listen to the recorded sounds of Lagos's favourite performer/singer, Fela Kuti, and his jazz, funk and Afrobeat music from the 1970s amplified through nearby speakers.

Toks and I talked incessantly for all that time.

We picked apart the anonymous caller's message and what it might mean for the business. Was it true? What evidence did I have? Who was involved? Who was the anonymous caller?

We considered how the allegations matched the situation. They would certainly explain the out-of-control ink costs, the inexplicable ink usage, the failure to collect proper printing records and the loss of ink cartridges – all of which had been Chuks's responsibility. During the afternoon, I had called around other suppliers to compare ink cartridge prices, something I previously left to Chuks. His assertions that our recycled ink cartridge supplier was the cheapest easily proved false. Yet the evidence was only circumstantial.

And even if it was deliberate fraud, who else could be involved or responsible? How widely should I cast the net? Could Sonny and Molly, who also worked in the conversion processes, be involved? Or Yinka, our talented graphic designer, who had recently resigned following an argument with my salesman Kola? I didn't know what the dispute was about and had been disappointed to lose her, but the two had never got along. Gail had replaced her with an inexperienced young man who was likeable enough but whom I did not know well. Might he or the six casuals we currently employed in conversion be implicated? If the thieving stain was limited to the new staff or casuals I would not feel as badly as if some of my closest and longest-serving staff were involved. My head ached as I searched my brain for clues, and my heart ached at my doubts. The alleged fraud felt personal. Surely Sonny, one of my foundation employees, would not do this to me. How could I establish the truth?

'You won't ever get the evidence,' said Toks. 'You won't find out for sure and thinking about it will just make you ill. For the business to survive this loss you'll have no choice but to lay people off. The shock of the sackings will make the others behave—for a while.'

But what other losses and behaviours might actually be fraud? I thought about the rework and wastage on the notebook covers. Could Chuks or others in his team be getting kickback from the Mushin suppliers of strawboard and laminate? 'Mistakes' on cover sizes increased the purchases of these supplies, which might make rework worth their while. Could Mr Babatunde be offering kickback to Chuks and the others for punching and binding our notebooks? Would that make them waste notebooks to inflate numbers and their illicit payments?

My mind was a flurry of wild ideas moving as fast as the clouds above us. All trust had evaporated in the minutes of the anonymous call. Should I kill my baby? Was closure the better option?

Although customers liked our distinctive products and the business could be profitable if we could lower the costs of papermaking and conversion and reduce wastage, I knew I could not continue without trust in my staff. Whom did I trust?

I trusted Peter. I could imagine him suspecting Chuks of misdeeds and being too weak to challenge him or tell me directly. I thought he or perhaps Molly was the most likely to have insider knowledge and to have put up someone to make the anonymous call. Peter would do it this way because he wouldn't want to be seen making the accusations against people who lived in his area. Molly might do it as she was outside Chuks's circle. I also trusted Gloria, my PA and Patience, my accountant. I trusted my driver, Tayo, and Edward, my steward. Kola was difficult to manage but I was confident he was basically trustworthy. I wouldn't put Sonny and Remi past some petty skimming. Remi had annoyed me for his role in the papermaking 'go slow' and each could drive me crazy with repetitive mistakes, but I could not imagine either of them working in collusion against me in a determined and systematic way. Beyond these people, I was not sure.

I also could not continue if my passion for my social enterprise had been killed. At the moment it was seriously undermined. But underlying everything was my commitment to help Peter and my two other original employees, Sonny and Remi. I remembered us sitting under the tree in my garden nearly two years before. We made a pact to make Ekologika Papers work, together. Remi and Sonny might be rascals, but I was fond of them and Peter had a solid honesty. I still felt an obligation to them and to the twenty-five staff that Ekologika Papers employed. Most were seasonal casuals, but they were gainfully employed and learning skills. Was I going to let this incident kill our dream and their life chances?

My short-term decision was also complicated by pre-existing orders, the largest of which was for Kevin, my banking client, whose consulting income now underpinned the viability of my Lagos existence. The cost overruns meant this order could only be fulfilled at a huge loss. Yet a declaration of bankruptcy by Ekologika Papers would be highly visible in the local market. In Kevin's shoes, wouldn't I doubt the viability of Strategyworks to deliver the year's-worth of consultancy services he and his change manager had already commissioned? Wouldn't the past and future clients of Strategyworks feel the same? I felt I could not close Ekologika Papers without serious ramifications for my personal reputation in Nigeria and harsh consequences for my consulting business.

Toks was patient as we re-examined every aspect of the Ekologika Papers business, as if it were still possible to re-cut a below-grade diamond for new, dazzling brilliance. Killing my baby was something to consider in the medium-term, but for now I had the motivation to continue, albeit on a smaller scale, as an adjunct to the profitable and successful Strategyworks. But I could only do this with people I trusted until I could feel confident about investing and hiring anew. For Ekologika Papers, the next year would be for refocusing, regrouping and surviving.

Things were bad, but not unsalvageable.

'So, what do you need to continue?' asked Toks, forcing me to focus on pragmatic short-term steps.

We began the hard work of making a recovery plan to execute the company's existing orders and consult my lawyer about how to manage the necessary layoffs. Gail's new graphic designer had made a lot of mistakes and needed hand-holding, something the business could not afford. Toks promised to help find a mature graphic designer who could also manage production.

'Patrick is very experienced,' she suggested. 'He is from the printing industry. I am sure he can manage the production of your existing orders and find ways to economise. He works freelance for me but I'm sure he'll make himself available to start as soon as you want him, Pamela. But don't expect him to be loyal—he works for himself.'

I was later to remember that advice, but tonight was for focusing on immediate plans.

O

But that weekend doubts once again spread like an aggressive oxalis weed, indiscriminately but expeditiously exploding its seed pods into fertile ground. Over and over I wondered who was involved in this alleged conspiracy and who should be trusted now. I told myself it was futile, a waste of time and profitless worry, but my mind would not let go of a deep sense of betrayal and a new wariness with my team.

Despite these emotions, I worked feverishly towards a clear objective: to save what I could of the Ekologika Papers dream. I gathered further information about ink usage, the current status of orders and our financial position. I crunched numbers to establish how much the company had lost and how much it would cost to complete our orders. I assessed how deeply I should cut with the knife. How many staff could I afford to keep on? How many did I need? Would we have any capacity for any more orders? How could I prevent further fraud or reduce my exposure to it?

My work that weekend made me also consider my plan for Strategyworks. I had paid off the loan to Haresh and the consultancy already had a full year's order book from several clients. My consultant Sophie, after just seven months' employment, had resigned the week before. It had been a further source of heartache. My analyst Edith remained and I decided to recruit another analyst. No longer would I seek to build a sustainable firm of partners. Instead I'd deliver advisory work with minimal professional staff support, more like the strategy I had recommended to Michelle.

Patrick, Toks's graphic designer, turned up at the office on Saturday morning. His number two haircut was shaved to within a few millimetres of his skull – perhaps he thought it made the hints of grey less noticeable. He was older than the other members of the Ekologika Papers team, quietly spoken, quite plump and a little low on energy. He reminded me of a koala munching on soporific eucalyptus leaves. But he seemed competent and quickly understood the printing and cost issues.

'We can save money only by using offset printing,' he advised.

I explained that we had done tests with our high-moisture-content paper and found offset printing delivered unacceptably muddy colours and blurred images, but he demurred.

'I will start the tests with offset printing on Monday, Madam.'

I accepted his plan. After all, I remembered, Chuks had led the previous tests.

On Saturday afternoon, I had a long meeting with Mr Atta, my lawyer. He was an elderly man whose eyesight had deteriorated since I'd last seen him. 'I have glaucoma,' he said matter-of-factly. He held documents at arm's length or handed them to me to read, but he had arrived by car and, rather worryingly, was the driver. Mr Atta had not become rich through his legal advisory service; he was too scrupulously honest, from the Nigerian 'old school' and I liked and respected him. I never imagined that my lawyer should prove such an indispensable part of my support team in running businesses in Nigeria.

'Sack most of the conversion team but cite difficult operating conditions,' he advised. 'Never mention fraud, Pamela—you don't have enough proof. Just say that the company has to make difficult decisions to survive, that some staff need to go, and then pay them their full entitlements.'

Those last conditions were hard. However, I agreed to comply with Mr Atta's advice.

'Make sure you have Gloria with you to record the conversations and minute them,' he said.

What a change from the informal, collegial culture I had hoped to forge. Were we reduced to this?

O

On Monday morning I laid off five staff – Chuks, the new graphic designer Gail had recruited and three casual staff from the conversion team. I also brought in Peter from paper production to help with conversion, and because of her good performance I confirmed Molly's position.

Patrick took our paper to a printer hoping to deliver our existing jobs as cheaply and quickly as possible. Within a day he proved offset printing was feasible, albeit with some loss of quality. He suggested further tests to improve the spot colour and sharpness and, having agreed on an acceptable quality for each job, that we outsource to several printers simultaneously. Even with this sensible plan, Kevin's calendar order would have to be delivered in batches through January.

Later that week, I briefed Kevin about our technical problems and delivery delay, but not about the alleged fraud. He grimaced at my news.

'Well at least my team can advise our customers and plan the despatch.' He was understandably unhappy.

He was lucky he was getting calendars at all – but I kept this thought to myself.

I had another tough call to make that week – what to do about new customers. In a meeting with my team, Kola argued passionately to close sales he had worked hard to create while Peter doggedly explained we did not have capacity to take on new orders. When Patrick supported Peter, I agreed that we should cap this year's orders, disappointing Kola who would now miss out on commission.

'Blame your colleagues,' I told him. I had opened up about our precarious financial situation but cited the former conversion team's incompetence. Thinking of Mr Atta, I took care not to use the word fraud. 'Their over spending, wastage and slow production has let us all down. But if we take on new orders, and we don't have the capacity to deliver them, we'll make everyone unhappy.'

Kola nodded but seemed withdrawn.

Later in the office bathroom, I leaned against the basin and took a deep breath. Emotional exhaustion had replaced my former agitation.

I considered Gail's future role. She had been shocked and sympathetic throughout the past week, but I was the one having sleepless nights and not her. What value she was adding?

As I washed my hands I wondered if her *laissez-faire* management style might indirectly have led to this fraud. I wondered whether her presence had stopped me keeping a tighter rein on the team.

I dried my hands, deep in thought. The business could not afford her. She should go, but when?

Although it was bad timing, I felt compelled to fly to Australia next month for Christmas. My father's frailty during my last visit in August had frightened me and now I learned he had fallen and broken his hip. I also needed to nurture my strained relationship with Alec before it was too late.

Back at the basin to brush my hair, I looked in the mirror and saw haunted eyes, straw-like hair and worry lines. The last year had aged me as much as the previous decade. I needed time out for me, too. Gail could manage the business until I returned, and then she should go.

During the afternoon, I called her into my office to negotiate her departure.

But she had an announcement of her own.

'I am resigning, effective the middle of January,' she said. 'My husband is buying me a bar.'

It was Splendido, the Italian restaurant and bar where Jean, Max, she and I met for Friday night drinks.

'He thinks it might help bring us back together.'

I was surprised, as she had already confided to me that she did not love him anymore.

'Will it?' I asked.

'No,' she said, 'But I'll have the bar'.

It was fair enough not to forgive her husband's philandering, but her manipulative behaviour made me wonder how she'd used her time at Ekologika Papers.

Her timing, however, was perfect so I congratulated her instead.

O

As demanding as a Lagosian beach trader for my attention –
'Madam, I give you good price' – my businesses claimed the lion's
share of my focus. To escape, the following Sunday I went to Agaja.
Dapo, who was resiliently rebuilding his home, joined me.

'Better to have trustworthy but incompetent staff,' he remarked.
At the beach hut bar with a glass of cold Gulder in his hand, Dapo
was ready with pithy words of wisdom and it was good to have the
old Dapo back. I told him that I decided to rely more heavily on
my original staff, Peter, Remi and Sonny. He was right. What they
lacked in expertise they made up for in passion, capacity for hard
work and trust, rare as gold dust.

Thankfully, he did not say, 'I told you so' about Chuks.

'Follow the money,' he said. 'If an investment seems ridiculous,
a decision inexplicable, a mistake inexcusable,' he said. 'There is only
one sure way to get through the opacity, to get clearer about motives
and who is in charge. Follow the money.'

I didn't quite understand so he continued, shaking his head at
my lack of percipience.

'The money, Pamela, the money. Things in Nigeria happen for
the money. See who benefits financially by following the money trail.
It might be one or two layers under the surface, but then you will
know why things have happened the way they have. It's true in your
business, in every business and it's true in politics and the village.'

If I had followed the money trail on the high and rising costs
of production, the wastage and rework, and drilled down to the
ink costs and volumes maybe I would have considered fraud as a
possibility. Was Dapo's cynical realism based on experience?

This rule could be applied elsewhere, I thought glumly.
Politicians, business people and public figures the world over made
sometimes bewildering decisions, seemingly not in the public

interest or with common sense, but later the exposed cosy relation-ships, illicit payments or political support from business or trade union pals explained why. Corruption and fraud certainly were not exclusive to Nigeria, but I had never been so close to them before.

I felt enveloped in and buffeted by a corrupt system whose wide reach and impact was becoming more tangible as I bore its brunt, financially and emotionally. I felt bruised by the allegations and the wariness with which I now viewed my team. Was I simply naïve or did it take time to learn all the ways in which human beings can betray each other?

I was determined not to be caught out again.

CHAPTER SIXTEEN

It's Complicated

The mouth that eats pepper is the one the pepper influences.
– Nigerian proverb

Another Friday night. It was late January 2007 and I had recently returned from Australia. I went to Splendido, now under Gail's management, where the music was loud and the crowd boisterous, and found it hard to talk. But I was with Jean and Max and we were drinking imported Italian beers straight from the bottle. It felt good to be back in Lagos, where I had friends, challenge and purpose. And now that I had returned, I could get on with trying to improve things at work.

I'd glued a favourite cartoon to my office wall. It had been sent to me during my trans-African bicycle ride and I'd received it at a low ebb. It showed a pelican with a frog in its mouth – with the frog using its legs to prise open the bird's beak, desperate to avoid being swallowed.

'Never give up,' was the emphatic maxim. It was now mine.

My break in Australia had been fraught. Despite leaving Gail and Patrick in charge, I'd found myself again managing from afar. New issues had emerged around the delivery of Kevin's calendars and other Christmas orders. My father had been in hospital with a broken hip throughout my stay, and while there had been some days of fun together, Alec and I had bickered over small things. The irritation was amplified by his lack of connection with what I was doing and our lack of a shared vision for our future. Still upset by the allegations, I had spent time reflecting on how to secure the future of Ekologika Papers and I'd surprised myself by coming back enthused to try again.

'Long-term recycling partnerships,' I announced to Jean and Max.

From customer feedback, I'd realised customers were more excited that our paper was recycled than that it created jobs for the under-skilled and under-employed. Helping companies recycle their waste and sensitise their staff to environmental issues seemed socially responsible ideas for which the time had come.

'I'll ask companies to sign up with Ekologika Papers for two- or three-year agreements. They'll supply us with shredded office paper and order a guaranteed annual volume of our products. That will give us a supply of raw material, better cashflow and sales forecasting, and more confidence to invest. Meanwhile we'll agree to provide recycling stations in their offices and materials to show how paper recycling is environmentally responsible—as well as a great product, of course.'

'You sound like a Lagosian,' said Jean drily. With his shock of black curly hair and dark designer stubble, I couldn't make up my mind whether he looked dashing, piratical, or both. 'Always optimistic about the next big thing.'

'We've been shortlisted for an environmental award,' I countered.

It was true. The article last year in the Nigerian environmental magazine had resulted in our nomination which, in itself, would further enhance Ekologika Papers's green reputation. The announcement of the award was due in April, three months away.

'Many companies say they want to be socially responsible,' I continued. 'A recycling partnership could be just up their alley.

It will engage their employees, help retention, improve their green credentials.'

'What does your salesman think about it?' asked Max. Once again, he was dressed for a stroll on the Champs-Élysées rather than through gritty Lagos. But when he asked about my salesman, I thought about Kola. He was still downhearted about losing the commissions on sales he had worked for last year and was not yet very enthusiastic about my recycling partnerships idea.

'He's a bit sceptical,' I admitted. 'His network is with the external communications people who buy cards, and this deal would have to be made with the corporate social responsibility department or the board. But he'll still get commission and I've told him I'll help him.'

'The external communications manager will be eating well from the card budget,' said Max.

I knew he meant earnings in backhanders. It was one of the reasons I wanted to go around that department.

'They won't easily give it up. Kola's probably scared of missing his cut too.'

'Well, I'll try … ' I already had an appointment with the head of corporate social responsibility at my telecom client, so I was still optimistic. While Kola had probably engaged in offering kickbacks to clients with the support of former employers, he knew I expected him to be as straight as a Lagos workday was long. I had no worries there.

I looked up and saw Gail standing near the entrance. We had exchanged brief greetings on arrival, but she was busy tending to the bar. After all, she was working. She had finished up at Ekologika Papers as soon as I got back and this was her first official week running Splendido. A coterie of roughnecks and white-collar workers surrounded her, and she greeted and joked with all comers then turned to chat with her barman and kitchen staff. She seemed to be in her element – everyone's pal and the *maître d'hotel*. But I found it odd to see her in this role.

The clientele was already changing from the old Splendido faces. Instead of mainly Italians and Brits there were more Nigerian and South African customers and overheard conversations suggested Gail's North American compatriots had also come out to support her. Had the news of a change of ownership and promise of a different style of management filtered through the American and Canadian community, or had Gail leveraged her enormous network in a way she had been unable to do in my business? With the amount of alcohol – beer and wine, but also prosecco and Campari – I saw consumed, I was sure profitability would be improved and I wished her success.

I turned back to our table. Max was taking a call and Jean was texting on his phone.

'André and Vanessa will join us—and some of the people you met at the party,' Jean announced. 'We're going clubbing later. Join us?'

Why not, I thought? After the lonely months of work, it was good to have a social life. My circle of friends had grown; apart from Dapo and Esther, the gang was almost entirely new since Alec left. Regardless of age or nationality, I had more in common with people who also ran their own businesses like Dapo, Toks, Haresh, Jean and Max. I valued their advice as we seemed to view Nigeria through a similar lens, shaped by our shared experiences. Also, we all sought some much-needed stress relief.

Our pizzas were served but they were soggy and unappealing – Gail had some work to do to improve the food – and we started talking about the forthcoming election. In April, Nigeria would go to the polls, for the third time since its return to democracy. President Olusegun Obasanjo, a Christian southerner, had served two terms and was ineligible under the constitution to stand again. He had been reluctant to relinquish power to a bitter northern rival, but northern Muslim factions had insisted that it was their turn to hold power.

Obasanjo had eventually engineered a compromise and influenced his party to choose a relatively unknown northern Muslim presidential candidate, Umaru Musa Yar'Adua. The dominant ruling party had money, even more after two terms in office, so it was likely Yar'Adua would win, but all Nigerians and interested foreigners anticipated the election with some trepidation. Never before in Nigeria had one civilian administration successfully handed over to another through the polling station. In the past a coup had intervened to give power to a military head of state. Would this time be different?

Jean, Max and I had more prosaic considerations of our own.

'Nothing will happen until after the election,' said Max grimly.

'We were lucky to have some orders from last year to carry us through,' said Jean. 'But we're not expecting clients to release budgets until they know the outcome.'

Just like last year and the year before, the first quarter's business activity would be slowed down. One year it had been a fuel strike, the next the census, and now it was the election.

There seemed to be a rhythm to the Nigerian business year, I thought. Some source of uncertainty blocked business decisions in the first quarter, things started to pick up in May, then slowed down again mid-year as executives fled the wet season and took summer holidays abroad.

'It seems only in September that things really take off,' I said. 'It's always so busy in the last quarter.'

'It's when budgets have to be spent and goals met,' said Jean. 'Sometimes I wonder if I might as well work during those four months alone.'

He had a point.

For once, though, I could feel a little less agitated. I had guaranteed cashflow to tide my hungry businesses and myself over. The customer service work at Kevin's bank had been agreed and scheduled last year and a first train-the-trainer programme was starting soon. For the moment the Strategyworks analysts, Edith and new recruit Reti, and I, were fully occupied. My brain was working over-time wondering how I could create action-learning experiences for Kevin's banking staff to help them become more responsive and proactive. It was creative work, which I enjoyed.

But a shadow lingered over my plans. The telco and chemicals strategy work had been delayed, the latter probably indefinitely. I knew the signs of indefinite delay now too – lack of response to calls and emails. I was learning. I told Max and Jean.

'Don't be downhearted,' said Max. 'We will muddle through— like Nigeria. Nothing here is ever as bad as it seems or as good as it could be.'

We chuckled and raised our beers to that.

'Of course, nothing here is straightforward either,' added Max in his serious tone. 'It is always complicated.' This new friend was starting to sound like Dapo too.

O

Before the critical events of last year had unfolded, I decided to host an Australia Day event at the end of January. I had invited the Australian High Commissioner although, as I knew the High Commission's resources were limited, I hadn't much hope of his coming. But might there be some financial support this time?

Mike, ever jovial, had called me from Abuja on receiving my request.

'Your email enquiring about financial support crossed with an email from Canberra instructing that honorary consul posts were not eligible for funding of social events,' he said. 'Isn't that funny?'

Very funny, I thought. I also learned that, with further budget cuts, the High Commissioner only had funding for his annual Anzac Day visit to Lagos. It made me wonder again if this level of representation could achieve anything for Australian business and geopolitical interests. It certainly did not make me feel supported.

I decided to go ahead with my celebrations anyway and managed again to get some corporate sponsorship. Invitations went out to Australians in the Lagos community, prominent Nigerians and other nationals, including my friends.

Now that the new year had arrived, I regretted the extra workload, but was committed. Instead of a cocktail party, I figured there was no better way to demonstrate Australian values and lifestyle – the point of Australia Day – than to hold a beach barbecue. My hut at Agaja, still standing, would be the venue.

Following a brief welcome speech at the start of the party, we got down to cultural events: beach cricket. There were insufficient Nigerians to form a national team, so the Australians played the Rest of the World. Despite his advancing years, Wale proved a devastating bowler.

'I was captain of my school cricket team in Surrey,' he said, surprising me.

Against his onslaught, the Aussies lost.

I mingled with my guests and noticed Michelle talking intensely to a new friend she had brought – he looked young. I broke into the conversation to greet her and introduce myself to him.

The man turned his intelligent gaze squarely onto me, probably assessing me as much as I did him. He was dressed in khaki shorts and a tropically patterned short-sleeved shirt. He was clean-shaven and thick tresses of nutmeg hair fell artfully across his brow and left eye. With a charming smile that crinkled his eyes, he reminded me of Hugh Grant. Was he another diplomat? Some of the diplomatic community were impressive in their command of a wide number of issues; others were impressive in their lack of curiosity and insensitivity to the country they were in. If he was a diplomat which camp did he fall into, I wondered?

'Josh is a journalist,' said Michelle, as if reading my thoughts. She named the international news service he worked for. 'He's the new West Africa correspondent.' Josh was based in Lagos, which was promising. Some news services based their reporters 5000 kilometres away in Nairobi in East Africa and expected them to cover West Africa from there. I admired him taking a journalistic assignment in Nigeria as there were easier places to report from.

'What are you covering?' I asked.

'The usual,' he answered. 'The election, the oil industry, violence in the delta and environmental damage.' His service was focused on business reporting so this was not a surprise, but it felt a clichéd list. 'I've been invited by one of the local communities down in the delta to see the pollution from a leaking pipeline on their land.' He named a big oil major's installation as the source.

'That's courageous,' I said and meant it. Some journalists relied on the conversations to be had with politicians, diplomats, company officers and NGO leaders in Abuja and Lagos, and didn't get out to the rougher places to see things first-hand. But I wondered if he understood the complex dynamics of the delta and the oil industry.

'Local youths or criminals might have tapped the pipeline and caused the mess,' I said. 'The communities might be inviting you down to use you for publicity and to help their compensation claims.'

'What's wrong with that?' he said. 'These multinationals need to clean up their mess.'

Things were more complex than Josh described, but he seemed smart and I assumed he had done his research.

The instability had become worse in the delta over the past few years and international criminal gangs, as well as local opportunists, were now at work. It was estimated that 100,000 barrels of oil a day were being illegally bunkered. 'Bunkering' of oil referred to 'hot tapping' a live pipeline, a process requiring advanced knowledge and tools, and installing a hose to siphon off oil into barges. The barges were then often used to move product through creeks to small, decrepit oil tankers anchored in nearby channels. Further out at sea, loads from several small tankers were transferred to an international class 'mother ship', possibly topping up a legal cargo, or filling up an empty ship; often the ship's name and country of registration were changed while it was at sea. In the early years, the illicit cargoes were sold only to refineries along the West African coast. Now, as operations expanded and international gangs became involved, the laundered cargoes were sold to refineries in the US, the Balkans, South America and Asia.

Running such large-scale and sophisticated operations required trades, skills and roles ranging from welders to divers, oil industry personnel to traditional rulers and local godfathers, politicians, military commanders, security contractors, accountants, lawyers, corrupt officials, bankers, ship owners and oil commodities traders – inside and outside Nigeria. What was really going on, and who was involved, was as murky as black crude.

One example of the wide and opaque web of complicity was the 2004 case of a fully laden Russian oil tanker taken into custody in Port Harcourt. A few days later, it disappeared with its thirteen Russian crew members and stolen cargo, never to be seen again. Another was the Movement for the Emancipation of the Niger Delta (MEND), portrayed internationally as a political organisation that pressured for a greater share of oil revenues and social and environmental justice, but was accused of being involved in oil theft and providing cash and arms to other militant groups.

I silently wished Josh luck to uncover the reality.[1]

'It's not that straightforward,' I said instead. 'The pollution might be from deliberate sabotage, the illegal refineries that spill oil everywhere, or from explosions of oil stored in huge, open pits. Or it might be from impoverished local communities taking advantage of a tapped pipeline. They go out with buckets to catch the leaking oil, someone lights a cigarette and the whole lot blows up.'

These were sadly common occurrences that led to many deaths. For many delta indigenes, working with the gangs or following their lead with smaller-scale tapping was the only way to eke some benefits from the black gold running through their midst.

'That might happen sometimes, but the oil companies do rip off these communities,' said Josh.

'Exactly,' chimed Michelle, who appeared at my side. 'Big oil companies just can't be trusted.'

Michelle's comments were rather superficial and hackneyed, and matched those of many casual observers with preconceived notions. But I was surprised by Josh's comments as I expected him to be more curious and nuanced and be open to multiple viewpoints and data. Yet he was lazily ascribing blame, identifying predators and victims, and didn't seem to realise that at the same time people can be both.

I looked around. Steve had joined a group of his Australian colleagues nearby. I thought he would be better placed to help Josh broaden his perspective and called him over. After all, as an oil and gas industry executive he would know about the community and the pollution.

'Josh is headed to the delta at the invitation of one of the communities,' I said after the introductions were made.

'Good on you, Josh,' he said in his usual direct manner. 'But make sure you challenge the stories they feed you. In my experience, the idealism of you reporters can be more than matched by the self-interested motivations of people pushing their point of view.'

Josh looked taken aback, perhaps even offended. As I knew from hard experience, Steve was skilled at rubbing people the wrong way. But having seen him take charge of Agaja, I was revising my views about Steve and I hoped Josh would listen.

'I'm not saying it's just the deprived people in the delta who might be motivated to distort the truth,' he continued. 'They have suffered the rough end of the corruption in this country. But there are people – their leaders, politicians, admirals, youth leaders – who also use them, their poverty, the oil, pollution from any cause and the chance to make big bucks. Just don't take anything at face value.'

'That's an interesting view,' said Josh. 'But I've seen videos about the pollution.'

'And I've seen it too—in person. We have our own polluted sites and whether we think the pollution is caused by vandalism or genuine accident or pipeline degradation, we take responsibility for cleaning it up,' he said. 'But the community won't let us in. They want compensation first—so we are asked to pay them for the privilege of getting access and while we cannot get access the problem grows.'

'So why don't you compensate them?'

'Firstly, we do, but the money goes missing. I've known youth leaders who have held up work and demanded payments for their poor community's schools and health centres. The money was paid and teams were sent back, but the community barred them. It turned out the youth leaders kept the money. Eventually we had to pay a second time.'

'Secondly, the multinational operators sometimes cannot get budgets approved for the clean-ups or the community development work they want to do. As operators of a joint venture they can only spend in line with annual budgets approved by their shareholders,' Steve said.

Shell, Exxon Mobil, Chevron and other multinationals were contracted as operators of joint ventures with Nigeria's national oil company, the Nigerian National Petroleum Corporation (NNPC) in which they were minority shareholders. To complicate matters, the joint ventures were unincorporated, meaning they had a limited capital structure. Revenues from the operators' oil production and exports flowed into the Nigerian government's own federal accounts and the operators were dependent on annual cash calls from the shareholders for their funding.

'The majority shareholder bears the majority of the clean-up costs – and that's the Nigerian government,' continued Steve. 'Due to political pressure, the government uses NNPC to delay approvals and ties the hands of the operator.'

'I thought a lot of the worst pollution was due to pipeline degradation and a lack of routine maintenance,' said Josh.

'It's one of the issues, but the disrepair is also caused because the operators haven't been allowed in to do routine maintenance,' he said. 'I'm not saying that there isn't work for us to do. It's a difficult environment – one of the most densely populated parts of Africa in the middle of a network of creeks, not to mention the armed gangs running large-scale illegal bunkering operations. Another of our problems is the collusion of some of the people inside the oil companies. Many of our employees come from the delta. They think it is their duty or they are pressured by the communities to conspire with them or the criminals.' These were the cliques that Steve had mentioned to me in his home.

'Surely you've got the resources to do audits,' said Josh. His charm was not working on Steve and he was beginning to sound testy.

'Josh, the world is not as it should be, or as you'd like it to be. It's not the way I'd like it to be. But multinational bad guys outmanoeuvring the downtrodden good guys did not create or sustain the current dire situation. It's a tired plot and it's also inaccurate.'

'While you're working on this, challenge people like me, the government, the communities you talk to and do your research,' Steve continued. 'Then write more balanced articles capturing all the complexities and points of view and expose the vested interests. You'll risk making enemies and that might shorten your stay in the country, but at least you will know you have not been their stooge.'

As Steve spoke, I remembered a well-regarded foreign correspondent based in Lagos at the turn of the millennium. His visit to the delta came at the invitation of a leading group that portrayed itself as fighting for the emancipation of the people of the delta. In a rare exception to the usual narrative, he wrote a critical report exposing their less-noble side: the in-fighting, violence, extortion, corruption, greed, political links and self-interest. He was invited back to the delta again – but security sources advised him not to go as the group's leaders had put a contract out to behead him.

'To my mind something fairer would be a report that multinational oil companies are doing a pretty good job given the difficult circumstances,' said Steve. 'And it's a bunch of local and international criminals and vested interests who are actually causing all the trouble.'

'That's not much of a story,' snorted Josh. It seemed sad that describing a complicated reality was considered dull.

'Well, if it's sensation you're after, how about investigating oil bunkering?' asked Steve. 'The Nigerian navy is said to be involved and the current Governor is the biggest crook of all.'

He named the State Governor and I thought that a great suggestion. What a Pulitzer prize-winning opportunity that would be.

Josh laughed. His eyes crinkled charmingly but there was cynicism in his voice. 'You want me to write a story about Nigerians being corrupt?' he said. 'That's not a story. I'd never get my byline printed. And my editor wouldn't pay for me to be a foreign correspondent writing about that.'

O

Josh and Michelle went for a swim and I remained with Steve by the bar. The sun was low in the sky, a red ball above the line of palm trees lining the creek. There was mist around the mangroves and the creek had become a silver snake. It was my favourite time of day but soon we would need to pack up and head back to Lagos. The waterways were not safe after dark when fuel and drug smugglers headed out. But before I called my guests to their boats, we refreshed our beers; one more for the journey.

'So, Josh is basically saying that the truth and honest reporting takes second place to his own personal interest. It doesn't seem to matter what he reports as long as he's published and paid,' said Steve angrily. 'Where is his integrity?'

I was also disappointed at Josh's attitude.

'We forget how much we've learned living here and how much is still opaque. It changes you,' I answered. 'Maybe he'll become more courageous once he knows more.'

I was still modifying my view about Steve. He was crass but he showed greater open-mindedness and awareness of the complications of this environment than either Michelle or Josh.

I turned towards the crashing Atlantic Ocean waves so I could keep an eye on the guests in the water. I was relieved to see Luke had stationed some villagers as lifeguards and had the long safety rope at the ready in case of trouble.

'Any progress on tackling Agaja's erosion?' I asked Steve, pointing out that the thunderous sea had washed another line of palm trees away.

'We've secured funding from the other major oil companies,' he said.

I congratulated him enthusiastically.

'But we've decided we need a local NGO to tender the project, sign the government approvals and manage the contract,' he finished. 'We don't want to lead this or sign anything.'

I was puzzled. After all, with the reputation of oil companies sunk low by activists and journalists such as Josh spinning their simplified morality tales, shouldn't this be a good news story to improve their image? I asked Steve.

'Hell, no!' he exclaimed. 'The last thing we want is to be linked to this work. Once they thought a multinational was involved everyone would be after money. The budget would increase ten-fold and the government approvals required would multiply. Everyone would find fault with the project and we'd have spurious damage claims galore, from the government and the community. We want to keep a low profile.'

The situation in the delta and the complicity of the big oil companies and other actors was very complicated, I knew. But so too were my little endeavours. On Friday I'd had a meeting with the Ekologika Papers team to explore the idea of building recycling partnerships to help to clean up the Lagos environment.

'The shredded paper from offices is already recycled,' Remi responded.

I was surprised but Remi sourced our paper so he should know.

'The cleaners sell the shredded paper to dealers. The paper is sorted and sold to toilet paper manufacturers.'

The company managers I'd talked to assumed, like my customers and me, that their waste was incinerated or sent to dumps. We were learning new things all the time.

Now I took a swig of beer and considered the idyllic beach scene in front of me.

Environmental catastrophe was still at hand. Luke stood nearby, probably wanting to discuss new and exorbitant maintenance work before I left. Village children, some with heart-breaking polio-withered limbs, gathered on the sand in front of the hut and started to sing for our group. One child carried a plastic bowl and asked for 'dash'.

The complexity of this beach scene was different from what anyone might perceive at first glance, and understanding the real truth was difficult. It was the same with so much else.

Josh wanted to distort the truth to fit a stereotypical narrative and get his byline published. Steve distorted reality by hiding good deeds to protect his company from litigation and extortion. And my idea that Ekologika Papers created environmental benefits distorted the fact that it would cost cleaners their entrepreneurial side income from recycling shredded paper.

As Max had said, nothing here was straightforward and everything was complicated.

I sighed and fished some notes from my pocket to give to the children. It was one difference I could make today.

CHAPTER SEVENTEEN

Good Days and Bad Days

When the leopard has a broken paw, the antelope comes to collect an old debt.

– Igbo proverb

'Alec thinks you are killing yourself,' said Haresh. Time had passed slowly and, although it was late March, we were still in a lull waiting for the election to pass. Decisions on Strategyworks projects and Ekologika Papers environmental partnerships were delayed and only Kevin's customer service work enabled me to pay my bills. Then, for the first time in nearly a year, Alec came to Lagos for a three-day visit.

I was eager for us to have a good time together and for Alec to feel more connected to my life here, so I had organised a round of dinners, including one with Haresh and his wife, whom I now counted as friends. That had taken place last week and today I was meeting Haresh to hear more about his business expansion plans – but he turned the discussion to the more personal.

'I think he still cares for you, but he does not support what you are doing,' Haresh continued.

I found Haresh's observations discouraging but I couldn't disagree. I cared for Alec, too, but we lived separate lives. While I felt disappointed by his lack of interest in my work and dreams, I had to admit I didn't have much interest in his.

But was I killing myself?

This observation brought me up short. I remembered how naïve Josh had been – full of energy and enthusiasm for his new role and so fresh-looking. Had that once been me?

My thoughts wandered as Haresh talked. What did he see when he looked at me? My local Lebanese hairdresser only created two looks for his clients – blonde and straight or dark and straight. He attempted the latter with me. He could deliver the dark, covering the parting line of my grey roots (a dismal new feature of advancing middle age) with hair dye, but increasingly drier hair and humidity put paid to his attempts at straightening. I permanently wore 'big hair' in a mushroom cloud of frizz. My face seemed blotchy with dark rings under my eyes and my sober business suit was time-worn and shiny from being pressed by an overly hot iron. I needed a new wardrobe at the very least, but I couldn't find anything locally. When I had travelled, I hadn't made time to shop either.

These external signs of wear and tear were matched by inner turmoil. My attempts to turn Ekologika Papers around were stalled by a hiatus in decision-making by clients, and by having to design and deliver Kevin's project and several proposals for Strategyworks with just two analysts. I constantly dreaded that I hadn't done enough and sensed a personal and professional tsunami approaching.

Most of all I recognised now that running two businesses alone was too much. Yet I stuck with my plan to generate enough cash from consulting so I could finally give Ekologika Papers my full attention and its best shot. Could I hold on for one more year?

I turned my attention back to Haresh. As usual, his swift brain had moved on and he now told me that he planned to move his group headquarters to Dubai, his vision to build operations in multiple African countries. I thought his expansionary business strategy was as much a result of his wife's desire to live in a more functioning first-world city, with better schools and closer to her parents, as his own ambition. It was a novel way to achieve work–life balance.

Haresh startled me again. 'I'm building up my senior management team and I need someone to lead on strategy and change,' he said. 'How about coming to work for me?'

O

Tippy rubbed herself against my leg and purred. I had opened the balcony's sliding doors to let in fresh air but sunlight falling on my computer's screen made it hard to read. The lunchtime call to prayer broadcast from a loudspeaker on a nearby mosque's minaret made concentration difficult. I moved to the dining room table and gazed at the piles of papers. The table had become my desk and the open-plan dining and living rooms my new office.

The extended lease on my old office had ended in April. During the business lull, I had spent months searching for new premises for Strategyworks and Ekologika Papers. I was again stymied to find a single location that suited both businesses.

'Bring Ekologika Papers to Ikotun,' Max had kindly offered during one of our Friday evening get-togethers. 'We have plenty of room.'

Peter and I went to see his compound and warehouses. Unfortunately, it rained the day Tayo drove us out and, although Ikotun was not that far beyond Mushin, the tedious journey through endless Lagos suburbs took three hours.

'It is too far, Madam,' said Peter.

I felt more positive. Behind high walls that blocked out the teeming commercial and residential area surrounding it, the compound was perfect for a small industrial operation. We could locate the papermaking workshop at the rear and use a small office for conversion work. But Peter was unimpressed.

'We will spend too much money on transport,' he said. 'We should find somewhere in Mushin.'

In the end, with Ekologika Papers unable to fund its own premises and worried to let the team out of my sight until I could supervise full-time, I decided to have both businesses work out of my three-storey townhouse.

The compound contained three terraced townhouses, of which mine was the middle. Also within the grounds was a studio apartment and separate tiny office the size of a small bedroom, which I now rented for the use of the Strategyworks analysts. The Ekologika Papers conversion team, with my landlord's permission, now worked in the staff quarters on the ground floor of my townhouse near the laundry and garage. Paper stocks were safe in a storage room nearby, my office was in the open-plan dining and living room on the first floor and my spare bedroom on the top floor was filled with office paraphernalia. After last year's disappointing Ekologika Papers sales, we had substantial paper stocks, so for the moment could run the business without setting up the papermaking workshop. The equipment was stored at Max's warehouse at Ikotun.

It was a temporary fix, like so much else, but it had the benefit of eliminating time spent on my commute and easing my financial burden.

It was surprisingly satisfying. My mood was improving daily.

Musa Yar'Adua had won the April 2007 Presidential election, and although the election was universally acclaimed as the most corrupt yet, at least his installation ended our business paralysis.[1] Strategyworks clients, as impatient as I was to get on with the year, now wanted their projects started immediately and I had their advances in the company's bank account.

Kola was cheering up as, with Patrick's design help, he had sold modest volumes of wedding souvenirs and had developed promising leads for significant seasonal calendar and card sales that would be finalised in the next quarter. Although our proposals for environmental recycling partnerships had not yet been officially confirmed, many of the company's social responsibility goals were being dusted off and I had hopes we would attract a partnership deal soon.

There was still one decision hanging over my head. What should I do about Haresh's job offer?

I had thought hard about whether to cut my losses and run. After all, it was tempting to escape my money worries. But could I now work for someone else? And the passion I held for my vision, while battered by the events of last year, was not something I felt for Haresh's business. His plans were bold and the work would be interesting, but was I ready to trade pragmatic reality for my roller-coaster business adventures?

I had delayed giving Haresh my answer, partly swayed by the sense he was offering a lifeline, and one that might also save my relationship with Alec, but he needed a decision soon.

The call to prayer ended and I refocused on the work at hand, the next phase of work for Kevin. My mobile rang, startling me. When I hung up, I went straight down to the Ekologika Papers office.

'We won,' I said to the team.

In the cramped space, Peter stood with a sample notebook in his hand and Patrick looked up from his computer, open-mouthed. Kola turned around from where he had been leaning over Patrick – probably issuing design instructions – and Sonny and Remi stood motionless beside their guillotine and a sizeable stack of papers. Molly was out, probably in Mushin getting notebooks bound, but Gloria and Patience looked up from their computers. My driver Tayo, who had seen me run down the stairs, had left his vehicle and now peered through the doorway behind me. It was a trimmer team, with many casuals laid off until peak season later in the year, but it was the best of them.

'Ekologika Papers has won the environmental award.'

Grins broke out and we whooped and crowded together in the tiny, dusty office where the desks were less than a metre apart. We squeezed past each other, patted each other on the back and high-fived. It was a small win on our rocky road. Perhaps our fortunes were due to change.

Back at my dining room desk and returning to my real world of Powerpoint and Excel a short time later, elation buzzed inside me. The magazine sponsoring our prize was new and relatively unknown. The cynic could say a dinky award didn't mean much, but the recognition meant something to my team and me. We had taken the knocks together and today we felt proud of our work.

As I logged back onto my computer, I made my decision. I would turn down Haresh's generous offer. This small success was hard-won and I still relished the freedom to make my own mistakes and gain little triumphs. The year, I thought, had changed for the better.

O

'Madam, I've won the order,' exclaimed Kola, bustling into my dining room office several weeks later. 'It is for 1000 notebooks.'

It sounded good news until he told me the client; a major tobacco company with operations in Nigeria. I was stunned. How could I be pleased?

I had repeatedly told the teams of both Ekologika Papers and Strategyworks that I would not work with tobacco companies.

Tobacco companies, having had their markets curtailed in western countries due to the health issues smoking caused, had aggressively entered Nigeria in the past five years. It sickened me to see a society with low levels of smoking suddenly targeted. Cigarettes were handed out free to get people hooked, advertising made smoking cool on the airwaves and billboards, and cigarettes were sold singly to make them affordable to the poorest in society.

'But you work for alcoholic beverage companies,' teetotal Gloria had countered. 'People die from drinking too much.'

'They are spending so much,' said Tayo. 'Can we afford to turn them down?' Even my driver had an opinion if it meant more work.

They made valid points but, as far as I was concerned, smoking was an unnecessary problem being added to Nigeria's list of woes. Having witnessed the tactics to get people hooked when I was growing up and the ruthless targeting of young girls especially, I felt it was the unfettered, unethical seventies all over again.

I had made my attitude clear, but it seemed Patrick had already developed artwork, Molly had made a sample, and Kola had negotiated the deal.

Why was I being ignored? Was I speaking a language they did not understand?

Recently, the corporate souvenir-buyer at an insurance company had sent signals to Kola that we'd get an order if we inflated our invoice so he could cop a share and I had refused. That decision was clear and accepted by the team, but I knew they were puzzled by my stance on tobacco.

Maybe my policy was unreasonable when our business was so precarious. But what kind of message would it be to the team if I allowed them to ignore me?

'I'm sorry, Kola,' I said. 'But I will not accept that order.'

Kola looked sullen.

I was not moved; he should have known my answer.

O

In May Tippy fell critically ill. She had stopped eating and drinking and I had Tayo drive us both to the nearest veterinary practice. The clinic was hot as the generator was not running and neither was NEPA. Cats are not popular pets, perhaps because some Nigerians fear them, and vets had few feline patients. Guard dogs were this vet's specialty and the barking from the caged inpatients was incessant. Tippy had gone from listless to terrified in quick succession. But the vet was her best chance of survival.

'Your cat is dying,' the young vet said as he stroked my cat's clammy, weak body.

Blood and urine samples would go to the laboratory for tests and until then there could be no diagnosis. The tests would take a week to return.

'She will be dead by then,' the vet announced. 'I can give her a wide-spectrum antibiotic to try to tackle whatever infection she has in her system. That will give her a good chance, but you must bring her morning and evening for a saline drip to keep her hydrated.'

I feared the worst and knew I'd find the loss of this precious companion hard to bear. We went dutifully morning and night for the hour-long drip. During the day Tippy lay next to me, her body hot in our air-conditioned home. It was difficult to focus on work and I cancelled several meetings and asked one client for an extension to submit my proposal. My staff found my distress strange, but they tried to understand.

'Is Tippy any better?' Gloria asked each morning.

'The staff send their get well wishes to Madam Tippy,' said Peter on Wednesday.

Yesterday Sonny had presented me with a Get Well Soon card, made on our paper, and everybody in Strategyworks and Ekologika Papers had signed it. I was touched; my staff could still sometimes make me feel part of something bigger than me.

Tippy soldiered on. A week later she pushed weak legs against me and wanted to get off my lap. On the floor, she took unsteady steps towards her bowl and lapped at her water. It was her first drink since I'd taken her to the vet.

I raced downstairs to tell my staff.

'Congratulations, Madam,' said Tayo, grinning from his car.

'Congratulations, Tippy,' laughed Gloria.

It was another crisis over. Surely now, I reasoned, after this difficult time things could only get better.

O

The following week, I awoke to an email from my brother.

'Call our mother,' he wrote in his usual curt manner, without providing an explanation.

It was afternoon in my hometown in Australia, so I called her immediately. She sounded small; there were tears in her voice as she answered.

I waited for her to speak.

'Your father is dying,' she said.

I booked a flight immediately. Things were not going to get better.

My father died three weeks after I arrived home. Cancer did not deliver a peaceful death and he was not ready to go. Watching him die was harrowing.

O

After a month in Australia and my father's funeral, I returned to hold an Ekologika Papers team meeting around my dining room table, which still served as my office.

Just carry on, I thought. Stay on the treadmill. Work would serve to keep bad memories at bay – for a time.

'I need mock-ups for my jobs today,' Kola demanded of Molly.

'Well, I need the final artwork,' Molly gestured impatiently to Patrick. 'I can't do the mock-ups until I have the artwork. And then the covers have to be made quickly, not like last time.'

This was a jibe at Sonny who had recently made mistakes on the covers, causing rework, which in turn led to an order delivered late.

'I need some paper,' Sonny barked at Molly and Peter. 'I can't make up the covers until I get more stock.'

Despite the drama I found it difficult to stay focused. I kept seeing my gaunt father at the hospice.

'Fix it,' I finally snapped at Peter. I was also not as good at staying calm.

Work had not stopped in Nigeria while I was away. From afar, I had even prepared a workshop for a major new Strategyworks client while I had monitored my team's activities. But when the team failed to respond to emails, I got very angry. My temper was on a short leash.

'Peter,' I said more gently. 'I'm sorry.' I had made him acting general manager, but he seemed to still be more focused on paper than on products. 'Get me the artwork so I can check it then get some paper for Sonny from the store.'

The meeting broke up and the team dispersed to their offices on the ground floor.

It seemed surreal to be dealing with these business issues. Having been through the worst period of my life, they now seemed petty.

Tippy, completely recovered although thinner, meowed at me from the doorway. A week after her recovery the blood test results had come in – she had had a major infection and all her organs, including her kidneys, had been affected. The vet's intuitive diagnosis and twice-daily drips had saved her and I was grateful. I picked her up and stroked her fur and looked out my window. I could see a minaret of the neighbouring mosque and brightly dressed women gathering for prayer. Whereas the men gathered inside or under canopies when crowds were large, faithful women were relegated to an area near the latrines, without cover whatever the weather.

Alec had taken extended leave and visited my father with me. It helped a lot to have him by my side during those traumatic days. I missed him and could have done with him in my corner now that I was back in Lagos with a team that seemed fractured and out of sorts, just like me. I had not yet got to the bottom of what was going on with them. I reminded myself to ask Peter, but I didn't yet feel up to managing his answer, which would probably involve more drama.

I heard footsteps on the stairs leading to my open-plan dining and living room and I turned, expecting to see Edward, my steward.

It was Peter, back again. He looked serious.

'I have just been to the store,' he said, 'To get paper for the mock-ups.'

'OK. I don't need the car today – can you tell Tayo to help Molly get out to Mushin …' I stopped. 'What's wrong Peter?'

'It's our paper stock,' he said. 'It's gone.'

CHAPTER EIGHTEEN

Paper Chase

When a person is not as she used to be, she does not behave as she used to behave.

– Igbo proverb

'There are fifty wraps missing,' said Peter.

A lot of Peter's time had gone into sorting the handmade paper by size, grade and type into blocks of 200 sheets, called wraps, which were secured in brown paper and labelled with their contents. Peter knew his inventory well.

'At least 10,000 sheets have gone.' He looked shocked, eyes wide.

I felt numb and disbelieving. It was well over half of Ekologika Papers's stock.

I went downstairs and peered into the storeroom. Before my most recent trip to Australia, just a month ago, there were stacks of wraps teetering to the ceiling. Now the left-over wraps were scattered around the open space.

'The remaining paper seems to be our coloured stock,' said Peter. The thief had selected the more marketable plain paper. This was a serious theft that threatened the business.

No longer disbelieving but shocked, I faced the question I abhorred: who had done it?

'When did you last access the store, Peter? Who else had access? Where did you leave the key?'

'I took out some paper last Friday to give to Sonny for the covers,' he replied in a shaken voice, and told me only he had had access. 'I leave the key in my drawer—but the drawer is not locked.'

So anybody could have had access after-hours, while I was away.

'Let's ask Moustafa what he knows,' I suggested.

Moustafa was the friendly gateman at my compound and his simple quarters, which also housed his wife and young baby, were by the gate. He reliably attended to the opening and closing of the gate at all hours, even rising from his prayer mat if necessary. It seemed the only time he handed over the responsibility to someone else – a gateman from a neighbouring compound – was when he attended the mosque for Friday prayers. He was a gateman rather than a security guard. If he didn't know a vehicle or its occupants he called through to get permission, but he did not challenge people he knew.

Now he rose rather stiffly from the mat where he'd been resting. His long, thin body was clad in a faded blue robe. It took a little while for him to understand my question as his English was poor.

'Kola came to the compound last Saturday,' he said, while adjusting his embroidered skullcap. 'He drove his vehicle and came with his wife and baby. They were here some time loading the boot.'

Could it be that simple? Was Kola that brazen? I could not believe it of him but Moustafa said no one else had come at strange times or left with an unusually large load.

I immediately called a meeting and we gathered together in the small Ekologika Papers office on the ground floor. It was so like the time I had come to tell them about winning the environmental award. Patrick turned his chair from his computer and Kola stood nearby. Gloria and Patience sat in chairs and made room for Molly, Remi and Sonny to perch on their desks. Tayo peered through the doorway and the Strategyworks analysts also stood nearby. But this time my face was grim, and I had never seen Peter look so angry.

I let Peter take the lead and he told everyone that our paper was missing.

'I came last Saturday,' said Kola immediately. He was fidgeting with a dirty handkerchief. It made him seem nervous, but I knew it was also his habit. 'I took just two wraps – I wanted to get a mock-up made; it was taking too long.'

'Moustafa says you were here for some time, with your wife, loading the boot of your car,' said Peter. The accusation was out but Kola continued with his denial.

'No, Madam,' he said, appealing to me. 'Please, it was not me. Someone else must have taken the wraps. I only took two.'

I felt confused. Moustafa's evidence was strong, but Kola was a funny, likeable rogue, not a thief. He wouldn't steal from the business while I was burying my father.

Would he?

'Let us examine everyone's phone,' said Peter, sounding unusually authoritative. 'Put them on the hall table,' he said without waiting for my answer. 'We will check who you have been calling and the messages.'

I was not sure how this intrusion of privacy would be accepted in a European workplace, but it seemed a good suggestion. I wanted to catch the thief whose actions threatened all our jobs and investment.

As the phones were gathered, I went upstairs to my dining room office to try to focus on this issue that I did not want and to untangle emotions erupting inside me. But I had barely got there when I heard a commotion from the compound.

'Madam,' called Peter running up the stairs. 'Kola just grabbed his phone and left the compound.'

Unsure I would ever see Kola or the papers again, I thought about what to do.

Who should I call?

'Mr Atta,' I said down an echoing phone line. 'I have a problem …'

O

Mr Atta was in court and could not come until the evening. As I waited, I mulled over my options.

I regularly saw advertisements in local newspapers, which had a photograph of an accused employee, generally a grainy mugshot making the individual look very guilty, together with a list of his or her alleged offences and a reward. I shook my head. No, I was not going to become a vigilante employer.

Another idea occurred to me. If I ever saw Kola again, should I threaten him with exposure to his church, one of the large evangelical churches, in which I knew he had a prominent role? His actions had been anything but Christian – but blackmail? Another bad idea, I decided, and not a route I wanted to go down.

So what did I want? Our papers. What else?

Did I want Kola? Without a salesman at this critical time of year, Ekologika Papers was sunk, but if I took Kola back, however remorseful, I knew I could never trust him again and it would send the wrong signal to others. Had my generosity to staff during tough times, even as I made them redundant, made Kola think I was a soft touch?

That evening an unexpected visitor arrived. Moustafa rang from the gate to tell me Kola, with his wife and baby daughter, had pulled up in his car.

'Tell him not to come in,' I said to Moustafa. I knew I was too wrung out emotionally to cope with facing him now. I wanted my papers or my lawyer to take charge. I put the phone down.

'Please, Madam.'

It was Kola. He was upstairs, in my living room – I must have left the door unlocked.

'Get out of my home,' I shouted, anxious as well as upset by this intrusion.

'Please, Madam,' he entreated me, getting down on his knees. 'In the name of God, you must believe me, Madam, I didn't take the papers.'

'I don't believe you, Kola,' I shouted. 'Just bring back my papers.'

'You can check all our suppliers,' he continued. 'You won't find any papers there. I did not take them. I still want to work for you. Please, Madam, please.'

His diminutive wife had come up the stairs behind him with their baby wrapped securely against her back. She added to Kola's pleading.

'Please, in Jesus' name, my husband is innocent,' she cried.

It was a dreadful scene.

'Kola, I know you took them – just bring them back and we can talk. Now, get out of my house.'

Moustafa appeared on the stairs, with Patrick behind him. He must have been working late, I thought briefly, but didn't have time to ask. I was simply relieved at their help. Together they quieted Kola, calmed down his wife and crying baby and then shuffled them from my home.

Soon afterwards Mr Atta arrived. He could see I was shaken. When I'd finished telling him the full story, his advice was simple.

'You must report the theft to the police,' he said.

Why didn't I think of that?

The Nigerian Police Force's motto was 'The Police Are Your Friends' but the widespread suspicion that the police were corrupt and inept meant that many Nigerians took the law into their own hands to seek justice. Now it seemed I had made the same assumption. I had been drilled so long to avoid run-ins with Nigerian authorities that I had not even considered this option.

But I still hesitated wondering what would happen to Kola. Mr Atta seemed to sense my continued reluctance.

'Kola knew what he was doing and what the consequences could be.' He was sombre. 'He might have thought you were an *oyibo* and wouldn't go to the police,' he continued. 'But it is the only way to get the papers back and it is too serious not to report it. We shall go together in the morning.'

On Saturday, Mr Atta and I drove to Ikoyi police station. Located on the busy Awolowo Road, I had passed it often enough – a compound surrounded by a yellow-painted block and rendered wall. Today we drove through the gate into the busy forecourt in front of the single-storey colonial building. The Nigerian Police flag fluttered in the breeze. We climbed three steps to the veranda and then walked into the building's dark interior.

In the dim foyer Nigerians, all men, were slumped on benches. Some wore jeans and grubby T-shirts, others were in traditional outfits. It was hard to tell if they were here to report incidents or criminals awaiting formal charges. Officers in blue uniforms bustled purposefully around. Eventually we were called to a desk and a neatly dressed officer took my statement. Done with pen and paper, it was a professional, if long, process.

That weekend I shut everything out. I did not go out for a drink with Jean and Max as we'd arranged. I cancelled plans for the beach but did not share my problems with Dapo or Toks. I buried my thoughts and emotions in a project for a Strategyworks client, filling my time with research, analyses and planning. At night, however, all of it returned to assault my bruised brain – the devastation of another fraud, the disbelief that Kola could do this to me, the sorrow that I had given up precious time I could have spent with my father. Was it grief for my father or grief for lost trust that did not allow sleep to come?

I did not let Alec know about the second theft. What was the point?

At midday on Monday I heard that Kola had been arrested.

At mid-morning on Tuesday I had a phone call from Mr Atta. 'The station inspector called me,' he said. 'Kola has confessed.'

Confirmation of his guilt was not a surprise, but I still resisted believing it. I felt bewildered. What had they done to Kola to make him confess so quickly?

'The police have no fuel to go to the place where Kola says the papers are,' continued Mr Atta. 'They want fuel money.'

'Is this a bribe?' I asked.

'No, no,' said Mr Atta quickly. He knew my position on bribes. 'The station inspector is in charge and he will not take money.' I thought it must be because this senior officer was honest, but Mr Atta enlightened me. 'He cannot take bribes because an *oyibo* is involved.'

Determined to get my papers back and not be a patsy this time, I gave money for fuel to Tayo to take to the station.

Mid-afternoon Mr Atta called again.

'They have recovered some of your papers, Madam,' said Mr Atta. 'You need to identify them.'

A little later an officer met Mr Atta and me in the foyer of the police station where I had made my statement. The officer led us down a dim corridor into a small room that contained an old wooden desk, a single rickety metal chair and two long benches.

'Sit on the chair,' said the officer, his only words to me.

But I insisted the elderly Mr Atta, dressed in his blue suit and tie, take the chair while I sat on a bench.

The officer left, shutting the door behind him.

The room was bare of ornamentation except for framed photographs of the inspector general of police, the State Governor and the President. The walls might have once been yellow but were now faded and speckled with black mildew. Open shutters allowed an occasional wispy breath of air to enter, as well as the cough-inducing smoke from a charcoal stove burning nearby. The desk was carved with notches and stained. Everything seemed as battered and empty as I felt.

Mr Atta and I waited in silence.

After half an hour the door opened, and a policeman came in carrying a heavy load. It was a large pile of our paper.

Until that moment I still had not quite believed that Kola had taken it. Now I saw the evidence. There were perhaps 500 sheets in the pile, unwrapped and loose.

Another policeman followed also carrying paper and wordlessly, they both deposited their loads on the floor. A few minutes later they returned with more, and then more. The floor gradually filled with piles of our paper.

I was relieved and grateful to the police for solving this.

'Can we take the paper?' I asked Mr Atta. I was anxious for this horrible episode to be over and to escape the police station. I did not have any thoughts or feeling for Kola – not yet.

'We must wait,' said Mr Atta, and we did.

Eventually another officer arrived, and without preamble went straight to the point. The papers were at a printer in a place I did not recognise.

'It is far from Mushin and the islands,' explained Mr Atta, sensing it was a part of Lagos I did not know.

So much for Kola's and his wife's assurances on Friday night, I thought sourly. The officer spoke to Mr Atta in Yoruba.

'They will bring Kola in now so that you can formally identify the paper in his presence,' said Mr Atta to me.

I did not want to see Kola, but the wheels of Nigerian justice were in motion.

Minutes later Kola was brought in. He was shoeless and his trousers sagged as the police must have removed his belt. His shirt was open, loose and filthy. He begged me to forgive him. He was crying. He was also moving slowly, shuffling really, and I realised he was in leg chains.

I was aghast. Leg chains.

My heart raced but I didn't know what I could do. I felt sick and was shaking. This was dreadful but I was not in charge now.

I rapidly wrote the necessary statement to identify the papers and I agreed that Peter would come to count the papers in front of a policeman that afternoon. Kola was taken away.

I wished Kola had just brought the bloody papers back. I wished once again that this was all over.

Mr Atta and the officer again exchanged words in Yoruba and then the officer left.

'What is going on?' I asked. 'What have they done to Kola? Where is he being kept?' I was confused – now I felt concerned about Kola's welfare.

'Kola will be in a cell here. It will be crowded but not too bad,' he said. 'The family have offered money to get his release and you will be expected to pay to get your paper back. The police want to know if you want to press charges.'

'I'm not paying for my own paper,' I said angrily. Then the second part of what he had said sunk in. 'What do you mean about me deciding whether to press charges?' I neither wanted to make this decision nor thought it should be mine to make. 'I don't understand. Doesn't the prosecution service decide whether to make a charge against Kola? Aren't I just a witness? Why do the police want my opinion?' I felt overwhelmed.

'The police want to take the money from the family to release him,' said Mr Atta. 'But because the evidence is so strong, if they don't charge him, they are worried you will lodge a complaint.'

Mr Atta now advised that I should not want the matter taken to court.

'It will be tied up for years in the courts. Not only will you not get the paper back, but the police and lawyers will be looking to get things on you as leverage and it could get very unpleasant as well as expensive.'

'But what will happen to Kola? Will he be released?' I was still grappling with this unfamiliar approach to justice.

'I think he has learned his lesson,' said Mr Atta. 'If you press charges Kola will be transferred to Kirikiri.' This was the main Lagos prison, notorious for overcrowding and dreadful conditions, far worse than a holding cell. 'I don't think you would want Kola to face that.'

Mr Atta knew me well and I appreciated his candour. As long as I had most of my paper, I wanted Kola released and back with his family.

In the end, I stuck to my guns and refused to pay the police for the return of my paper but assured them, through Mr Atta, that I would take the matter no further. With that assurance, the police returned the recovered sheets of paper – about 5000 – to me. Having signed an undertaking to recompense the company for the thousands of sheets still not recovered, Kola was released.

But I could not get the image of Kola weeping, in leg chains, out of my head.

CHAPTER NINETEEN

Something Wrong with This Picture

If one imitates the upright one becomes upright; if one imitates the crooked one becomes crooked.

– Igbo proverb

I wandered down Agaja's coastline towards the wreck. The black hull had broken in two but only one jagged half protruded above the waves. The ugly metal shards seemed a symbol of the power of corruption and incompetence to destroy people's dreams and lives.

I had guests with me, but I left them at the bar; I wanted to be by myself for a few moments. I splashed in the waves that washed gently upon the shore. The wet season and its aggressive seas were past, and November had arrived – nearly another year over.

I felt out of my depth, something I had felt frequently since the episode with Kola. Why was I still so confused and agitated? I knew that grief for my father was destabilising me but there was more. Was it Kola's betrayal? Or was it the shocking consequences I had unleashed for Kola? Questions pounded inside my head like the giant waves of an Agaja wet season, dumping and churning until I could not see straight.

So many questions remained. Why had Kola stolen the papers in the first place? How could he steal from me while I was away burying my father? Was it my fault – because he didn't get commission on the sales he might have made? Was he trying to supply the tobacco company with notebooks despite my refusals?

His theft had been so brazen. How could he not expect to get caught? Did he count on my not going to the police? Did he see me as a soft touch? Were other members of my team involved?

My head would not let go of questions to which I had no answers.

By reporting the matter to the police, I had started a process that had led to his abominable leg chains. But while I felt Kola had brought them upon himself and I could not blame myself for a system outside my experience and control, I remembered something Mark Twain had written in *Following the Equator*: 'Everyone is a moon, and has a dark side which he never shows to anybody'.

Had I uncovered my dark side?

Certainly, something had been unleashed inside of me. I was angry at how I had been treated by Chuks and Kola, and at the entire team's repeated misdemeanours, and my futile efforts. And I was angry in my grief for my father. It was a simmering hot-pepper soup of rage and I wondered when it might finally cool. When I became frustrated by some repeated small incident or a larger calamity, my temper flowed from my lips like a pyroclastic flow. It worried me. How could I get my equilibrium back?

I looked forward to a family break in Scotland. Alec and I were planning our Christmas there with our elderly widowed mothers – mine was flying in from Australia – and with Alec's younger brother Hew. I thought it might help my mother and me to celebrate Christmas in a different setting, but I was not hopeful that such a brief reunion would help Alec and me. Although his presence during my father's final illness had been very comforting, the stress of our respective lives, the separation and the bickering was taking its toll. We were drifting further apart. I preferred not to think about that.

A fisherman wearing ragged shorts hailed me as he picked his way through the debris-strewn high-water mark nearby. I returned his greeting with a smile and a wave. I turned to look at the cluster of simple bamboo and thatched huts set back amongst palm trees behind the eroded coastline. A few mangy yellow dogs nosed among accumulated rubbish. My thoughts wandered back to how things had worked out in the office.

I had visited Kola's major clients and discovered that he had been wildly optimistic about volumes or our chances of winning Christmas card contracts. I was dubious about the transparency and fairness of buying practices in many large firms. Perhaps Kola had sensed his sales forecast and his hoped-for bonuses were a mirage, and had taken action to supplement his income. Perhaps. But he had a very generous base salary, and through his act he had let the team's years of hard effort down.

Smaller, professional services firms who wanted our table calendars or special Christmas cards seemed more likely targets. Molly, who had been roped into sales, had proved unexpectedly good at winning these smaller but profitable orders. I had been frustrated in my negotiations for recycling partnerships with several firms, but a new telecommunications company was to take the decision to its board. It was a decision for inclusion in next year's budget and would not have an impact on this year's sales.

Abandoning my view of the coastline entirely I thought back to my Friday meeting with the Ekologika Papers team.

O

'Next year we will move to Ikotun,' I had told them.

Peter, Remi and Sonny had seemed morose at the news, although it should not have been a surprise. We were too crowded working out of my townhouse compound and had discussed relocation options and their relative merits extensively in the preceding weeks.

'Ikotun is too far from our homes,' protested Remi, the team's new chief grumbler. Yes, it was far and I knew I risked losing some of the casual staff. But both Patience and Gloria lived in the area and coped with travelling in from there each day. And, as the experienced paper staff were on high salaries and could afford transport to their work, I hoped they would stay.

'Transport costs to Mushin will be very high,' warned Sonny, who was now responsible for most of the market purchases. Mushin was about the same distance to Ikotun as to the islands, so I had already dismissed this as an issue.

'The team are not happy,' said Peter, looking glummest of all. At times, he came across as a union representative rather than an acting general manager.

Ikotun had its location drawbacks – but Max's staff, who included people from all over Lagos, seemed to cope with the location. Papermaking was messy and needed space for air-drying and there were no viable options in places as densely built up as Mushin. Max's compound was already well served with a generator and other services and the small office we could use for our conversion work was neat and ready for moving in. It was a cheap option fit for the purpose.

Privately, I had also decided I would neither invest more in a business that had been defrauded twice by its staff, nor invest in staff whom I now suspected of enhancing their own income at the expense of the company. So, the team's mood probably reflected not only their disapproval of my decision but also the general foetid whiff of distrust in the air.

Lost in my thoughts, I used my big toe to prise loose an intriguingly large shell half-buried in the sand. As I bent to pick it up an unexpectedly large wave broke near me, soaking my shorts and T-shirt. A young child running down from the huts pointed at me and laughed. I chuckled to myself; the shorts would soon dry, but I needed to watch out – the tide was coming in. I dropped the broken shell, moved further up the beach and thought more about my suspicions.

Patrick had started misbehaving. On several occasions he had been slow to deliver the graphic designs and mock-ups for prospective clients and missed production deadlines for confirmed orders. Sometimes he did not turn up for days at a time and his phone was switched off. After hours, like a suspicious spouse seeking evidence of a partner's cheating, I had searched his system and found he had designed a business card for Kola and possessed private notebook designs that had nothing to do with our clients.

'I have my own clients,' he said when I confronted him. 'I am only working for you part-time.'

This was true; he was a freelancer and contracted part-time. But his contract included a non-compete clause and he should not be using my premises and equipment for his own activities. Were these designs for clients who would otherwise come to Ekologika Papers?

'I will always put Ekologika Papers first,' he said earnestly, but I had been deceived too many times to trust him.

I cracked down on rising costs by developing purchasing procedures and tracking reports. I made Sonny the chief purchasing officer for increased accountability. I pasted memos on the walls of the conversion office and sought Patience's help to coach the staff about wasting money.

Patience, who was responsible for spot market-price checks, went to Mushin and reported that card stock prices were significantly lower than those claimed by Sonny. He had receipts that he argued were genuine.

'Paper prices vary a lot,' he countered. 'It is not just by shipment – the traders watch the world paper prices and adjust their market prices.'

He was right. With the help of Google, texts and email, the smallest wholesale trader working from a shabby market in an emergent urban economy in a far-flung corner of the world could adjust his stock's price to reflect world prices, especially if it meant a price rise.

Patience demurred.

'The trader will give him a second invoice, Madam, and he can fill it in with any price he likes.'

Patience knew the less-honest tricks of the trade and was irked by them as well, but she seemed to have no suggestions on how to stop it. Without proof, I simply hoped these new and ongoing price verification exercises might restrain his greed.

As part of the measures to tighten up our procedures I also developed minimum stock levels and order quantities for commonly used items. Shortly afterwards, Patience had reported that transport costs charged to the firm were rising and she showed me some of the expense claims. I called in Peter to explain.

'Why did Sonny go to Mushin for one pot of glue?' I was hot under the collar. '500 *naira* for the glue and 1500 *naira* for transport.' It was ridiculous.

'Sonny ran out and the team had to finish the notebooks,' he said, citing an urgent order that had come in.

'But why do we need to purchase a single pot to complete an order?' I demanded. 'We agreed minimum stock levels and order quantities on standard items. Why are we still emergency buying?'

'I have been trying to save the company money,' he said. 'I know cashflow is tight.'

What I thought was that unreceipted transport expenses provided a chance for staff to inflate their expense claims, so each additional trip topped up their income.

With each repetition of feckless spending and waste, my temper became more frayed, but after my outbursts I felt embarrassed and in a quandary. My temper was damaging our relationships, but was it truly my temper – or their behaviour?

After Friday's meeting, I had taken Peter aside.

'I am worried, Peter. The team do not seem to understand that we have to reduce costs to survive. Instead they seem to resent my expense crackdown and waste even more, which makes me angrier and I have to crack down further. We need to be able to break out of this vicious circle.'

Peter had promised that he would talk to Remi, Sonny, Molly and Patrick and make sure this misbehaviour would stop. I felt relieved to know I could count on him.

As I continued walking towards the wreck, my mind went back to a more recent conversation this afternoon at my beach hut.

'He should pay me for enduring his stupidity,' Toks had insisted, exasperated by her PA's purchase of the wrong equipment. 'I know he does it to get a share. He might earn 10,000 *naira* from the supplier, but the company wastes one million *naira*. He's biting the hand that feeds him, but he doesn't care.'

Toks, Dapo, Jean, Max and I sat on stools around the bar. I had most of my favourite people as guests today. We had already been for a swim in the newly calm seas and everyone looked windswept and salt-kissed. We all shared the same issues at work; it was part of what bound us together.

'This waste kills us, literally,' Toks continued. A recent medical had revealed her blood pressure was too high again and she put it down to the stress from her staff. 'I am really going to have to get rid of him.'

I had heard her say this before, yet her PA remained in his post.

'It's better you manage the devil you know,' Dapo insisted while helping himself to another Gulder from the cool box.

I thought the same; it was why I kept my rascals on. Anyway, we had history together, I had convinced myself. I refused to give up on them.

Tola, a friend of Dapo's, had joined us at the bar. He shared a tale of costly incompetence he had suffered in his hospitality business.

'I just didn't know if the guy was stupid or thieving from me,' he had begun. 'I used to keep staff until they thieved again—that's how I knew. But I can't afford that anymore.' Dapo offered him a glass of Gulder and he took a swig before continuing. 'So I crossed myself, prayed to God that if I was wrong He would look after the guy and not be too harsh on me. And then I sacked him.'

I still could not do that, I thought. Remi, Sonny and even Patrick might make stupid mistakes. They might also top up their salaries through a touch of greed and a fistful of ignorance about its impact on the company's future, but I believed they still loved Ekologika Papers and wanted it to succeed.

It was my turn to describe how my Ekologika Papers staff now all looked more prosperous than me. Peter, Remi and Sonny, the targets of my social conscience, were all plumper than two years ago, now wore smart clothes and had personal gadgets – smartphones, iPods, good watches and the like.

'My car broke down last week – it's battered from being used to transport paper to Mushin,' I said. 'The potholed streets of Mushin are hard on its old body. I'd love a new car but I can't afford one.'

'They are probably saving up for their own vehicle,' said Max.

'So your business is bleeding while your staff are getting richer,' Jean observed mischievously.

He was right.

Then, adopting an American drawl, he added, 'There's something wrong with this picture'.

O

I eventually arrived at the site of the wreck. I had come to see the progress on its break-up and removal. Work had commenced several months earlier, led by an international dredging company. For a while there had been busy activity – a temporary road was laid across the island from the creek to the foreshore and a mechanical digger had been brought in to dig out the half of the wreck that had been closest to shore. Teams of workers with oxy-acetylene cutters had effectively broken it up and the scrap metal had been removed to a barge in the creek, but the other half remained further out to sea. I wondered how they were going to tackle its removal.

I waved to the foreman, a Dutchman I knew. The dredging company employed him, and since the mobilisation he had lived at Agaja on a floating accommodation barge moored in the creek. I had visited him and he had come to lunch at my hut several times.

'I'll be finishing next week,' he called out as he walked towards me. I looked around and realised most of the equipment was gone. Only the mechanical digger remained.

'But what about the rest of the wreck?' I asked, dismayed that he could leave the job half done.

'The funding has run out,' he explained. 'Someone ate the money.' He shrugged. He was an 'old Africa hand' and this was just a job to him.

'But if the wreck isn't completely removed will the erosion continue?' I was worried all our efforts for Agaja would be in vain.

'We're going to dig a channel over there,' he said, pointing to the wide, sandy point built up to the west of the wreck. 'If we can get the water to flow through the channel in front of the remaining part of the wreck, then nature should take its course. The flow will remove more sand and eventually the natural wave pattern will return.'

It had been part of the original plan, so I hoped he was right.

'We think the sand that gets lifted from the channel will get deposited further east and build back the beaches,' he said. 'Anyway, it's all we've got budget left to do.'

I was discouraged and turned back to walk along the beach to my hut. Why could nothing ever go smoothly? Why did corruption always get in the way?

I was lost in my thoughts and did not see an elderly man walking down from his hut towards me.

'Pamela,' he called and waved to get my attention.

'Good morning, sir,' I said as he approached me, wondering how he knew my name and what he wanted. We shook hands.

'You must be Pamela,' he said. A small boy had skipped alongside him and now peered at me shyly from behind his robe. 'The Australian ambassador who has saved Agaja.' He grabbed my hand again and shook it vigorously. 'Thank you.'

I was rather taken aback; Agaja was not yet saved. While I had certainly done some legwork, being Honorary Consul had not helped one jot. I couldn't take credit for all the work done. I wondered if Steve was also getting some thanks but doubted it. I knew that he and his company, as he had promised, were keeping a low profile.

There was 'something wrong with this picture' – in the villager's simplistic perception of my role. But in this difficult environment it took many attempts and many hands to get things done. I felt happy to have played my part and it felt good to be behind something worthwhile – if it actually succeeded.

CHAPTER TWENTY

Wahala!

Man is like pepper, till you have chewed it you do not know how hot it is.

– Hausa proverb

'Tell Dapo about your Christmas,' said Toks. It was mid-January 2008, another New Year passed, and soon it would be three years since my independent life in Lagos had begun. In fact, I had just returned to Lagos following my Christmas break. My gang had gathered at the boat club for the usual Friday evening drink and discussion session.

'My worst Christmas ever?' I joked through thinly veiled pain. It had been a disastrous vacation capping a very unhappy year and I was not sure I wanted to talk about it.

The family Christmas in Scotland had sounded like a good idea. It would take my grieving mother away from her familiar surroundings in Australia. We would celebrate with Alec's elderly mother and only brother, Hew, in a rented cottage in the Scottish Highlands.

But two days before Christmas, Hew died unexpectedly in a household accident.

Alec and his mother, and my mother and I, spent Christmas together in a remote, muddy and grey environment. We sat around the fire and drank many cups of tea; grief was thick in the air.

When Christmas was over, my mother took a train back to London and we held Hew's funeral in Glasgow.

During the night drive south, a furious hailstorm struck. Hailstones the size of golf balls hit our car and I slowed to a crawl as we came through the mountains on the motorway. But the road had become so treacherous that when I added a little acceleration to get up a steep incline, the vehicle skidded uncontrollably on the hailstones. We slid across three lanes and back again to crash into the safety barrier.

Alec and I were lucky to survive.

'Here in Africa we'd say it was Hew saying goodbye,' said Dapo when I'd finished the tale. 'He was looking after you both that night, Pamela.'

I might think stories about spirits were tosh, but I smiled at Dapo's comments, reflecting that this dark Christmas had one surprising upside.

After the accident, Alec and I had leapt out of the car onto a pitch-black mountainside and stood in screeching winds and pelting rain without coats and clung to each other. We shivered as we waited for emergency services to arrive, and slowly realised we were uninjured and safe. In the subsequent days, something had shifted in both of us, changing our relationship for the better.

But this was private; I wasn't about to tell Dapo.

'It was your *annus horribilis*,' said Toks with feeling.

I could not disagree. But I now knew there were more important things than paper companies.

O

Later in January I organised another Australia Day barbecue at Agaja and there was a large turnout of Nigerians as well as Australians. Steve was not there – like Alec he had been unexpectedly transferred back to his company's headquarters – but the legacy of his intervention at Agaja was developing. The channel had been dug and sand was coming back. The villagers and I were in a celebratory mood.

Michelle came alone but exuberant with news.

'I have a Nigerian business partner and we're going to import portable mini generators from China,' she said. 'He's got the connections and I can fund him,' she continued.

That sounded a strange choice of business. It was certainly a departure from educating children and running a software consulting firm.

'It's just a side business for me,' she said. 'But he thinks he can sell a lot out east—there's no power and these tiny generators will make a difference. And he has government connections so we're getting contracts to supply schools.'

I knew the mini generators she was talking about – portable ones that could be used to run a small refrigerator or keep lights burning while charging a phone or laptop. They were colloquially called 'I better pass my neighbour' and were bought by people who couldn't afford a large generator and its fuel costs. I had one for occasional power at Agaja. The lack of power made life very difficult for much of the population and presumably schools would use them for light and small appliance power. But how could she square the importation of generators with her environmental principles? After all, they were highly polluting, a fire hazard and caused lung damage. Why wasn't she getting into the solar power business, I wondered.

'It is very profitable,' she continued blithely. 'We've already made a lot of money.'

It was also a highly competitive business, which you would be unlikely to succeed in without paying bribes. Just as I had revised my opinion about Steve, I was revising my opinion of Michelle too – but not as positively. It was certainly an about-turn – on many fronts – but I had seen this moral flexibility before and pondered that she would probably end up being more successful than me.

Ekologika Papers was struggling. Once again, we were in the slow season with time to conclude the move to Ikotun, but the business outlook was uncertain. People were edgy about the economy and growth prospects. Corporate social responsibility budgets, always at the frontline of savings, were being frozen. It seemed a recycling partnership was a socially responsible idea whose time had not yet come – my contact at the telecommunications company was no longer returning my calls. Without a partnership, sales were too uneven and the scale too small to justify significant further investment.

Strategyworks had several possible projects in view, although getting the green light was also affected by economic uncertainty. My analyst, Edith, had resigned before Christmas and now Reti had resigned as well. Still disappointed by staff defection, I was nonetheless grateful to be relieved of the burden of their salaries, and I'd see how the year developed before replacing them.

I had called Mike at the High Commission to let him know about the barbecue.

'Canberra still isn't allowing budget for your events,' he said cheerfully. 'But I'm glad you called – the new High Commissioner will be appointed soon.'

I learned about his background and later told Toks.

'Another civil servant,' she exclaimed scornfully. 'Your country is not really investing in its relationship with Nigeria.'

Sadly, I agreed.

In my view the Australian government was underestimating this country's trading and geopolitical potential. I could appreciate that having made choices about geographic focus that did not include Nigeria, they would cut budgets and scale back our representation. But was that an adequate excuse to send bureaucrats as diplomatic representatives? I did not think so. Nigerians seemed to take my position as Australian Honorary Consul in Lagos more seriously than my country's government.

Just before my dreadful Christmas I had a further run-in with the Nigerian authorities, this time during a late-evening drive from the border back to Lagos. I had been in Togo visiting a friend and, to avoid heavy traffic, had taken her advice to travel back along the West African coast by night. I discovered, upon entering Nigeria, that travelling in a hired car along the expressway at four in the morning was not a wise decision.

Roadblocks abounded – I later learned there were more than twenty mobile roadblocks set up on this stretch of highway after dark. Smugglers travel by night, but the roadblocks were also a way for the officers to earn some dash. At each stop, policemen and agents for the Nigerian Drug Law Enforcement Agency shone a torch into the vehicle. During daylight my pale skin conferred a nod and wave through any checkpoint as their conclusion was, I was either on legitimate business or an unsatisfactory target for dash. At night, on seeing a white woman in the back seat, their conclusions were exactly the opposite. I couldn't really blame them.

'Tell her to get out of the car,' a stern woman said to my driver. By the way others deferred to her I realised she was the senior officer – but was not in uniform. She had a blanket around her shoulders and was dressed in civilian clothes. I asked for her identification but by way of reply she pulled open my door.

'Get out and let me inspect your luggage.'

This was going to be a long inspection and this woman was going to make my life hell. Should I give her a bribe to get through?

I had one last option.

'I am diplomatic staff,' I said haughtily, handing her my Consulate business card.

Her sceptical gaze clearly communicated that she wondered why diplomatic staff would be in a beaten-up Mercedes hire car coming from the border in the middle of the night.

'I am on private business,' I said rather lamely. I held her gaze and she held her silence. Finally she shrugged.

'Thank you, Your Excellency,' she said in a tone that was anything but deferential.

Then, she smiled – human after all – and added: 'Do you have anything for me?'.

'God's blessings,' I said cheerfully.

I chuckled at the memory. It was one of the few fringe benefits of being Honorary Consul.

Now in the shade of my beach hut I called the guests together to deliver a speech. The group was diverse in background and status, a far cry from what I knew of the cloistered, homogenous diplomatic cocktail party circuit in Abuja and my invitations had reflected this deliberate choice.

'By getting to know each other we can learn from each other,' I said in my welcome. 'Australians might do well to absorb some of the exuberance, entrepreneurialism, ambition and vision of Nigerians.'

There were a few raised Australian eyebrows.

'Nigerians might learn to appreciate egalitarianism and fairness in their society.'

I wanted to provoke some discussion.

'However, it is in the face of adversity—often climate-led in Australia's case, often government-led in Nigeria's—that our people show their remarkable shared inner strength and resilience.'

I believed this.

When I finished, Toks unexpectedly jumped up to take the floor.

'Pamela is not only Consul General for Australia,' she began.

I smiled – promoted again.

'But she is Consul General for Nigeria. She knows us Nigerians well, our weaknesses and our strengths, our vast opportunities and the issues that get in the way, but she is one of our strongest supporters.'

Sometimes with the evidence of corruption's stranglehold, it challenged even my optimism. But it was when people like her dropped everything to help me that I felt embraced by the country's natural humanity and warmth. And when I benefitted from human experience, insight and wisdom that could hold its own anywhere, I could not help but be energised and positive.

Now, I blushed and raised a toast to Australia and Nigeria.

O

The next day Dapo rang me at the office. 'The staff have won,' he said lugubriously. He had phoned to tell me about an upcoming social event, but I thought the real motive was to let off some steam. 'I know they always take something but now they are threatening my business.'

Dapo had caught the dismal contagion of being blighted by one's staff. His end of year seasonal sales had been down and the inflated costs caused by his staff's 'mistakes' were leading to painful losses. I thought he was exaggerating, but of course I, too, suffered staff-born cost manipulation and carried its scars in my own soul.

But I thought I was through the worst.

The papermaking equipment had been set up in a small workshop at Ikotun, and at the weekend all the conversion operations of Ekologika Papers would finally move there too. We would soon be less dependent on Patrick, as a new graphic designer was joining us. Only Molly and a new salesman would hold an office downstairs.

With Patience's sleuthing and Peter's coaching, I had successfully foiled many inflationary practices over the past few months. These included inflated claims for transport, deliberate wastage resulting in additional orders of glue, ink and cardstock and invoice inflation. I estimated that both our notebook costs and some of my staff's illicit sources of income had been halved. I had been especially disappointed that many of the bad practices pointed to Remi and Sonny. Their disruptive grumbling about the move had become louder as the sources of their extra income became fewer.

One afternoon in February I was working at my dining room office but could hear a lot of noise downstairs. Peter had supervised the wrapping, counting and recording of our paper stock and setting up the papermaking equipment for its move to Ikotun. Now he was in charge of packing the business files, sample archive and boxing up computers, printers and cables in readiness for Saturday's move. But his work was happening amidst the chaos of delivering a large notebook order for a society wedding, also due for delivery this Saturday. I had authorised taking on some high-season casuals, but I stayed out of the way of the people, cardboard and paper clippings downstairs.

I could not wait to get the team out of my home. Angry shouting was not unusual in these more strained days. I vaguely wondered what they were unhappy about now. But I only looked up when Peter came to see me.

'The team have gone on strike, Madam,' he said with a worried frown. 'The casuals say they want an increase to their daily rate and overtime. And Remi and Sonny want their salary increased too.'

The casuals were being paid well above the normal rate for unskilled workers and from benchmarking I knew Sonny and Remi were being paid nearly three times the rates normally offered to workers in the printing industry. Dapo thought I was crazy, but I was not crazy enough to give in to these demands. I knew what this threat of strike was really about – their lost illicit extra income and the unwanted move.

'I will come to hear their demands,' I said to Peter. 'But tell them that this order is the one that will pay their salaries this month so stopping work now is not going to do anyone any good.'

With Peter gone, Patience came to see me.

'It feels like extortion,' I said to her. I shook my head, at the end of my tether and my goodwill.

'You must understand, Madam,' she said. 'They do not see what you bring to them or think about the long term. They think you can afford it and they will always try to take more from you.'

It was such a long way from the kind of relationships I had tried to build with my team. I told Patience I felt frustrated.

'But you are a white, Madam—an *oyibo,*' she said. 'They will always see you as richer than them.'

This was sobering.

'We are not all like this,' continued Patience. 'They are worthless, Madam.'

I had been an automatic cash point for too long. But no longer. I hardened my position; there would be no negotiations. I met my team but told Remi, Sonny and the casuals that the rates and salaries were final.

Later that day, the compound was silent.

Remi, my strong-man papermaker, and Sonny, my hippy craft worker, had led their team of casuals in walking off the job. It was no longer a strike. They had quit.

O

It was a panic to deliver the wedding order but with Molly and Peter's help, and long hours, we delivered it on time. Of course, we were obliged to postpone the move by a few days.

Peter seemed upset by Remi and Sonny's defection, more so than I was. I realised I had emotionally detached from them in the prior months as I had come to accept their complicity in costly bad behaviours. Their departure opened up the more exciting possibility of a new team.

Max sent three casual workers he had once employed – two young men and a woman – to see if they might be interested in training to be members of the conversion team or as papermakers. He recommended them as hard-working, but Peter had reservations.

'They are deaf, Madam.'

'Let's give them a go,' I said. I wondered how they'd communicate but at least we'd employ another woman.

A week later, I visited our new Ikotun office and wondered at my old team's resistance. It was perfect.

But Peter had news. We sat down at the round wooden conference table, now scratched and worn.

'I am sorry, Madam,' he said. He looked wretched. 'I have been offered a job as a quartermaster for a Chinese company and they will pay me very well. You know I only came to you when I could not make enough money as a skipper. But the water is my real love. Please, Ma'am, understand that I have to take this chance.'

This was truly the end of an era for Ekologika Papers. To lose Peter, my ally in the face of so much disloyalty even from his fellow foundation staff, was a massive blow. But I did understand that his great passion lay elsewhere. He had been exhausted by all the intrigue, too, and now he had to take his chance and start afresh.

O

Peter behaved impeccably before leaving. I implored him to stay on a couple of weeks and he agreed. He had trained the new deaf papermakers and conversion workers who had picked up the work well. They used sign language amongst themselves and a mixture of writing and gestures with other team members and were more productive than their hearing counterparts. At my request Peter had also documented our paper recipes and our paper and equipment inventories. He was assiduous in his work and I said goodbye to him with real fondness and regret.

Not long after his departure, I visited the papermaking workshop and noticed that no newly moulded papers had been pressed. When I enquired, I was told that the 'jacks' (car jacks) used on the press were missing.

This was odd.

So I checked Peter's records and noted a full complement of jacks in his inventory.

Simultaneously, I was told we had a shortfall in the special type of paper needed for a new order we had won.

This was puzzling.

Peter's inventory records suggested we had huge stocks and I had the accounting records of the expenses for raw materials and labour that had created them.

'How can we not have enough paper, Patience?' I asked.

Patience and Molly, as well as my driver Tayo and steward Edward, were all that were left of the old team. Patience now had a dual role as accountant and stand-in manager of Ekologika Papers. She was coping well.

'We have opened the packets that Peter packed,' she said. 'He wrote on the outside the quantity, type and thickness of the paper within.'

I knew this. Peter's key quality control and supervisory role was to sort and pack the inventory. That was why he was so upset by Kola's theft. And he had been paid overtime for hours spent sorting and counting paper.

'Madam, I don't know how to tell you,' she said. 'They have just been packed anyhow. Many have mixed papers and nowhere near as many as suggested by the label.'

There must be a mistake. I asked Patience to do an inventory count and an equipment check.

A little later she reported that more than half the stock did not exist or was poor quality and a lot of papermaking and conversion equipment was missing.

So now I knew where all those boots and rulers were going. Peter had been deceiving me too.

'It is always the people you trust the most who let you down worst,' Patience said.

Had she taken over from Dapo in delivering unwelcome homilies?

Peter too, I thought bleakly. What a cunning actor he was. I was utterly gutted.

O

It was a few weeks later and I was in my home office. 'One of your former papermakers is at the gate to see you, Madam,' said Patience. 'He is looking for work.'

Following the bitter-tasting discoveries about Peter's lies and theft, I had decided that I would focus on my Strategyworks consulting practice. I had no more ambition for recycling partnerships that would help drive Ekologika Papers's future growth. Staying closer to my original vision, Ekologika Papers would remain a micro-social enterprise creating jobs for disadvantaged young men and women – but there was a rub. I would only employ individuals as long as they proved themselves worthy. After training, I made it clear I had zero tolerance for any mistakes or nonsense.

And I certainly did not want anything to do with Peter's team.

'It is James,' continued Patience.

I remembered James – the pleasant papermaker I had liked, the one who had been sacked by Peter. Perhaps his work had been better than I had been led to believe and there were other reasons for his dismissal. Still, I was reluctant to see him – I was not in the market for staff.

But Patience had already spoken with him and wanted me to hear what he had to say. James came in.

He was not plump and well-groomed like Peter, Remi and Sonny. He had not been feeding on my unintended largesse like them. He was a cheerful presence – as I remembered – but after greetings and an update on his family he grew more serious.

'Peter sacked me because I would not join their plan. I tried to come to tell you before, but they told me you would not see me.' I remembered the time he had tried to see me. 'They are working in competition with you, Madam.'

'*Who* is working in competition with me?' I demanded.

'Peter and Sonny and Remi,' he answered. 'They were working on it for a long time stealing your paper and selling notebooks. Then, last year, Peter set up a company with Sonny and Remi. They stole your equipment and have employed your former papermakers.'

I listened in stunned silence as I processed what he said. His claims would mean that my founding team had run a shadow company alongside my own for at least the last year of their employment. Were they a clique doing business for themselves all the time I had invested and worked to help them? Many times, I had given up my own monthly salary to make sure they never went without. And I now knew Peter was as culpable as the others.

But James had not finished with his shocking allegations.

'A white woman has funded them,' he said.

This stopped me in my tracks. Who? James did not know who she was. But to my knowledge, the team knew only one white woman other than me.

I think all the blood had drained from my face and by the time he left, I was unsteady on my feet.

'Don't worry, Madam,' said Patience coming in to my office. She tried to reassure me. 'They do not know how to market the product and their quality will be poor. There is no honour amongst thieves. They will steal from each other.'

I found no comfort in her words and her voice echoed through the billowing cavity of my mind. She left and I still felt dazed.

If James's story was true, then the purportedly disadvantaged founding team of Ekologika Papers had together conspired against me and become a lethal cancer within. It would mean I had been betrayed on every front by nearly everyone I had tried to help. If so, I had never really had a chance.

As ever, Dapo's observation was apt.

The staff had won.

Gibbous Moon Over Lagos (2019)

Gibbous Moon refers to a moon in an intermediate phase between half moon and full moon. There are two phases of gibbous moon—a waxing gibbous growing in brightness to full moon and a waning gibbous becoming less visible to us, on its way back to showing us only its dark side.[1]

Epilogue

Return to old watering holes for more than money; friends and dreams are there to meet you.

– African proverb

'They had confiscated seventy bags of ballot papers with votes already cast,' said Dapo. 'Thumb printed already!'

Toks, Max, Jean and Dapo had finally joined me at the boat club. It had been a long wait, but we had not expected this reunion tonight. Today, Saturday 16 February, had been scheduled as the day eighty-four million Nigerian registered voters would cast their votes in the 2019 Presidential election. On voting day no vehicular movement was permitted. On Friday, offices and markets had closed early to allow people to travel to where their voter cards were registered. People across the nation had gone home or travelled to their villages.

In the few days I had been back in Lagos, I witnessed a vigorous campaign between two septuagenarians. President Muhammadu Buhari of the All Progressives Congress (APC) was fighting hard for a second term, despite absences from Nigeria for treatment of an undisclosed but clearly serious illness during his first four-year term of office. Alhaji Atiku Abubakar, who had been Vice President to former President Olusegun Obasanjo, was put forward by the

People's Democratic Party (PDP) as the main opposition candidate. There were a lot of candidates – 73 in all – in this boisterous, immature democracy. From the moment I arrived, social media had been alive with ballot-rigging rumours and hints of possible violence, neither sourced nor verified. Yet I had felt the combination of real excitement, tension and anticipation in the air.

Then, at 2.30am on Saturday, there had been a bombshell. The Independent National Electoral Commission (INEC) responsible for organising and overseeing elections in Nigeria, had announced a one-week postponement of the Presidential poll.

'That's just "fake news",' said Toks. 'Who knows if it's true? The parties are coming up with accusations and blaming each other when they should be blaming INEC.'

During the afternoon INEC had issued a statement that, having realised some polling stations would not open on time with all materials and equipment available, they decided on postponement. They blamed bad weather – the unseasonal harmattan that was shrouding the country as well as Lagos – forcing them to send voting materials by road instead of by air – and recent suspicious fires in key offices, which had destroyed electoral materials and equipment.[2]

'You're right,' admitted Dapo. 'Their excuses might have been accepted if they had taken the decision two days ago—not six hours before the polls open. Their incompetence is embarrassing.'

'They have shown contempt for Nigerians,' said Toks. She was angry. 'The cost for the country and all the people who have stopped work, closed businesses and travelled will be huge.'

'INEC postponed the Presidential poll in 2011 and 2015,' said Jean. He seemed bemused. 'Maybe we were the fools thinking this time would be any different.'

'But I heard the delay will help Atiku,' said Max, using Abubakar's first name, which was how he was commonly known. 'He was ten per cent behind in the polls and so any reduction in voter turnout—which there will be after this fiasco—will help him.'

'Buhari will still win,' said Dapo confidently. 'It's the power of the incumbent.'

'Buhari will win,' agreed Toks, 'but it's because the masses don't want a return to the PDP's corrupt ways. And it's the masses who have voters' cards in this country – they don't mind the hard work it takes to get one. And they won't mind the hard work to get to a polling station next week.'

I listened to my friends' debate; so passionate and opinionated, so resilient in the face of such a display of official incompetence, or something more sinister.

It was two decades since I first arrived in Lagos and nearly a decade since I left. I had been back numerous times – unwilling to abandon either the city or good friendships – and, each time, there were signs of huge growth and change. There was a vibrant art, entertainment, bar and restaurant scene in Lagos that had not existed before, roads were wider, bridge infrastructure impressive and the skyline had grown. But some things, such as the chaos and opacity of government decisions and actions, remained the same.

President Buhari had promised change when he was elected to his first term in office in 2015. A former military leader and Fulani Muslim from the north, he had a reputation for honesty and a simple lifestyle, which appealed to an electorate fed up with spiralling security concerns and unequal distribution of the wealth overseen by his PDP predecessor, President Goodluck Jonathan.[3] Nigerians had voted overwhelmingly for Buhari and his promised anti-corruption drive. As it was the first time a democratically elected leader had conceded electoral defeat, facilitating the transition of power to an opponent, it was also a significant achievement in the evolution of Nigeria's democracy.

By 2019, Buhari's scorecard was mixed. He had embarked on his promised anti-corruption drive and had some notable successes although critics complained that he had focused on political enemies rather than attacking the system.[4] His administration had invested in needed national infrastructure, including improving interstate roads and building a railway line from Lagos to Kano but when months after his election, oil prices collapsed to thirty per cent of their 2014 highs, he faced economic crisis. He imposed import bans and currency controls, which enriched those who had access to scarce foreign currency and made local manufacturing industry suffer. He had deployed virtually the same policies when he faced similar low oil prices during his tenure as military leader in the seventies, and now he got virtually the same results.[5]

In 2016, Nigeria's economy had fallen into recession for the first time in two decades. Recovery had been slow and the economy was not growing faster than population growth. Recently, more Nigerians were classed as living in extreme poverty than Indians, a country with six times Nigeria's population.[6]

'If Buhari gets re-elected we've probably got four more years of economic stagnation,' said Max with a sigh.

'And if Atiku gets elected we'll see Nigeria's assets sold off to his cronies,' said Dapo. Atiku's campaign had promised more pro-business policies than Buhari, including privatisation of the national oil companies, the assets to which Dapo was referring. Atiku was a multimillionaire businessman who was alleged to have used his term as Vice President in Olusegun Obasanjo's administration to enrich himself and those close to him; allegations he dismissed.[7]

'Buhari is incompetent,' said Max. 'It would be better if his running mate took over—at least, he is hard-working and has shown he can manage the economy.' Vice President Yemi Osinbajo, a Yoruba lawyer and pastor from Lagos, had taken over during Buhari's absence due to illness from the country in 2017 and 2018 and had been admired for his unassuming but decisive leadership style and action taken on the economy and security.[8]

'Buhari is old and ill,' said Jean dryly. 'Where there's death there's hope.'

Toks looked a bit shocked but brushed aside Jean's comment.

'Buhari will win and the second term will be better,' she concluded. 'Anyway, the oil price crash was positive for young Nigerians. They saw that the old ways were too obsessed with oil and making easy money off contracts. Now they've got into agriculture and mining and started all kinds of new technology businesses. They don't need government help. It's exciting.'

Trust Toks to see the bright side. I had been feeling depressed by today's setback, but perhaps I had been out of the country too long.

Times might have been hard for the last four years, but the yachts of Lagos's wealthiest set still bobbed in the harbour. Low-key Afrobeat played over the club's sound system and it felt like old times. Within minutes of our reunion we had embarked on this passionate conversation about politics, economics and business. What else could I expect?

I looked back towards the clubhouse in search of the moon. It was higher in the sky, almost overhead, a ghostly glow still shrouded by haze.

My friends were focused on their debate about Nigeria's future, but I fell again into a reflective mood, thinking about all that had passed.

O

I continued Ekologika Papers for another eighteen months after hearing those final allegations of Peter's betrayal.

Like Dapo, who I had once thought was too cynical about his employees, I carried a heavy cloak of wariness and weariness. I could not prove whether my staff's actions had been errors and incompetence, or something more nefarious. But I was worn out by distrust.

There was insufficient evidence to prosecute any former staff for the theft of missing equipment and I knew trying to prosecute them for breaching the non-compete clause in their employment contracts would have been futile. My years of experience had taught me how hard it was to access justice in Nigeria, and even in the situation with Kola, where the case was clear, justice had felt tainted.

I didn't know how to find out the truth about who had funded them and couldn't see the point of fuelling a greater sense of outrage and betrayal by searching for information.

With immediate pressing financial concerns, such as paying salaries and keeping my business alive, it was time to move on.

I operated Ekologika Papers only on a very small scale. Patience, my loyal accountant, stepped up to help run the business and, at last, I employed women – young deaf women as well as hearing women – in all roles. Their enthusiasm and capability made me wonder how things might have been if I had employed more women from the start. I tried to sell the business, hoping the skills, jobs and original products would not all be lost, but eventually I closed it down. The trauma of betrayal was more distressing than the financial loss and a failed business endeavour.

In early 2009, I closed both businesses, resigned as Honorary Consul and, after ten years of calling this great city home, I left Lagos.

My focus in my final months in Nigeria before I left was on my consulting work and afterwards on reviving my faltering relationship with Alec. It made a difference that we would be fully committed to each other now. He took on a less demanding role and we based ourselves in London. Leaving Lagos after a decade had been a personal and professional wrench. But our relationship was refreshed, renewed by proximity and our independent sources of stress had been removed. With better alignment of our goals we rediscovered the things that had originally made us a great couple.

And he still looks dashing in a kilt.

Tippy came to London with me, but she had to endure a six-month quarantine. Her health deteriorated during that time of inactivity and she sadly died of kidney failure in 2012.

As time passed, I came to appreciate that my business adventure in Lagos had brought personal growth, deep friendships and valuable life wisdom. The greatest learning, I realised with chagrin, came from my mistakes, and not without substantial pain and sacrifice. Ekologika Papers was too small for effective and systematic governance – the same size trap I had observed in tiny NGOs. I had made naïve assumptions that people's motivations and ethics were the same as my own. My anger and frustration with my staff had probably fed their sense of resentment and their feeling of having a licence to thieve – it was a vicious circle that only I could have broken. Running one business was enough. I had been neither brave enough to choose Ekologika Papers and take the financial risk, nor ruthless enough to shut it down. As Toks had advised in colourful language, some business babies did have to be killed, quickly and humanely, with less pain and sacrifice for all.

Over time, as I continued to share my experiences with others, I learned that my story of business failure, due to corrupt employee cliques, was quite common. The problem is shared by Nigerians and foreign investors in Nigeria alike.

It seemed small business owners, recognising that viability made them more vulnerable to corruption-led losses, responded (amongst other things) by hiring fewer people and sacking them when any cloud of incompetence or suspicion arose. Larger businesses, whose deeper pockets allowed them to survive employee fraud and deception for longer, spent money on anti-corruption training, auditing and control processes.

My conclusion was that even the smallest Nigerian business should invest in control systems and processes, internal and external audits and constant checks and reports. Businesses should be run tightly with access to experienced managers and good training, so that repetitive untoward incidents could be avoided or resolved decisively. Although this made operation more difficult and increased the investment levels required, it was necessary because once incidents happened, everyone was distrusted. And that, I knew, was toxic.

These experiences are of course not unique to Nigerian business.

As Dapo once asked: 'I wonder if there is a bit of "the Nigerian" in employees elsewhere in the world?'.

I heard similar tales from European, UK, US and Australian small and large businesses. As westerners, we should not kid ourselves that we are free of such individual and collective acts of greed. Even in the small community of expatriates I knew, for some such as Michelle, the search for wealth became a higher consideration than ethics.

But corruption in Nigeria affects everyone at all levels and positions in society.

'Don't judge them too harshly until you live in their shoes,' another Nigerian friend who heard about my experiences responded. My team, or at least some of them, had betrayed a personal bond and I could not forgive them. But I understood what she meant.

In a corrupt system, the descriptions of poor victims, super-wealthy leeches and predatory multinationals are misleading and simplistic stereotypes. Corruption becomes more than payments made to win enormous contracts and the 'winners' some nefarious local business or public sector or aid-agency employee. It is more than the siphoning of government revenues by greedy politicians in positions of power. And it is more than an emailed demand for advance payment that challenges your credulity.

A corrupt system goes hand in hand with a lack of access to transparent and effective justice. People are frustrated by being powerless in the face of others' power and corruption. A corrupt system also poses challenges to individuals and organisations, every single day at every level of their existence. How do I get my child admitted to a school? How do I get my exam results certification? How do I get my lease extension? How do I get the right to vote? How do I get paid? How do I pay my staff salaries? There is always someone barring the way to achieving one's rights and dreams. To live in that sort of system with no escape (unlike me) is to be challenged every day to make a decision about whether to sacrifice a principle or the outcome.

Yet every person who decries the system is – possibly only in small ways but always in some way – complicit. They have little choice.

It seems a wonder that many people do still act ethically.

But with such intense pressure on ethical boundaries, is it such a surprise that the lines shift and some lose their way?

The costs of this corrupt system are high. It lays waste to individual endeavour, curtails business success and slows positive social change and economic growth. But worst of all, in my experience, a corrupt system poisons relationships, undermines trust and fuels anger.

'Our staff make us suspicious, paranoid even, short-tempered and angry,' said Toks during another conversation. She described her cheating PA whom she eventually sacked as an example. 'Like other staff members I've sacked, he might have won in the short term but in the long term he lost because his duplicity and treachery prevented him reaping the longer-term rewards he stood to gain.'

Another Nigerian put it even more succinctly. 'My employees bite the hand that feeds them even though I want to help them build a better life.' And like me, he was perplexed. 'I don't understand why they do it.'

Undoubtedly many employees were loyal and worthy of absolute trust, and it was not only employer/employee relationships that were affected. But the damage to mutual trust and the growth of resentment was a sad aspect of this corrupt system.

In my view, corruption remains a metastasising cancer that needs to be excised. I believe Nigeria's new leader[9] should make it a priority to drive anti-corruption measures on many fronts, not only targeting individual thieves of public sector financial flows, but also delivering broader systemic change.

As a country, Nigeria still has plenty of other problems to tackle.

Despite President Buhari's efforts to neutralise Boko Haram, a violent Islamist insurgency, during his first term of office, recent renewed violent attacks in the north of the country and the emergence of new breakaway groups, underline the fragility of the gains.[10] Since at least 2017, Fulani herdsmen militia have been unchecked in terrorising Christian middle belt farmers and long-standing instability and criminality in the delta continue. In addition, each of these conflicts was and is used as a cover for organised international crime, including people trafficking, drug smuggling and oil smuggling.[11] And this is to say nothing of how rapid, unchecked population growth and people flooding into already overstretched urban centres such as Lagos, make reversing shocking poverty and inequality a superhuman endeavour.

What a glutinous, bubbling brew. So what might the next decade bring?

Despite this gloomy picture, there is upbeat news for Africa. As a continent (comprising fifty-four nations), it is being touted as the 'Next China'.[12] I welcome the new narrative of an enterprising, energetic and youthful Africa, which should replace the tired stereotypes of aid-recipient, war-ridden basket-case Africa.

Yet with these opposing forces of conflict and opportunity, and in the chaotic and opaque political reality that I witnessed today, I wondered now if Lagos and Nigeria's moon was waxing or waning?

Max once told me that Lagos and Nigeria would muddle through. But while their fates were not as dire as one might think, he did not see either ever fulfilling its potential. Corruption remained the limiting factor.

Nigeria is still the African giant that matters, and a quarter of the country's GDP is generated by Lagos, Africa's largest city.[13] It has been predicted that, by 2050, seventy per cent of Nigeria's population will live in urban environments and that Lagos's population will reach approximately thirty-five to forty-two million, making it the world's third largest megacity. Indeed, it is also predicted that by the end of this century, Lagos will grow to become the world's largest megacity,[14] filled with humanity infected by Lagos verve and striving for personal success. If the continent and country is to move forward to its promised great future, I have no doubt that irrepressibly energetic Lagosians – some of whom would be role models in any society – will lead the way.

Living in Britain, where happily there is a social safety net, I also saw the unhealthy growth of a dependency culture – a seeming expectation by some that government should resolve all their lives' shortcomings, sometimes with little contribution in return. In Lagos, where there is a minimal safety net, people expect little from their government except perhaps corrupt self-interested action by elected and public officials. The positive outcome is that folk are far more self-reliant. While there had been improvements in state infrastructure, works and power supply during the previous two decades,[15] nearly all Lagosians look only to their own entrepreneurship and wits for a hand-up and many use their energies to create change for good, while offering a free hand to others along the way.

Toks was right to focus on the way young (and more mature) Nigerians are embracing opportunity and not waiting for government to act. The digital and telecommunications revolution has transformed business opportunity and in two decades fuelled the emergence of online retailing and fintech and the growth of the Nollywood movie industry. In the vibrant 'Yabacon Valley', young, tech-savvy Nigerians and investment incubators jostle to develop solutions to Nigeria's problems – and to create 'unicorn' billion-dollar start-ups.[16] Even Uber and Airbnb have come to Lagos, and there is a nascent tourism sector. There is a surge in entrepreneurialism, big and small, and the encouraging, not-before-time growth of female business owners. An astonishing investment in oil refining capacity by Aliko Dangote, Nigeria's visionary and transformational businessman – the Rupert Murdoch or Jack Ma of Africa – will deliver a Lagos refinery capable of processing two thirds of Nigeria's oil output by 2020–22 and eliminate Nigeria's dependence on imported refined oil products.[17] Like in other large, poor cities located on rivers and waterways, plastic pollution has become an invasive epidemic in Lagos waterways, beaches and land environment. Bad news, but environmental issues such as this are now top of the state's, entrepreneurs' and social entrepreneurs' agenda making me proud to have been one of the Lagos pioneers.[18] All these changes were very exciting to witness.

And as for Australia? Did the government ever demonstrate it was serious about its relationship with Nigeria and, in particular, serious about understanding business opportunities and building commercial connections in Lagos? Representation is still by an Honorary Consul, but I understand the Abuja-based Australian High Commissioner visits Lagos more regularly and Austrade representatives, now based in Ghana, come to Lagos too. I understand the number of Nigerians studying in Australia has quadrupled in the last few years,[19] so that's a start. Yet, if Australia wants a bigger stake in Lagos's future it needs a permanent Deputy High Commission and trade office in the city where the commercial opportunities are and where the risks and complexities of doing business can be properly assessed. I hope Australian business people will start exploring the potential for exciting ventures in Africa's wild west for themselves but do it wholeheartedly – no toes in the water will work – and, like Nigerians, not wait for government to lead.

In an earlier conversation, Dapo had told me that he had moved out of the printing business and been invited to join the board of a large industrial company, but one that had recently struggled to deliver good financial results.

'Have they got corruption problems too?' I asked.

'Of course, Pamela,' he laughed. 'That's why they asked me to join.'

I also knew the ever-imaginative Toks remained active in managing her property empire and had overseen some new property developments and profitable sales. Amongst several philanthropic endeavours, her most impressive achievement was perhaps that she channelled her grief at the loss of her daughter to help spread grief and trauma-counselling services throughout Nigeria.

And despite her optimism for younger Nigerians, when she saw that people bearing the brunt of the oil-price crash and Buhari's mistakes – those desperate to make a living and without hope for work – were jumping off Third Mainland Bridge and being fished from the lagoon daily, she acted. Her grief-counselling NGO now partnered with Lagos state government for funding and a United Kingdom NGO for frontline operator training to provide innovative and ground-breaking first-level mental health support through a twenty-four-hour call centre service for these desperate individuals.

Toks acted on problems she saw. She is just one of the Lagosians I know who is contributing to their country by building a new vibrant Lagos, one building block, one business, one social enterprise, one NGO at a time.

Would the next administration deliver necessary infrastructure, economic growth and freedom from the destructive corrupt system that had embraced Nigerians so tightly for so long? And when would brave Nigerians from every part of society get the energetic and visionary political leadership they deserve? [20]

O

Returning from my reflections, I now refocused on my friends. They were still discussing today's postponement.

'It's the X in Nigeria,' said Max, laughingly. 'You can never count on anything being certain.'

'But look at how people reacted,' said Dapo. 'They are angry, and they are sad. But instead of getting violent, they get on with their lives because they have to.'

'It is always two steps forward, one, two or three backwards,' said Jean.

'It will pass,' said Toks. 'The next four years will be brighter.'

I had come to Lagos, upbeat about the election and today I had felt depressed. Now tonight, I saw the bright side in my friends' attitudes. Indeed, this morning's news had created a huge collective disappointment. It was a show of incompetence or contempt by their leaders against the people, and tonight the country gave a huge collective shrug. Stoicism, resilience and optimism were some of Nigerians' best attributes.

Max was now looking at his smartphone. Business did not stop and likely he was having a conversation with a supplier in China or sending a quote to a customer. His business partner, Jean and he had suffered setbacks during this recent prolonged downturn, including the failure of a new line of business, but they remained committed. Jean changed the conversation and explained he was considering a number of new independent business opportunities. Now he was sizing them up with the help of Toks and Dapo.

'How about a restaurant business?' Dapo suggested to Jean. 'There is always money in food.' He was right. Victoria Island had once offered a meagre choice of restaurants but now many modern restaurants, bars and clubs buzzed with customers.

'I wouldn't go into anything in hospitality,' replied Jean. 'It would be all right while I felt sociable and enjoyed customers' company but when I didn't, I'd tell them to go away.'

Max looked up from his phone.

'Closed due to bad mood,' he winked.

We laughed.

Pursuing my dream alongside them had been an intense experience. Like any adventure it brought wisdom and disappointments, great joy and pain. It meant experiencing the complexity of life and getting inside the lives of others and enjoying their company – my friends, and even the villains, made it worthwhile.

I knew I was not yet finished with either Africa or Nigeria; I had more travel and business adventures planned. I still had an unquenchable thirst for wide skies, dust in my nostrils and uncertainty about how the day would end.

The haze cleared and the moon was suddenly visible above our heads, and I saw it was neither full nor a crescent. More than a half moon, it was a pearl pebble, a glorious, liberated gibbous moon. It might be waxing into a full moon or waning back to the dark side. I didn't know. Like my years in Lagos, like this disappointing day when an anticipated step forward was stopped in its tracks, like Lagos and Nigeria moving into the future, I thought, it heralded ambiguity. It cast doubts but simultaneously, raised enormous, glorious hopes.

Acknowledgements

Many people helped in the tricky, long, but rewarding journey to create this book.

There are the people I knew during my adventurous days in Lagos, many of whom I count as valued friends. There are also the kind folk who helped with writing the book in the UK and Australia, and with checking it for factual errors and a wandering, complicated storyline. There is also the team of professionals who have supported and will continue to support the book's publication, distribution and marketing. Despite their combined best efforts, I am sure some errors remain. They are my responsibility.

To all, I send my heartfelt appreciation and thanks.

In listing some names, I fear I might forget some dear friends and supporters. Or some detective readers might search the list to identify those on whom my characters were, to varying degrees, based. This list, let me be clear, is not a 'Who's Who' – some folk I knew back in the first decade of this century, others I have come to know since. And some people remain unnamed, for various reasons.

Thanks for your various contributions through friendship, support and help to Ijeoma Abara, Bayo Adaralegbe, John and Omolara Adeleke, Olubunmi Adeleye, Sylvester Aguddah, Edward Akpevba, Ogie Alakija, Polly Alakija, Teju Alakija, Deytika Amegee, Sam Ammar, Gloria Amosu, Habiba Balogun, Myma Belo-Osagie, Jay Clark, Ekaba and Alan Davies, Johnson Djorhogba, Ernest Dragoo, Dele and Eyono Fatayi-Williams, Chris and Doreen Finlayson, Maneesh and Meenakshi Garg, Brian Garrington, Nick Hardie-Grant, Anne Harte, Jane Heatherington, Paul Igwebuike, Zainabu Jallo, MaryAnn McCabe, Bill McCreadie, Simon Millett, Courtney Nicholls, Thomas Olabintan, Blessing Olateju, Sandra Obiago, Deola Osinuga, Amina Oyagbola, Laïla and Eric Peysson, Ann Pickard, Pastor John Roberts, Tiffany Sayers, Joke Silva,

Lanni Smith, Margaret Swinson, Chief (Mrs) Taiwo Taiwo, Sir Philip Thomas, Kate Thompson, Leanne Tolra, Edith Unuigbe, Claude Vogel, Mutari Wada, Mujib Waziri, Madeleine Wilson and Imad Yazigi.

In Lagos, I attended many long dinners, some a bit tedious and speeches often began with long lists of VIPs to be named. To cut time down and avoid the embarrassment of missing someone important, there was a useful way out. I shall employ it here.

To all others who supported me during my ten years in Lagos, Nigeria and during the writing of this book: thank you and all protocols observed.

I thank my mother, Gwen Watson, now ninety-three years old, for being my longest-running supporter. You shaped me as the person I could be and supported me to become the person I am.

And now to AJ.

'A bit harsh on old AJ?' he said on reading the manuscript. Possibly. Back then, we were out of synch and it was hard to be supportive across bad phone connections and thousands of kilometres. Fortunately, we got into synch again. Thank you AJ, for supporting me through the writing of this book – at times you believed in it more than me and kept me going. And thank you for being my wonderful, supportive partner in life's exciting and always turbulent adventures. I look forward to more adventures together to come.

Notes

1   'Presidents and Military Leaders of Nigeria Since Independence', *World Atlas* <www.worldatlas.com/articles/nigerian-presidents-and-military-leaders-since-independence.html>

Prologue: Phases of the Moon (2019)

1   <www.moonconnection.com/moon_phases.phtml>
2   Population numbers for the city of Lagos and Nigeria are hard to come by and often disputed. Until 2006, the 1991 census data was considered the most credible, even though it was thought to have underestimated the total country population by as much as 20 million. The 1991 census figures put the population of Lagos at only five million while the controversial 2006 census put the population at nine million by federal government and 17 million by the Lagos state government. In 2017, the population of Lagos was estimated at between 14 and 21 million. More information is provided about the history and politics of the Nigerian census in Chapter Ten. 'In the News: The Nigerian Census', Population Reference Bureau, April 2006 <www.prb.org/inthenewsthenigeriancensus> United Nations Population Fund <www.unfpa.org/data/world-population/NG>; Alastair Leithead, 'The city that won't stop growing: How can Lagos cope with its spiralling population?', BBC News Resources, August 2017 <www.bbc.co.uk/news/resources/idt-sh/lagos>

Part One: Earth Shine (2005)

1   Moon Glossary: Lunar Terms and Definitions <www.moonconnection.com/earthshine.phtml>

Chapter One: Fresh Meat

1   In 2013 the power sector was privatised and Power Holding Company of Nigeria (PHCN) closed. The Nigerian Electricity Regulatory Commission (NERC) monitors and regulates the 18 successor companies. In 2018, daily power production capacity was approximately 12,500 megawatts, although daily production languished at about 4000–5000 megawatts for a population of almost 200 million. By contrast, in 2018 South Africa had domestic power generation capacity of over 50,000 megawatts for

a population of about 60 million <www.usaid.gov/powerafrica/nigeria>
<www.usaid.gov/powerafrica/south-africa>

2 Since then, an ambitious reclamation project has begun to create an
8.5 kilometre sea wall off Bar Beach and reclaim 10,000 square metres of
land, the size of New York's skyscraper district, to create a new residential
and financial district for Lagos. With aspirations like Dubai, Eko Atlantic
City, as it is called, is taking shape, funded by the Chagoury Group of
companies in partnership with the Lagos State government and supported
by the Federal Government of Nigeria <www.ekoatlantic.com/about-us>

Chapter Three: Everyone Worked Hard

1 Rev. Samuel Johnson, *The History of the Yorubas from the Earliest Times to
the Beginning of the European Protectorate,* London: Lowe and Brydone,
1921, republished 2012 <www.forgottenbooks.com>; This Yoruba oral
tradition contradicts the Benin oral tradition. See also: Basil Davidson,
Africa in History, London: Paladin Books, 1978; 'The Story of Africa: West
African Kingdoms', BBC World Service <www.bbc.co.uk/worldservice/
africa/features/storyofafrica/4chapter7.shtml>

2 The recalibration exercise was completed in 2014 and Nigeria's GDP was
rebased at $510 billion, an increase of 89%, making it 1.5 times the size
of South Africa's economy. Baobab, G.P., Give Yourself an 89% Rise, *The
Economist*, 7 April 2014 <www.economist.com>
Since the collapse in oil prices in the fourth quarter of 2014, Nigeria's
economy has shrunk. In 2017 Nigeria's GDP was estimated at
$372 billion. South Africa's economy had also struggled and in 2017
its GDP was estimated at $313 billion. Nigeria's economy is now about
1.2 times bigger than South Africa's. World Bank development indicator
comparisons between Nigeria and South Africa, Google Public Datasets
<www.google.com/publicdata/directory>

3 Thomas J. Hutchinson, *Impressions of Western Africa with Remarks of the
Climate and a Report on the Peculiarities of Trade up the Rivers in the Bight of
Biafra*, London: Longman, Brown, Green, Longmans & Roberts, 1858.

Chapter Six: What Have You Got for Me?

1 Peter Cunliffe-Jones, 'How Indonesia overtook Nigeria', Focus on Africa,
BBC World Service, 28 September 2010.

The trend has continued to 2019. See World Bank development indicator comparisons between Nigeria and Indonesia at Google Public Datasets <www.google.com/publicdata/directory>

2   In February 2019, Nigeria was estimated to have 91 million people living in extreme poverty, the highest concentration of people living in extreme poverty in the world – far more than India's 49 million and Indonesia's nearly 13 million. This represents 15% of all people living in extreme poverty in the world.
The World Poverty Clock, World Data Lab, Vienna, funded by Federal Ministry for Economic Cooperation and Development of Germany <www.worldpoverty.io>

3   Indonesia and Nigeria: Maternal mortality in 1990–2015, WHO, UNICEF, UNFPA, World Bank Group and United Nations Population Division Maternal Mortality Estimation Inter-Agency Group <www.who. int/gho/maternal_health/countries/idn.pdf> <www.who.int/gho/maternal_ health/countries/nga.pdf>

4   For a profound and sympathetic attempt to understand the dilemmas average Nigerians face every day in a society riddled with corruption read: Daniel Jordan Smith, *A Culture of Corruption: Everyday Deception and Popular Discontent in Nigeria*, New Jersey: Princeton University Press, 2008 <www.press.princeton.edu/titles/8266.html>

5   The Nigerian civil war was a tragedy with complexities I neither claim to fully understand, nor can do justice to in this book. Accounts of the war and analyses of its causes and impact can be subjective, shaped by personal experience. For wider reading go to <www.republic.com.ng/library/ reading-biafra>

6   A list of Nigeria's leaders since independence is provided on page xvi.

7   'Former leader of Nigeria Babangida to run for President', BBC News, One-Minute World News, 12 April 2010 <news.bbc.co.uk/2/hi/africa/ 8615529.stm>; Tobi Soniyi, Onyebuchi Ezigbo, Laleye Dipo, IBB at 75, says 'I'm Not an Evil Genius', *This Day*, 17 August 2016 <www.thisdaylive. com/index.php/2016/08/17/ibb-at-75-says-im-not-an-evil-genius>

8   Power reform accelerated from 2013 when the power industry was privatised and restructured. Yet despite considerable investment by both the public and private sector since then, the creation of a power ecosystem that meets the needs of industry and people remains years away. David Wijeratne, Pedro Omontuemhen, *Powering Nigeria for the Future*, PWC,

Growth Markets Centre, July 2016 <www.pwc.com/gx/en/growth-markets-centre/assets/pdf/powering-nigeria-future.pdf>

9 Paul Kenyon, *Dictatorland*, London: Head of Zeus Ltd, 2018.

10 For depressing but well-documented accounts of the nature of oil smuggling in Nigeria (and of other transnational crimes in West Africa) see *Transnational Trafficking and the Rule of Law in West Africa: A Threat Assessment*, United Nations Office on Drugs and Crime, 2009; Christina Katsouris and Aaron Sayne, *Nigeria's Criminal Crude: International Options to Combat the Export of Stolen Oil*, London: Chatham House, 2013 <www.chathamhouse.org/nigeriaoil>

Chapter Eight: Black Goats

1 Duncan Green and Matthew Griffith, 'Dumping on the Poor: The Common Agricultural Policy, the WTO and International Development', Institute for Agriculture & Trade Policy, 2002 <www.iatp.org/documents/dumping-on-the-poor-the-common-agricultural-policy-the-wto-and-international-development-1>

2 Green and Griffith, 'Dumping on the Poor'.

3 'UN Official: The EU should consider the global impact of its farm policy', Euractiv, 2013 <www.euractiv.com/section/agriculture-food/news/un-official-the-eu-should-consider-the-global-impact-of-its-farm-policy> In 2018 it was reported that European producers of subsidised powdered milk products were flooding the West African market, outcompeting local herdsmen and farmers and again leading to severe criticism that the EU's support of its own farmers and producers worked against its stated goals of promoting development in Africa, reducing migration flows and combatting terrorism. Emmet Livingstone, 'How EU milk is sinking Africa's farmers', Politico, 4 August 2018 <www.politico.eu/article/eus-milk-scramble-for-africa>

4 Lobbying by civil society had resulted in commitments by the European Union (EU) to what it called 'policy coherence in development'. This was a commitment that all policies, and not just development aid, promoted growth in developing countries. However, research by the Overseas Development Institute showed that CAP instruments remained, distorting damaged developing countries, and the EU remained the main beneficiary; *The Guardian*, 2011 <www.theguardian.com/global-development/poverty-matters/2011/oct/11/eu-agriculture-hurts-developing-countries>

Despite changes to the 2014–20 CAP, developing country farmers
continued to face unfair competition from heavily subsidised EU exporters;
Fairtrade, UK 2015 <www.fairtrade.org.uk>
A European Parliament review of the impact of the Common Agricultural
Policy on developing countries concluded it 'implied risks for sustainable
development and food security' and 'can also have a negative environmental
impact'; Maria Blanco, 'The impact of the European Common
Agricultural Policy on Developing countries', European Parliament,
Policy Department, Directorate-General for External Policies, February
2018 <www.europarl.europa.eu/RegData/etudes/STUD/2018/603862/
EXPO_STU(2018)603862_EN.pdf>

Part Two: Palus (2006)

1　　Moon Glossary: Lunar Terms and Definitions <www.moonconnection.
com/moon-glossary.phtml>

Chapter Ten: The Warrior Pose

1　　The 2006 census was no exception in being disputed. No further
census has been undertaken since. See: 'In the News: The Nigerian
Census', Population Reference Bureau, April 2006 <www.prb.org/
inthenewsthenigeriancensus>
In 2017, the Nigerian population was estimated at 196 million. The
population of Lagos was estimated to be between 14 and 21 million.
United Nations Population Fund <www.unfpa.org/data/world-population/
NG>; Alastair Leithead, 'The city that won't stop growing' <www.bbc.
co.uk/news/resources/idt-sh/lagos>

Chapter Eleven: Never a Dull Day

1　　David C. Noonan, 'War Losses (Australia), 1914–1918 Online',
International Encyclopaedia of the First World War, June 2016
<www.encyclopedia.1914-1918-online.net/article/war_losses_australia>

Part Three: Dark of the Moon (2006–2008)

1　　Moon Glossary: Lunar Terms and Definitions <www.moonconnection.
com/moon-glossary.phtml>

Chapter Sixteen: It's Complicated

1　　'Nigerian crude is being stolen on an industrial scale ... Nigeria's oil
industry is one of the world's least transparent in terms of hydrocarbon

flows, sales and associated revenues. Industry watchers and policy makers often think they know more about oil theft than they actually do … The specifics of who steals oil are elusive, even in Nigeria … At present, oil theft is a species of organised crime that is almost totally off the international community's radar,' wrote Christina Katsouris and Aaron Sayne. Their excellent source, written in 2013, describes the situation then and now. Christina Katsouris and Aaron Sayne, *Nigeria's Criminal Crude: International Options to Combat the Export of Stolen Oil*, London: Chatham House, September 2013 <www.chathamhouse.org/nigeriaoil>

Chapter Seventeen: Good Days and Bad Days

1 Lagos state government elections for Governor and House of Representatives were also held in 2007. Bola Tinubu, who had an early career with Arthur Andersen and Mobil Oil, had been Governor of Lagos State from 1999 to 2007. He had improved state tax collection to use revenue for improved education, roads and housebuilding. He also embarked on public-private partnerships for large projects including bridges, shopping malls and gated communities. Tinubu developed a reputation as a political godfather and he handpicked his successor Babatunde Fashola, a lawyer, who became Governor in 2007. David Pilling, 'Nigerian economy: Why Lagos works', *Financial Times*, 25 March 2018.

Epilogue: Gibbous Moon Over Lagos (2019)

1 Moon Glossary: Lunar Terms and Definitions <www.moonconnection. com/moon-glossary.phtml>
2 Address by the Chairman, Independent National Electoral Commission (INEC), Professor Mahmood Yakubu, to the Stakeholders' Meeting on the 2019 General Elections, International Conference Centre, Abuja, on Saturday 16 February 2019, Independent National Electoral Commission, Nigeria, Press Release, 16 February 2019 <www.inecnigeria.org/resources/press-release>
3 President Goodluck Jonathan was described as an 'ineffectual buffoon who let politicians and their cronies fill their pockets with impunity' during his six years in office between 2010 and 2015. 'Nigeria's Economy: Crude Tactics', *The Economist*, 30 January 2016 <www.economist.com/middle-east-and-africa/2016/01/30/crude-tactics>. Damian Zane, 'Nigeria's Goodluck Jonathan: five reasons why he lost', BBC News, World Africa, 31 March 2015 <www.bbc.com/news/world-africa-32136295>

4   'Muhammadu Buhari, Nigeria's "new broom" president in profile',
     BBC News, World Africa, 6 February 2019 <www.bbc.com/news/
     world-africa-12890807>

5   'Nigeria's Economy: Crude Tactics', *The Economist*, 30 January 2016
     <www.economist.com/middle-east-and-africa/2016/01/30/crude-tactics>

6   David Pilling, 'Popular Verdict Looms for Nigerian Leader Buhari',
     Financial Times, 18 September 2018.

7   Stephanie Busari, 'The old men vying to lead Africa's youngest population',
     CNN, 14 February 2019 <edition.cnn.com/2019/02/13/africa/buhari-
     atiku-nigeria-elections-intl/index.html>

8   Ishaq Khalid, 'Yemi Osinbajo—why Nigeria's favourite leader won't
     become president, yet', BBC Africa, Abuja, 19 August 2018 <www.bbc.
     com/news/world-africa-45206970>

9   The postponed federal elections were held on Saturday 23 February 2019
     and suffered from further logistical difficulties and low turnouts. On
     Wednesday 27 February 2019, APC's President Muhammadu Buhari
     was officially declared the winner of the presidential election with
     15,191,847 votes, defeating PDP presidential candidate Alhaji Atiku
     Abubukar with 11,262,978 votes. President Buhari said he would run an
     inclusive administration to 'strengthen unity' and 'to ensure no section of
     the country is left out'. He also repeated his 'commitment to intensifying
     efforts in security, restructuring of the economy and fighting corruption'.
     Taiwo Amodu and Leon Usigbe, 'My victory God-given—Buhari',
     Nigerian Tribune, 28 February 2019.
     Meanwhile, his vanquished opponent announced plans to challenge the
     election outcome in the courts, calling the election a 'grand theft of the
     people's will'. Alhaji Atiku Abubukar questioned how voter turnout in
     APC strongholds like the northeast state of Borno increased by 82%
     – despite considerable insecurity – while plummeting in more secure
     PDP strongholds like Akwa Ibom in the southeast by more than 50%.
     Minister of Information, Prince Tony Momoh, amongst other political
     leaders, advised Alhaji Atiku Abubukar to concede defeat and congratulate
     President Muhammadu Buhari. Leon Usigbe and Olatunji Segun,
     'Election day witnessed grand theft of people's will, Atiku says', *Nigerian
     Tribune*, 28 February 2019; 'Emulate Jonathan, congratulate Buhari, Tony
     Momoh tells Atiku', *Nigerian Tribune*, 28 February 2019.

10 'Boko Haram in Nigeria', Global Conflict Tracker, Council on Foreign
    Relations, 31 January 2019 <www.cfr.org/interactives/global-conflict-
    tracker#!/conflict/boko-haram-in-nigeria>; 'Muhammadu Buhari, Nigeria's
    "new broom" president in profile', Stephanie Busari, 'The old men vying to
    lead Africa's youngest population'.

11 Mark Amaza and Commentary, 'A widening conflict between
    herdsmen and farmers is redefining Nigeria's geopolitics',
    Quartz Africa, 12 February 2018 <qz.com/africa/1204744/
    nigeria-fulani-herdsmen-clashes-are-redefining-its-geopolitics>

12 Acha Leke, Musta Chironga and George Desvaux, 'Africa's Business
    Revolution: How to Succeed in the World's Next Big Growth Market',
    Harvard Business Review Press, 2018.

13 'Lagos Population 2019', World Population Review, World Cities,
    <worldpopulationreview.com/world-cities/lagos-population>; David
    Pilling, 'Nigerian economy: why Lagos works', *Financial Times*,
    25 March 2018.

14 Jeff Desjardins, 'By 2100 none of the world's biggest cities will be in
    China, the US or Europe', World Economic Forum, Agenda, 20 July
    2018 <www.weforum.org/agenda/2018/07/by-2100-none-of-the-worlds-
    biggest-cities-will-be-in-china-the-us-or-europe>

15 Lagos state government had been controlled by the APC and its
    predecessor ACN since the return to democracy in 1999. Bola Tinubu
    remained the powerbroker and political godfather both at the state
    and federal level. State government had increased state tax collection
    and consumption taxes and had used improved revenues to deliver
    substantial improvements in infrastructure, works and power supply. Since
    1999, successive governors had embarked on significant public-private
    partnerships, but it was hard for the government to keep up with the city's
    rapid population growth. Governor Babatunde Fashola (2007–2015) was
    seen as an effective governor with many infrastructure projects commenced
    during his tenure, including the Eko Atlantic City reclamation and
    development project. Akinwunmi Ambode, a civil servant and accountant,
    was Governor from 2015 but retired in 2019 after not being endorsed
    by Tinubu. See David Pilling, 'Nigerian economy: why Lagos works';
    Oluwatoyin Bayagbon, 'Tinubu chides Ambode, endorses Sanwo-Olu for
    Lagos governorship', *The Cable*, 30 September 2018 <www.thecable.ng/
    tinubu-lagos-experienced-deviations-enlightened-governance-recently>

16 Emily Feng, 'Nigerian Tech Start-Ups Proliferate despite hurdles', *Financial Times*, 18 September 2018.

17 Neil Munshi, 'Bold Refinery Plan Aims to Transform Nigerian Oil', *Financial Times*, 21 November 2018.

18 Examples of state government policy and private sector initiatives on plastic pollution.' LASG intensifies campaign against plastic pollution', *Lagos State government news*, 24 April 2018 <lagosstate.gov.ng/blog/2018/04/24/lasg-intensifies-campaign-against-plastic-pollution>; 'We'll phase out plastic bottles in 2023—Lagos government', Friends of the Environment, March 2018, <fote.org.ng/2018/03/well-phase-plastic-bottles-2023-lagos-government>; Efe Uduigwomen, 'Tackling ocean plastic pollution with key infrastructure', *The Guardian*, 6 May 2018 <guardian.ng/interview/tackling-ocean-plastic-pollution-with-key-infrastructure>

19 Kanayo Umeh, 'Australia offers scholarship to 340 Nigerian students', *The Guardian*, 29 March 2018 <guardian.ng/features/australia-offers-scholarship-to-340-nigerian-students>

20 On Saturday 9 March 2019, state level elections were held nationwide. In Lagos, the APC candidate won the governorship for the fifth consecutive election since the return to democracy in 1999, confirming APC's and Bola Tinubu's stranglehold on the state. The incoming Governor, Babajide Sanwo-Olu, announced in his victory speech that he would focus on infrastructure, enhancing social services and planning specific businesses and investment to provide growth and jobs. 'Electoral Victory Speech Delivered By Mr Babajide Olusola Sanwo-olu, Governor-elect Lagos State', Proshare Economy, 11 March 2019 <proshareng.com/news/Politics/Electoral-Victory-Speech-Delivered-By-Mr.-Babajide-Olusola-Sanwo-olu--Governor-elect-Lagos-State/44341>